TRAVELS WITH GEORGE

Nathaniel Philbrick is the author of *In the Heart of the Sea*, winner of the National Book Award; *Mayflower*, finalist for the Pulitzer Prize; *Valiant Ambition*, winner of the George Washington Prize; *Bunker Hill*, winner of the New England Book Award; *In the Hurricane's Eye*; *Sea of Glory*; *The Last Stand*; *Why Read* Moby-Dick?; *Away Off Shore*; and *Second Wind*.

ALSO BY NATHANIEL PHILBRICK

The Passionate Sailor

Away Off Shore:
Nantucket Island and Its People, 1602–1890

Abram's Eyes:
The Native American Legacy of Nantucket Island

Second Wind:
A Sunfish Sailor's Odyssey

In the Heart of the Sea:
The Tragedy of the Whaleship Essex

Sea of Glory:
America's Voyage of Discovery;
The U.S. Exploring Expedition, 1838–1842

Mayflower:
A Story of Courage, Community, and War

The Last Stand:
Custer, Sitting Bull, and the Battle of the Little Bighorn

Why Read Moby-Dick?

Bunker Hill:
A City, a Siege, a Revolution

Valiant Ambition:
George Washington, Benedict Arnold,
and the Fate of the American Revolution

In the Hurricane's Eye:
The Genius of George Washington
and the Victory at Yorktown

George Washington at Trenton by N. C. Wyeth.

TRAVELS
with
GEORGE

*In Search of Washington
and His Legacy*

Nathaniel Philbrick

PENGUIN BOOKS

PENGUIN BOOKS
An imprint of Penguin Random House LLC
penguinrandomhouse.com

First published in the United States of America by Viking,
an imprint of Penguin Random House LLC, 2021
Published in Penguin Books 2022

Map illustrations by Jeffrey L. Ward.

Owing to limitations of space, illustration credits may be found on page 359.

ISBN 9780525562191 (paperback)

THE LIBRARY OF CONGRESS HAS CATALOGED THE HARDCOVER EDITION AS FOLLOWS:
Names: Philbrick, Nathaniel, author.
Title: Travels with George: in search of Washington and his legacy /
Nathaniel Philbrick.
Description: New York: Viking, [2021] | Includes bibliographical
references and index.
Identifiers: LCCN 2020054623 (print) | LCCN 2020054624 (ebook) |
ISBN 9780525562177 (hardcover) | ISBN 9780525562184 (ebook)
Subjects: LCSH: Washington, George, 1732–1799—Travel—United States. |
Philbrick, Nathaniel—Travel—United States. | United
States—History—18th century. | United States—Politics and
government—1789–1797. | United States—Description and travel. |
Historical reenactments—United States.
Classification: LCC E312 .P55 2021 (print) | LCC E312 (ebook) |
DDC 973.4/1092—dc23
LC record available at https://lccn.loc.gov/2020054623
LC ebook record available at https://lccn.loc.gov/2020054624

Printed in the United States of America
1st Printing

Book design by Daniel Lagin

To Melissa (and Dora)

CONTENTS

Part IV: SOUTH

The chariot at the John Brown House in Providence.

The Chariot

I like to probe the darkness at the edges of our nation's history. Instead of the triumphs, I'm most interested in the struggle. Whether it's the twenty crew members of a whaleship that's just been rammed by a whale or a group of religious refugees left on an unfamiliar coast by an old leaky ship called the *Mayflower*, I'm compelled to explore what happens to people in the worst of times, especially when it comes to issues of leadership.

Given my predilection for mayhem and moral ambiguity, I had, until about ten years ago, little interest in George Washington. What could be more *boring* than a stuffed shirt known as the father of his country? Then I started to write a book about Boston in the American Revolution.

The story was going just fine through the Battle of Bunker Hill; there was plenty of torment and suffering as the incredible pressures of a revolution descended on the citizens of Boston. But then, a few weeks after that epic confrontation on a hill in Charlestown, a new commander of the American forces showed up: George Washington. This was not the stern old man who stares at us from the one-dollar bill; this was a surprisingly young and aggressive leader with reddish-brown hair and a need to prove himself after a checkered career as a provincial officer in the Seven Years' War. How was someone so impulsive and inexperienced going to evolve into the leader who won the Revolutionary War? I needed to find out what happened to Washington next, and two more books were the result.

By the end of my American Revolution trilogy, I had come to realize that Washington did not win the war so much as endure an eight-year ordeal that would have destroyed just about anyone else. In the early years of the conflict, he'd been repeatedly second-guessed by the Continental Congress, even though that legislative body proved powerless to provide the food and supplies his army desperately needed. After the entry of France into the war, Washington spent three frustrating years pleading with his obstinate ally to provide the naval support that ultimately made possible the victory at Yorktown. And then, in the months before the evacuation of the British from New York City, Washington was forced to confront a group of his own officers who threatened to march on Philadelphia and demand their pay at gunpoint. By persuading his officers to remain at their encampment on the Hudson River, Washington prevented the military coup that would have destroyed the Republic at its birth. When he surrendered his general's commission to Congress in 1783, Washington did not declare, "Mission accomplished." He knew that an even greater challenge—establishing a lasting government that fulfilled the ideals set forth in the Declaration of Independence—lay ahead. Once again I needed to find out what happened to Washington next, never suspecting he would lead me into a world as fraught and contentious as our own.

By the time I finished my third book about the Revolutionary War, I was desperate for a change. For more than thirty years my wife, Melissa, and I had lived on Nantucket, an island thirty miles off the coast of southern New England. It was on Nantucket, once the whaling capital of the world, that I, an English major in college, had first fallen in love with history. But now, ten books later, the island that had served as my conduit into America's past was beginning to feel isolated and cut off from the giant land to the west.

I had grown up in Pittsburgh, Pennsylvania, where (thanks to summer vacations at my grandparents' house on Cape Cod) I'd developed an improbable love of sailing. Being effectively landlocked meant that I needed to travel just to find a place to sail. First there was the little lake about an hour outside Pittsburgh. By the time I turned eighteen, I was car-topping my Sunfish to races all over the country. I loved the sailing, but I also loved the driving— the interstates, the back roads, and especially the maps.

Nantucket had been just what we needed to raise a family and move along in our careers, but it took just twenty minutes to get from one end of the island to the other. I was getting itchy and impatient within my circumscribed life on an island at the edge of the sea. Then, during a research trip to Providence, Rhode Island, I saw the small horse-drawn carriage (technically known as a chariot) once owned by John Brown.

John Brown was one of the founders of Brown University and a notorious slave trader; he also revered George Washington. He named several of his ships for Washington and is thought to have based some of the details of his own magisterial home in Providence on Washington's Mount Vernon. The house, now owned by the Rhode Island Historical Society, contains a mural depicting Washington's inauguration in New York City. And in a wing in the back is the immaculately restored chariot in which Brown is supposed to have taken Washington for a ride when he visited Providence in August 1790. What, I wondered, was the newly inaugurated president doing in Rhode Island?

When Washington became president in 1789, America was already a divided nation. There were no formal parties as of yet, but there were two distinct factions: those who embraced the Constitution (Federalists) and those who distrusted the strong central government the Constitution had created (Anti-Federalists). During the state conventions to ratify the Constitution, the battles had been ugly. At the ratifying convention in New York, it had been Alexander Hamilton, a Federalist, versus Governor George Clinton, an Anti-Federalist. Clinton viewed the United States as too large a country for a single, democratic government to be effective, insisting "that no general free government can suit." At the convention in Virginia, Patrick Henry, the originator of the phrase "Give me liberty or give me death!," echoed Clinton's concerns, claiming that the new federal government would trample on white Virginians' God-given property rights. "They'll free your [slaves]," he warned—a prediction that would come true seventy-five years later when Abraham Lincoln issued the Emancipation Proclamation.

It could be argued that the only reason the Constitution was ultimately ratified by the nine states required to trigger a national election was that no matter what a person believed about the merits of the new government, everyone could agree that only Washington should lead it. That said, two states—North Carolina and Rhode Island—had not yet ratified the Constitution by the time of Washington's inauguration.

In addition to the political divide separating the American people, there were long-standing regional differences. When the governor of Virginia said "my country," he didn't mean the United States, he meant Virginia. Washington needed to unify this loose amalgam of virtually independent states into a nation. So in the fall of 1789, less than six months after his inauguration, he set out from the country's temporary capital of New York on a tour of New England.

It would take him a month. Studiously avoiding Rhode Island, Washington visited Connecticut, Massachusetts, and New Hampshire. He carefully observed every facet of the countryside, noting agricultural and building techniques. He talked to farmers, mill owners, and political leaders. He experienced firsthand the miserable

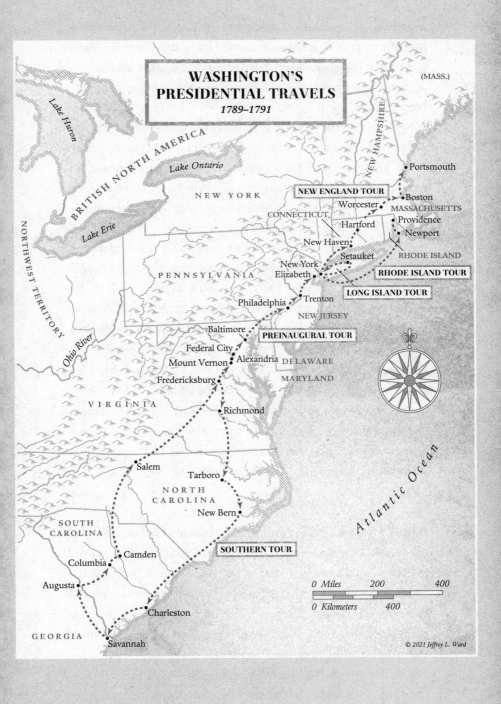

WASHINGTON'S PRESIDENTIAL TRAVELS
1789–1791

BRITISH NORTH AMERICA

Lake Huron

Lake Ontario

Lake Erie

NEW YORK

(MASS.)

NEW HAMPSHIRE

Portsmouth

NEW ENGLAND TOUR

Boston

CONNECTICUT

Worcester

MASSACHUSETTS

Providence

Hartford

Newport

New Haven

RHODE ISLAND

Setauket

NORTHWEST TERRITORY

PENNSYLVANIA

New York

Elizabeth

RHODE ISLAND TOUR

LONG ISLAND TOUR

Trenton

Ohio River

Philadelphia

NEW JERSEY

Baltimore

PREINAUGURAL TOUR

Federal City

Mount Vernon

Alexandria

DELAWARE

Fredericksburg

MARYLAND

VIRGINIA

Richmond

Salem

Tarboro

NORTH
CAROLINA

New Bern

Atlantic Ocean

SOUTH
CAROLINA

Columbia

Camden

SOUTHERN TOUR

Augusta

Charleston

GEORGIA

Savannah

0 Miles   200   400

0 Kilometers   400

© 2021 Jeffrey L. Ward

conditions of the country's roads, and because he insisted on staying only in public taverns, he learned more than he would have liked about the often flea-infested roadside motels of his day.

But the journey was much more than a fact-finding mission. From the first, Washington hoped to use the power of his immense popularity to foster a sense of unity and national pride that had not previously existed. So he resorted to a bit of political theater. Before entering a town, he'd step out of his carriage dressed in his general's uniform, mount his gleaming white horse, and ride down the main thoroughfare to thunderous acclaim. And sure enough, by the time he returned to New York, a new sense of nationhood had begun to infuse the American people. As a newspaper in Salem, Massachusetts, reported, the appearance of the president had "unite[d] all hearts and all voices in his favor."

The following year, Rhode Island finally ratified the Constitution, and Washington visited Newport and Providence. By then North Carolina had also come into the fold, meaning that the longest, most challenging journey of them all still lay ahead: an almost two-thousand-mile, three-month circuit of the South over the poorest roads in the country and through communities that had already voiced objections to the policies of the new federal government; and for that Washington needed a strong, meticulously built carriage just like the one owned by John Brown.

When I first saw John Brown's chariot, I couldn't believe how tiny it was: think the back seat of a VW Bug mounted on four skinny wheels. With a carriage like this, the fifty-seven-year-old Washington, whose health had begun to suffer almost as soon as he was sworn in as president, had saved both his country and himself by exchanging the confines of his presidential office for the boundless promise of the open road.

On that day in 2017 when I saw John Brown's chariot for the first time, I suddenly understood what I needed to do next. After two decades of writing about the country's past, I needed to see for myself what the country had become. And the ideal tour guide was staring me in the face: President George Washington. But *was* he the ideal tour guide at this particular moment in our nation's history—a time when so many once-celebrated leaders from our country's past have been discredited?

When Washington became president of the United States, he was still wrestling with the meaning of the American Revolution. He'd entered the conflict an unrepentant Virginia slaveholder. By the end of the war, he'd learned that his African American soldiers were as competent and brave as anyone else in his army. He'd also befriended the idealistic French nobleman Lafayette, who later claimed, "I would never have drawn my sword in the cause of America if I could have conceived that thereby I was founding a land of slavery."

Gradually, ever so gradually, a new Washington was emerging, one who realized that "nothing but the rooting out of slavery can perpetuate the existence of our union, by consolidating it in a common bond of principle." But even if he had come to recognize the direction the country must take in the future, he remained a slaveholder himself for the rest of his life. A struggle was being waged inside Washington between his ideological aspirations and his financial and familial commitment to slavery at Mount Vernon. Yes, Washington freed his enslaved workers upon his death, but it had been a very long time in coming. And yet, given where Washington had begun in life—as a slaveholder through inheritance at the age of eleven, when his father died—his eventual decision to free his slaves was no empty gesture. President Washington was, I began to realize, exactly the kind of tortured soul to whom I'm drawn—a leader whose troubled relationship with slavery embodied the contradictions and denials of our own conflicted relationship with the country's past.

Love him or hate him, Washington is a historical figure with whom all Americans must reckon. To ignore Washington is to ignore the complicated beginnings of the United States. We cannot remake our country's past, but we can learn from it, and all of us still have a lot to learn from George Washington. Yes, I would follow him across thirteen states and see what I discovered along the way. Thus was born (with due deference to John Steinbeck) *Travels with George.*

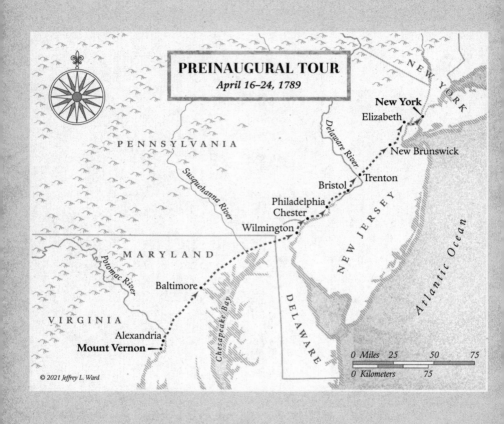

PREINAUGURAL TOUR
April 16–24, 1789

NEW YORK

New York
Elizabeth

New Brunswick

PENNSYLVANIA

Delaware River

Susquehanna River

Trenton

Bristol

Philadelphia
Chester

NEW JERSEY

Wilmington

MARYLAND

Potomac River

Baltimore

Chesapeake Bay

DELAWARE

Atlantic Ocean

VIRGINIA

Alexandria
Mount Vernon

© 2021 Jeffrey L. Ward

0 Miles 25   50   75

0 Kilometers   75

Part I

◇

INAUGURATION

Dora surveys the Great Falls of the Potomac.

CHAPTER 1

Loomings

I t's a maxim among travel writers that you've got to go solo—that a companion diverts you from the object at hand, that loneliness is essential to opening yourself to the experience of the road. In *Travels with Charley*, John Steinbeck insisted that "two or more people disturb the ecologic complex of an area. I had to go alone." Except, of course, he wasn't alone; there was his French standard poodle, Charley. "A dog, particularly an exotic like Charley," Steinbeck wrote, "is a bond between strangers. Many conversations . . . began with 'What degree of a dog is that?'" Steinbeck also insisted that he must camp along the way, sleeping in Spartan quarters in the back of his pickup truck. "I had to be self-contained," he wrote, "a kind of casual turtle carrying his house on his back."

But as has since been revealed, Steinbeck was hardly the stickler for solitude he pretended to be. Despite his claims, he routinely traveled with his wife, Elaine. Rather than campgrounds, they stayed at hotels, some of them so swanky that a jacket was required at dinner. Instead of being appalled by these revelations, I was relieved. Because I didn't want to go it alone. After spending the majority of the last two decades holed up in my office, I had no interest in wandering the country aching with loneliness. I wanted my wife to come along with me. A former attorney, Melissa was about to retire from her second career as the executive director of a local nonprofit. For ten years she had been at the center of the debate about how an island with a storied past should face the future. And now she was going to walk away from it all. Part of me worried that without her busy professional life we'd have less to talk about. The other part of me was downright gleeful that for the first time in thirty-five years she would be free from the demands of a full-time job. It was time we took advantage of her new-found liberty and hit the road. And like John Steinbeck, we were going to bring our dog.

A few months earlier we'd acquired a puppy named Dora (for the first wife of David Copperfield—the Dickens character, not the magician), who, like Steinbeck's Charley, was something of an "exotic": a red bushy-tailed Nova Scotia duck-tolling retriever, or toller for short. Unlike Steinbeck's Charley, who'd been a sedate ten years old, Dora was so rambunctious and freewheeling that we'd attached a GPS tracker to her collar. Whether or not Dora was going to be helpful in striking up a conversation with a stranger, she was guaranteed to make the trip a lot livelier.

Melissa and I took out a map of the Eastern Seaboard and began to plot our prospective trip. Washington's travels could be divided into five different legs: his trip from Mount Vernon to his inauguration in New York; his monthlong tour of New England; a four-day tour of the western end of Long Island; a sail from New York to Newport and Providence once Rhode Island ratified the Constitution; and a three-month tour of the South soon after the nation's temporary capital moved to Philadelphia.

We had some constraints to consider. We needed to stay in touch with our children and grandchildren, all in Brooklyn, as well as our two fathers, both in their nineties and both living independently on Cape Cod. The longest we could be away at a time, we decided, was two to three weeks, requiring us to divide each of the two longest journeys—New England and the South—in half. We also resolved that our two southern trips should be early enough in the spring to avoid the heat of summer.

We were following Washington, but I also wanted to find out as much as possible about the people he visited. Did he leave an impression? What traces—besides historical plaques and the seemingly omnipresent claim that "Washington slept here"—were left of his journey? I made a list of all the towns he'd visited and reached out to as many of their public libraries and historical societies as I could track down. In almost every instance, the librarians and archivists were eager to share what information they had, sending me pages from local histories, journals, diaries, letters, and newspaper clippings. In a surprising number of instances they even offered to show us around their towns, eventually climbing into our Honda Pilot and pointing out the houses Washington slept or ate in, the trees he tied his horse to, or in one instance the spot where he helped raise a rafter of the town's one-room school.

Even before we took to the road, a wholly different Washington began to emerge—not the general or the president or the plantation owner, but the human being, the traveler. And best and most revealing of all were the accounts left by the ordinary people—an eight-year-old girl on Long Island, a middle-aged lawyer from Virginia—who had seen the president from the side of the road.

Washington and Steinbeck were not my only sources of inspiration for this journey. There was also the example of Harry and Bess Truman, who set out on a road trip of their own shortly after the conclusion of Truman's second term as president. Without any sort of fanfare (let alone a security detail), they drove their black Chrysler from Independence, Missouri, to New York City and back over the course of three leisurely weeks. They ate at diners, slept in motels, signed the occasional autograph, and had a terrific time. If they could do it, so could Melissa and I.

But this wasn't going to be the same kind of carefree ramble enjoyed by Harry and Bess in the 1950s. We were, after all, following the travels of a slaveholder at a time when Confederate monuments were being removed across the South. The country's political divide seemed to be widening by the day. And yet I didn't want this trip to be about what separates us. I wanted to find out how Washington attempted to bind us together into a lasting union of states. Acknowledging and even delving into his weaknesses and failings, especially when it came to slavery, I wanted to know what Washington got right—what tools he and his generation had left us to begin to build a better nation.

Little did I know that in the months after our return from our travels, the country would be gripped by two extraordinary events: first, a global pandemic that made the freedom of movement we had once taken for granted impossible, quickly followed by a demand for social justice that inspired protests across the country and the world. Suddenly the original sin of slavery was no longer at the periphery of the conversation; it *was* the conversation. Even more than had been true before, the merits of the founding fathers were being questioned, which is all for the good. But questioning should never lead to forgetting.

Even in his own time, George Washington courted more controversy than most Americans know about today, or are taught in their American history survey courses. His belief in a strong federal government and his endorsement of the fiscal policies promulgated by his financial secretary, Alexander Hamilton, ultimately inspired a backlash led by his own secretary of state, Thomas Jefferson, abetted by his fellow Virginian James Madison, who wanted the states to retain more authority and power. Partisanship had been born, and by the end of his second term Washington was deeply embittered by the political divisions that threatened to destroy the country. And yet, because of what he'd accomplished during the first years of his presidency—both in the executive mansion and on the road—he'd established a government that was built to last.

Steinbeck wrote, "We do not take a trip; a trip takes us. . . . The certain way to be wrong is to think you control it." Every day on the road with George proved the truth of this claim. Just when we thought he was leading us on a journey of quirky and lighthearted adventure through the Middle Atlantic and New England states, we arrived in Newport, Rhode Island, the seat of the American slave trade. From that point on, as we made our way south to the Confederate monuments in Richmond, to the Rice Museum in Georgetown, South Carolina, and to the scene of a slave auction in Savannah, our journey proved more unsettling and more *unexpected* than I ever could have imagined. After one terrifying episode on our way to Newport, we are lucky to be alive.

Today, as I write this, I can't help but wonder whether our country will survive the next unexpected turn of events. More than ever before, Americans need to know what our first president did, at the very beginning, to bring this nation together.

Mount Vernon circa 1802 by William Russell Birch.

CHAPTER 2

Mount Vernon

Travel was essential to George Washington. As a surveyor in his teens and as a British provincial officer in his twenties he had ventured all over the American colonies—traveling as far west as the Ohio River and as far north as the Great Lakes. During his eight years as commander of the Continental army he had crisscrossed the country countless times, ultimately claiming victory with a five-hundred-mile march from New York to Yorktown. Even during Washington's supposed retirement to Mount Vernon after the war, he remained on the move, spending as many as six hours a day on horseback inspecting his sprawling plantation. Washington liked nothing more than to be *out there* and *seeing the world*.

There was one journey, however, he did not want to make. At about 10:00 a.m. on April 16, 1789, he walked out of the house he loved more than any place in the world and stepped into a carriage bound for New York City and the presidency of the United States. "I bade adieu," he wrote in his diary, "to Mount Vernon, to private life, and to domestic felicity; and with a mind oppressed with more anxious and painful sensations than I have words to express."

Instead of the culmination of a life in public service, the presidency seemed, to Washington, a kind of death sentence. He felt, he confessed to Henry Knox, his future secretary of war, like "a culprit who is going to the place of his execution." He had given up, he told Edward Rutledge of South Carolina, "all expectations of private happiness in this world."

He didn't have, he insisted, "that competency of political skill" the job required. Yes, he had worked miracles during the Revolution, but those achievements only created expectations that no man could live up to. "My countrymen will expect too much from me," he wrote to Rutledge. "I fear, if the issue of public measures should not correspond with their sanguine expectations, they will turn the extravagant (and I may say undue) praises . . . into equally extravagant . . . censures. So much is expected, so many untoward circumstances may intervene, in such a new and critical situation, that I feel an insuperable diffidence in my own abilities."

The Constitution had established an electoral college of sixty-nine electors, the number based on the states' representation in Congress, with each elector given two votes. In five of the states the electors had been chosen by the states' legislatures, while six states had employed a form of popular vote. Instead of a single day, the election was conducted over the course of several weeks, with each state's electors meeting at that state's capital; it then took another two months to count the votes in what was the first such popular election of a national leader in the world.

Everyone assumed Washington, a Federalist, would be elected president; the question was who would become his vice president—elected separately and not as part of a ticket. As it turned out, all sixty-nine electors voted for Washington, while Washington's fellow Federalist John Adams topped the seven-man field for vice president with thirty-four votes. Thanks to Washington's enormous nationwide popularity, America's first presidential election had been a victory for the supporters of the Constitution. And yet, as Washington knew full well, it was only a matter of time before the passions unleashed between the Federalists and the Anti-Federalists during ratification erupted once again.

For now Washington just wanted to get the 250-mile journey to New York over with as quickly as possible. Unfortunately, the American people, who had already begun to make plans for his reception along the way, had other ideas.

You may not believe it, but George Washington is bigger than Elvis—at least he was in 2014. In that year, Graceland attracted a whopping 600,000 visitors, while a *million* people visited Mount Vernon. And that's not counting the dogs, because, I'm happy to report, the grounds of Mount Vernon are dog friendly.

On an afternoon in the late summer of 2018, Melissa, Dora, and I were standing on the grass next to Washington's famous home. The rains associated with Hurricane Florence were predicted to arrive the next day, and the air was hot and sticky. Dora, being a furry red Canadian, was not enjoying herself. She could see the Potomac at the bottom of the hill and wanted desperately to go for a cooling swim. Under normal circumstances I would have been happy to oblige, but I was pretty sure they were serious about the "No Swimming" sign down at the river's edge. Dora would just have to tough it out.

A word about Dora, the duck-tolling retriever. The term "tolling" comes from the Middle English word *tollen*, meaning to attract or entice; church bells toll to lure parishioners. Since time immemorial foxes have been known to attract ducks by cavorting on the water's edge, even rolling onto their backs, with their bushy, white-tipped tail in the air. A curious duck swims to the shore, and the fox pounces on its prey. Nova Scotia's original inhabitants, the Micmacs, might have been the first to train their dogs to imitate this behavior. But it was the French, who settled in what they called Acadia in the early seventeenth century, who made the first recorded reference to the decidedly fox-like little dog that would become the Nova Scotia duck-tolling retriever. In the 1660s, Nicolas Denys told of how after luring the ducks to the shore for the hunter to kill, "the dog leaps to the water, and . . . is sent to fetch them all one after another."

That's the last anyone heard of the toller for more than two centuries, partly because the dogs and their masters were forced into hiding in 1751, when the conquering British did their best to purge the region of its French inhabitants. More than six thousand Acadians were rounded up and deported to places as far away as Louisiana (where the name Acadian became shortened to "Cajun"). There were some Acadians, however, who refused to leave. Rather than resist, they simply melted into the scarcely inhabited interior. Eventually, once a new group of English-speaking settlers had established their own communities on what was now called Nova Scotia (Latin for New Scotland), the British government lost interest in enforcing the expulsion. Acadians started trickling back to their homeland, where they rejoined the hardy few (and their dogs) who had survived decades in the backcountry. By the early twentieth century, the toller had begun to reemerge from the mists of time. There is a 1928 photograph of a dog named Gunner that is a dead ringer for Dora: the same high-alert expression, narrow snout, floppy yet expressive ears, tiny feet, and white markings on the face, the chest, and the tip of that big, bushy tail. But back to our story.

We turned down a pebbly path to the equivalent of George Washington's garage. There, far from the crowds and docents, with only a chain to keep back curious onlookers, was a carriage once owned by the first president—*George Washington had once ridden in there*. It wasn't the carriage in which he'd toured America, but it was a carriage just the same—red and black with the same skinny wheels as John Brown's chariot in Providence. As I stood there beside Melissa and Dora, an emotion began to stir within me similar to what I had once felt as a kid visiting the Pittsburgh Zoo: sadness tinged with anger at seeing a wild animal trapped in a cage. This was no museum object; this carriage, parked on the dirt floor of a brick stable, was meant to *move*.

Melissa's favorite part of Mount Vernon are the trees Washington planted around his mansion. There's one—a giant tulip poplar transplanted in 1785—that she actually likes to embrace. (Yes, I married a tree hugger.) Washington, I think, would have approved. He wrote fondly of "those trees which my hands have planted and which by their rapid growth at once indicate a knowledge of my declination and their disposition to spread their mantles over me, before I go hence to return no more—for this, their gratitude, I will nurture them while I stay."

Oh, how he wanted just to stay at Mount Vernon! Over the years, through a series of additions and adjustments—a large room for entertaining on the left, a piazza on the back, and a cupola on the roof—Washington had created a house that reflected the new, more expansive person he'd become during the Revolutionary War. Washington's postwar persona had found expression in other, less tangible ways. In addition to his evolving attitudes toward slavery, he seems to have reevaluated the role of religion in his life. Although he continued to attend church, he stopped taking Communion. No one is sure why.

Also gone were the days when Washington would foxhunt for days on end. Now he was too busy for that notoriously dangerous sport. In order to keep up with his correspondence, he employed two full-time secretaries—thirty-six-year-old David Humphreys from Connecticut and twenty-six-year-old Tobias Lear from New Hampshire. But there were other reasons for the cooling of his ardor when it came to foxhunting. His enslaved manservant and huntsman (the person who organizes the foxhunt) Billy Lee had shattered both his kneecaps (the first while helping Washington survey a portion of Mount Vernon, the second during a fall at the post office in Alexandria), making it impossible for him to ride a horse. According to Washington's step-grandson, George Washington "Washy" Custis, he had given up foxhunting completely by the time he was elected president.

Washington now had another obsession. Ever since the conclusion of the Revolutionary War, he'd been attempting to breed a new strain of mule. In a country poised to expand west to the Mississippi River and beyond, mules—the infertile offspring of a donkey (otherwise known as a jackass) and a horse—were the future. A mule was stronger, smarter, and had much more endurance than a horse. A mule also needed less to eat. The problem was that France and Spain had virtual monopolies on quality donkeys and were reluctant to share their valuable breeding stock with other countries.

In 1784, the king of Spain, hoping to win favor with the newly independent United States, agreed to send George Washington some male and female donkeys, known as jacks and jennies. These were followed by a shipment of Maltese donkeys from Lafayette in France. A cross between the Spanish and the Maltese breeds, named Compound, would become the Adam of American donkeys—the animal from which this country's donkeys (and their mule progeny) are descended. Yes, Washington was the father of his country, but he was also the father of the American mule—the creatures that pulled thousands upon thousands of pioneer wagons across the plains and served the U.S. military as late as the war in Afghanistan in the twenty-first century—and it all began here, at Mount Vernon.

By the time Washington departed for his inauguration in New York, his daily routine had been established: Every morning he was up before dawn. With a candle in hand, he descended the back staircase to his study, where he did more work before breakfast, it was said, than most people completed in a day. After a simple meal of corn cakes drowned in butter and honey, he mounted his horse and began a circuit of the five different farms that made up his property of approximately eight thousand acres. (Today Mount Vernon is down to a mere five hundred acres.) Ninety percent of the inhabitants of Mount Vernon were enslaved African Americans. Those who worked in what was called the mansion house tended to live in better quarters than the field hands, whose tiny, often one-room shacks—made of mud-daubed logs with a single wooden chimney running up the house's side—gave the outlying farms the look of rural villages amid the fields.

Once Washington had completed his rounds, he was back at the mansion house by three o'clock sharp for dinner. He never ate to excess and especially favored fish, drinking perhaps a beer and a few glasses of wine. More desk work followed in the latter portion of the day. Instead of supper he had some toast and tea, and after reading the newspapers, he was in bed by nine. On days when the weather prevented him from getting sufficient exercise, he devoted an hour to walking back and forth beneath Mount Vernon's ninety-six-foot-long piazza. As a result, he never suffered the gout that afflicted so many other members of what he described as his "short-lived family."

The sole exception to Washington's excellent health were his teeth, the first of which was extracted when he was twenty-four. Washington's cracked and decaying teeth were much more than a vaguely amusing historical tidbit. They were an agonizing and ever-persistent part of his daily life. At one point after the Revolutionary War, Washington grew so desperate that he attempted tooth transplants. This leads us to what many may consider an unforgivable act on the part of George Washington. But first, a little historical background.

By the middle of the eighteenth century, dentists in England and particularly France had developed the technique of using a healthy tooth harvested from one person to replace a diseased tooth that had just been extracted from another person—a procedure that quickly spread to America. One of Washington's officers in the Continental army, Richard Varick, who had overseen the compilation of his military papers, is known to have had an eyetooth and four front teeth replaced.

But why would anyone be willing to donate a perfectly good tooth? Well, if you paid them enough (forty-two shillings per tooth became the going rate), there were plenty of people willing to donate their teeth. The procedure went something like this: The "tooth surgeon" (I'm thinking the Nazi dentist played by Laurence Olivier in the movie *Marathon Man*) assembled his wealthy patient and several potential tooth donors in a room. First the surgeon extracted the bad tooth from the patient; then he asked one of the donors to step forward and extracted the corresponding tooth. With luck the replacement tooth (which was cleaned in warm water) fit snugly into the bloody hole in the patient's gums. If not, the next donor was called upon. This continued until the best match was found. Over the course of the next few months, it was hoped the transplanted tooth, much like one of Washington's transplanted trees, would bury its roots into the patient's jaw and take up permanent residence. Unfortunately, this almost never happened. Many tooth transplants didn't work at all. Others lasted for a year or so, five years tops.

In 1784, his first year back at Mount Vernon after the war, Washington paid several "Negroes" 122 shillings for nine teeth (about a third the going rate). That's all we know. Were the "Negroes" enslaved? Probably. Were the teeth used for transplants? Probably. The French dentist Jean Pierre Le Moyer, who ran advertisements for the procedure in the Alexandria newspaper, was a guest at Mount Vernon that spring. This suggests that Washington gathered together a group of his enslaved workers and had at least one of their teeth, maybe all nine of them, inserted in his jaws. This meant that while Washington's mouth was filling up with teeth, gaps were developing in the mouths of Mount Vernon's enslaved.

This is such a creepy scenario to contemplate that many of you might find it impossible to continue to view Washington with anything approaching sympathy. All I can say is that the past is not a pretty place—nor, I need remind you, is the present. Washington did everything he could to keep his embarrassing tooth problems private; if not for the labors of the researcher Mary Thompson at George Washington's Mount Vernon (on whose account my own has depended), we would never have known about the connection between his enslaved workers and his tooth transplants.

In this instance I agree with Herman Melville's narrator Ishmael in *Moby-Dick*, who at the outset of his own journey declares, "Not ignoring what is good, I am quick to perceive a horror, and could be still social with it—would they let me—since it is but well to be on friendly terms with all the inmates of the place one lodges in." If we don't allow ourselves to get to know an Ahab—and all effective leaders have a bit of the Ahab in them (as Ishmael also says, "All mortal greatness is but disease")—we will never begin to understand the true, frightening, and sometimes heartening variety of our world. So I beg you, let's not abandon Washington just yet. There will be plenty of time—and reason—for that later.

Whatever relief the procedure provided Washington proved temporary. It would not be long before his last remaining tooth had been extracted (his dentist, John Greenwood, kept the rotted tooth as a keepsake, which he wore on his key chain) and Washington was equipped with a full set of dentures made not out of wood but out of a combination of human and animal teeth, plus some carved hippopotamus ivory, set in two spring-loaded jaws of lead.

Melissa may dote on the 233-year-old tulip poplar, but the object at Mount Vernon that I find of the greatest interest is the set of Washington's almost equally old dentures—on prominent display at the estate's museum. There they sit, the yellowed upper incisors having the slightly bucktoothed look of horse teeth, which they may very well be, filed down to a human scale. No wonder Washington rarely smiled! In a time before Fixodent, the silver springs in back prevented the dentures from falling out when he opened his mouth. Because the springs exerted considerable pressure, closing his mouth required Washington to forcibly grit his teeth, contributing to the grim, determined look captured in so many portraits. Speaking, let alone eating, would have been difficult for Washington, especially in a public setting when all eyes were on him. And it wasn't just vanity on Washington's part. Without a set of dentures, it is impossible for a toothless person to properly enunciate his or her words. Washington needed those dentures if he was going to function in his elected role as president.

Call me crazy, but I think Washington's dentures, which could very well include the teeth of some of his enslaved workers, are not a bad metaphor for this country: all our anxiety, despair, embarrassment, rage, racism, fear, laughter, horror, and hope ingeniously cobbled together into a contraption once clamped between the jaws of our first president.

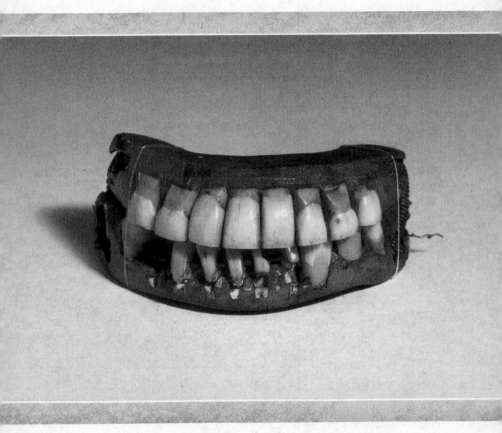

Washington's dentures.

Melissa the navigator.

CHAPTER 3

"Wreaths and Chaplets of Flowers"

Washington's first stop en route to New York City was at Alexandria. Mount Vernon was Washington's home, but Alexandria, a thriving port of thirty-two hundred people just nine and a half miles up the Potomac, was his hometown. He owned a house on Cameron Street and a pew at Christ Church and was the "worshipful master" of the city's Masonic lodge. Unfortunately, Washington also owed a lot of money in Alexandria.

He liked to cultivate the image of the wealthy country squire, but Washington was land rich and cash poor. After generations of tobacco farming, Mount Vernon's fields were exhausted. He had since switched to growing wheat and other crops that were better for the soil, but that did not change the fact that Mount Vernon, despite its grand appearance and state-of-the-art agricultural practices, lost more and more money every year. Now, on the cusp of the presidency, Washington was reduced to the indignity of hitting up his friend Richard Conway for a loan of five hundred pounds, which would enable him "to discharge what I owe in Alexandria." Failing to do this, he confided to Conway, "would be exceedingly disagreeable to me."

It was in Alexandria that Washington was formally addressed by the local citizenry for the first time, a ritual that would be repeated in every city he visited on his way to his inauguration in New York. As in all the other addresses, which were ultimately presented to Washington in a written form, the Alexandrians were effusive in their praise. But what made this one different was that it came from the people who knew him best. "Farewell! Go," they exhorted him, "and make a grateful people happy . . . , and after the accomplishment of the arduous mission to which you are called, may [God] restore to us again the best of men and most beloved fellow-citizen." The Alexandrians' good wishes left Washington, in the words of Joan Rivers, "a little verklempt." "Unutterable sensations must then be left to more expressive silence," he responded, "while from an aching heart, I bid you all, my affectionate friends, and kind neighbors, farewell!" And with that, he was gone.

Washington left Alexandria as quickly as possible, but when we arrived after the day at Mount Vernon, we decided to spend the night. That evening, before dinner, we went to the hotel's lounge for a drink. While Dora sat contentedly at our feet, Melissa looked around the place and sighed. I've long since learned to be wary of Melissa's sighs. Whenever I finish the draft of a chapter, I read it to her out loud—usually while she's washing the dishes after dinner. Not only does this get me out of doing the dishes, but it provides some extremely helpful, if on occasion devastating, feedback. After I've finished reading, Melissa dries her hands on a dish towel and delivers her critique, usually through a series of queries that seem harmless enough in the beginning but on further review start to call into question the entire premise of the chapter. But first, before she gets into all that, she sighs. That evening I could tell by the look on her face— a familiar crinkle around the eyes combined with a slight pursing of the lips—what I was in for.

"Isn't it kind of weird," she said, "that we're bringing a dog with us while following George Washington? Did he even like dogs?"

This launched me into a somewhat defensive disquisition about

Washington's devotion to man's best friend. Not only had he almost single-handedly developed what we call today the American fox-hound, but he had great affection for his dogs, giving them names like Sweet Lips, Drunkard, and True Love. I should have stopped there, but I could tell Melissa was not yet convinced that Dora was essential to our pursuit of the first president. I pointed out that just as Washington was the father of his country, the toller was the na-tional dog of Canada. This elicited what I can only describe as a smirk. Desperate, I decided to swing for the fences. Washington, I insisted, was the ultimate toller. Instead of ducks, he attracted a crowd of American citizens everywhere he went. Luckily, before Melissa could erupt into the dismissive laugh that I knew was coming, some-one sat down beside us.

Her name was Annie, and she, too, owned a dog. She said that Alexandria was "the most dog-friendly city in America." There were so many dog day-care centers in town that people asked each other, "So where does *your* dog go to school?" Melissa laughed and said that our dog was homeschooled.

On Annie's suggestion, we went the next morning to the epicen-ter of Alexandrian dog activity at Windmill Hill Park, where Dora was able to run off leash. John Steinbeck claimed that his conversations often began with the question "What degree of a dog is that?" I sin-cerely doubt it. Not once, not in Alexandria, not anywhere in all of our travels, did anyone want to know "what degree of a dog" Dora was. All they wanted to know was what *kind* of dog she was. Despite having been asked the question approximately two thousand times over the course of a year and a half, neither Melissa nor I ever came up with an appropriate answer. First we'd go with as brief a response as possible and simply say she was a toller. But that always required further explanation, which inevitably led to the confession that she was a Nova Scotia duck-tolling retriever. "Trolling?" "No, tolling." "Tolling?" "It comes from the medieval word . . ." By the time we'd completed the explanation, our questioner wanted to get as far from us and our pretentious dog as possible. So, no, Dora was not the conversation starter Steinbeck's Charley had apparently been. We probably should have said she was a border collie and left it at that.

Back in 1789, there was basically one major road leading up and down the Eastern Seaboard. The challenge was identifying what modern roads most closely corresponded to that ancient route. In many areas Route 1 is that road, but not always. To our aid came the ever-diligent National Washington-Rochambeau Revolutionary Route Association (NWRRRA). In the summer of 1781, knowing that the French admiral de Grasse was about to arrive in Chesapeake Bay with a large fleet of warships, Washington and his French counterpart, General Comte de Rochambeau, marched their armies all the way from the outskirts of New York City to Yorktown. Using the incredibly detailed maps drawn by General Rochambeau's cartographers and other documents, the NWRRRA has created an online resource that enabled us to come as close as is possible in the twenty-first century to following the road Washington traveled to his inauguration.

We were following Washington's route, but it was through a landscape that would have been unrecognizable to him. According to a traveler in the 1780s, the road from Virginia to Baltimore passed through "extensive woodlands, as if in a newly-occupied territory." Instead of virgin forests, we made our stop-and-go way through a megalopolis that extended all the way to Boston: a land of strip malls, car dealerships, and fast-food franchises. Melissa asked what we were achieving by sticking to this never-ending miracle mile when we could be on I-95 and making real time. Certainly Washington, who desperately wanted to get this journey behind him, would have approved. Every now and then Melissa would switch on the Google Maps app in a not-so-subtle ploy to get me to reconsider my commitment to supposed authenticity. By the time we reached Baltimore, I began to think of that program's disembodied voice as the modern-day incarnation of Washington's efficiency-obsessed sensibility, pleading with us to quit the sham of attempting to re-create the past, get on the interstate, and floor it to New York.

Washington traveled north with his personal secretary David Humphreys and Charles Thomson, the long-serving secretary of the Continental Congress who had been tasked with delivering official word of Washington's election to Mount Vernon. Although Thomson had been "much impeded by tempestuous weather, bad roads, and the many large rivers I had to cross," he completed his journey south in a week, and they were now returning to New York in the state carriage.

Serving as Washington's advance team were his secretary Tobias Lear and his enslaved manservant Billy Lee, who had departed from Mount Vernon the day before. Lee could barely stand, let alone walk, but he was desperate to be in New York for Washington's inauguration. In Philadelphia it became clear that Lee's condition had worsened to the extent that he could not go on. Lear left him in the care of a physician who fitted Lee with a brace for his knee that would "not only render his traveling more safe but enable him in some measure to walk." Although Washington thought it best that Lee return to Mount Vernon, he was unwilling to deny his "old faithful servant" if he still wanted to continue to New York. On June 22, more than a month after Washington's inauguration, Lee finally arrived in the city.

It was in Philadelphia, after stops at Baltimore and Wilmington, that Washington first began to appreciate the extraordinary lengths people were willing to go to honor him. It was also in Philadelphia that he mastered the art of making an impression.

First he had breakfast in nearby Chester, Pennsylvania, hoping against hope that he could somehow "elude the parade which necessarily must attend" his entrance into the city. When it became clear this was not possible, he ordered his carriage to the rear and mounted his "elegant" white horse.

Let us now pause to consider the vision of Washington on a horse. But before we get into that, I need to file a disclaimer. Ever since I watched my six-year-old brother, Sam, swing under the belly of a rampaging pony and get nearly trampled to death, I've been terrified of horses. Melissa, on the other hand, grew up on Cape Cod with an old nag named Yankee that she used to ride bareback along the beach. She loves horses and keeps trying to get me to go riding with her. I successfully resisted until it came to a research trip to the Little Bighorn battlefield. Reluctantly I realized that if I was going to understand what it had been like on Last Stand Hill in June 1876, I needed to ride a horse across the same terrain. That led to a petrifying encounter with a former rodeo horse named Tom Cat that still haunts my dreams. But back to George on his way to Philadelphia.

Thomas Jefferson said Washington was "the most graceful figure that could be seen on horseback." Our first president was also a big man for the eighteenth century—six feet two inches tall, with size 13 shoes and hands so massive that he needed to order specially sized gloves. Dress someone like that in a uniform with gold epaulets, put him on a big white horse, and you have a figure that commands attention. Today it doesn't hurt if a president looks good in front of the camera. Back then it was how you looked on a horse that made all the difference.

Before Washington and his entourage reached Philadelphia, they needed to cross the Schuylkill River over Gray's Bridge, a three-hundred-foot-long floating dock made of logs and decking with a railing on either side. Through the efforts of the artist Charles Willson Peale, what one Philadelphian described as "magnificent arches composed of laurel, emblematical of the ancient triumphal arches used by the Romans," were erected at the ends of the bridge, while colorful flags and shrubbery decorated the railings. As Washington passed under the first arch, he found himself in the midst of a production worthy of Broadway's *Peter Pan* as "a lad, beautifully ornamented with sprigs of laurel, assisted by certain machinery, let drop above the Hero's head, unperceived by him, a civic crown of laurel."

Washington, dressed in his buff and blue regimentals with his high three-cornered hat perched on his head, was preceded into the city by a troop of cavalry and light infantry. Upon his arrival at Market Street, a battalion of artillery fired off three discharges of thirteen rounds each as out on the Delaware River two ships decorated with signal flags fired their salutes. One observer estimated twenty thousand people (almost half the population of Philadelphia) "lined every fence, field and avenue between the bridge and the city." Soon the spectators were leaving the sidelines and joining Washington as he marched through the streets. "Thousands of freemen, whose hearts burned with patriotic fire, also fell into ranks almost every square [he] marched, until the column swelled beyond credibility itself."

For America, for indeed the world, in 1789, this was altogether new and extraordinary. This was not a king or an emperor who had achieved power through either birthright or a coup; this was someone the American people had freely elected to be their leader. "How different is power when derived from its only just source, viz., THE PEOPLE," proclaimed *The Federal Gazette*. "The first magistrates of the nations of Europe assume the titles of Gods and treat their subjects like an inferior race of animals. Our beloved magistrate delights to show, upon all occasions, that he is a man—and instead of assuming the pomp of master, acts as if he considered himself the father, the friend, and the servant of the people." There were, of course, about three hundred enslaved men and women back at Mount Vernon who could take exception to this statement. But there was also Billy Lee, who was in Philadelphia that day.

Washington had purchased Lee in 1768 for sixty-one pounds fifteen shillings from the widow Mary Lee. As Washington's manservant, Lee was the one who laid out his clothes in the morning, brushed his hair, and tied the queue in back with a ribbon. In addition to serving as his huntsman, Lee was with Washington throughout the Revolution, shadowing his movements on horseback and receiving and delivering messages. Off the field, Lee organized Washington's personal affairs. It's been argued that Lee's close relationship with

Washington during the war contributed to his owner's changing views about slavery. Now, hobbled by injury and yet determined to be with the general by whose side he had remained for most of the last twenty-one years, Lee knew Washington better than just about anyone short of Washington's wife, Martha. After Washington's death Lee remained at Mount Vernon, where he worked as a cobbler and regaled visitors with stories about his experiences with Washington during the war. One can only wonder what was going through Lee's mind on that day in Philadelphia as he watched the man heralded as "the father, the friend, and the servant of the people" riding his white horse through the crowded city streets.

Washington showed commendable patience throughout that long day, receiving and responding to addresses from the mayor and common council of Philadelphia, the trustees and faculty of the University of the State of Pennsylvania, the judges of the Pennsylvania Supreme Court, the Pennsylvania chapter of the Society of the Cincinnati (composed of officers who had served in the Revolutionary War), and the German Lutherans of Philadelphia. At a dinner for 250 at the City Tavern he endured a series of thirteen toasts, each followed by an earsplitting volley of artillery. That night there was a fireworks display, and it was long after his self-appointed bedtime of 9:00 p.m. when he finally retired.

Washington tolerated all the hoopla with genial stoicism, but there was one aspect of the preinaugural tour he could not abide. He hated it when a troop of cavalry insisted on leading him to the next stop. Not only was the military pomp unnecessary; all the horses in front of him kicked up choking clouds of dust, making life miserable in the confines of the carriage, which he shared with two others during the preinaugural tour. That evening in Philadelphia, Washington, the man who never told a lie, *lied*. He told his hosts he planned to leave the next morning at ten. When the company of light horse arrived to escort his carriage out of the city, they were shocked to discover that Washington had long since departed. It was a subterfuge he would employ more than a few times in his travels ahead.

We pulled into Bristol, Pennsylvania, about twenty-two miles outside Philadelphia, on a sunny Sunday morning. As we could tell from the many banners, Bristol had hosted a doo-wop festival the night before, and the town had a sleepy, pleasantly hungover feeling about it. We were soon ensconced on a park bench beside a canal, trying to enjoy our bagels as Dora lunged at the many squirrels in the surrounding park. The little furry rodents were everywhere, and Dora was desperate to chase each and every one of them up a tree. I'd just finished securing the end of her leash to the bench when a tall man in gray sweatpants and a T-shirt approached. He was smiling and throwing peanuts to the squirrels.

His name was Miguel, and he was a natural connector. As he soon explained, he'd emigrated with his family from Puerto Rico back in 1968 when he was twelve years old. He'd lived here for fifty years, and Bristol was, he said with affectionate pride, "my little town." He'd grown up in a neighborhood that was both Puerto Rican and Italian. "We all got along," he said. "This is a great place to live." His brother was at the park bench to our left, talking to an elderly neighbor with an old beagle named JD. After reporting to his brother and the neighbor that we were from Massachusetts and on our way to New York, Miguel brought JD over to meet us. JD came to Dora wagging his tail, but Dora was too obsessed with squirrels to notice. Miguel used to visit Puerto Rico with his dad but hadn't been back in years. He still had a stepsister over there, but most of his family was in Bristol, "my little town," he said once again. He talked about how he looked forward to retiring from his job at the local bank. "I'm done," he explained. I got the sense Miguel liked nothing more than to be here, on a park bench beside the canal, talking with relatives and neighbors and the occasional stranger on a lovely blue Sunday in September.

As you can probably tell by my earlier comparison of Washington to a duck-tolling retriever, I'd long since begun to see traces of

Washington just about everywhere. I didn't know if it was the gluten-free bagel I was eating that morning in Bristol, but I decided that Miguel had more than a bit of Washington in him. He was tall enough certainly, with the swagger of a former athlete, but most of all he had a disarming gentleness, an aspect of Washington that is often lost in the focus on his accomplishments as a general and a statesman. "He possesses a dignity that forbids familiarity," Abigail Adams observed, "mixed with an easy affability that creates love and reverence." Washington greatly enjoyed being around his step-grandchildren, Nelly, ten, and Washy, eight, whom he and Martha had adopted soon after their father's death when Washy was still a newborn. "Dear little Washington" was Martha's favorite, while her husband had a special place in his heart for Nelly, who as she grew older displayed a vivacious, sometimes cutting wit. She later told of how her grandfather's "grave dignity did not prevent his keen enjoyment of a joke, and that no one laughed more heartily than he did, when she, herself, a gay, laughing girl, gave one of her saucy descriptions of any scene in which she had taken part."

Nelly also testified to the "most considerate and tender" relationship between her grandmother and Washington. Every year during the Revolutionary War, Martha traveled to the Continental army's winter encampment and stayed for months at a time. In fact, Martha and Washington were together for almost half his time away from home during the war. Their relationship only grew closer on his return to Mount Vernon. Nelly recounted how when Martha, who was more than a foot shorter than her husband, wanted to "command his attention," she would "seize him by the button . . . [and] he would look down upon her with a most benignant smile, and become at once attentive to her and her wishes, which were never slighted." When Miguel stooped down to talk to his elderly neighbor on the park bench beside us, it was with the same indulgent serenity I associated with Washington's relationship with Martha.

We finished our breakfast and prepared to leave. I then made the mistake of asking two final questions. I explained that we were following George Washington and wondered whether they had heard anything about his passing through Bristol in 1789. The old man snorted and made some reference to Washington's wooden teeth. Then I asked Miguel what he thought about the country today. He looked at me in baffled despair. I had done something I didn't think possible. I had rendered Miguel speechless.

Later in the car, as we continued north along the Delaware, I realized how wrong it had been to ask Miguel about the current political moment. This journey wasn't about identifying the forces polarizing the country. I was hoping to discover just the opposite—what still holds us together. I was taking my cues from George Washington. Just before he left for New York in the spring of 1789, Washington wrote to Benjamin Harrison, the former governor of Virginia. He and Harrison had come to disagree about the Constitution, but Washington wasn't about to let that difference of opinion destroy their friendship. "Men's minds are as variant as their faces," he wrote. "Liberality and charity . . . ought to govern in all disputes about matters of importance." On the other hand, "clamor and misrepresentation . . . only serve to foment the passions, without enlightening the understanding." I think Miguel instinctively understood this and avoided answering my question because he sensed I might disagree with him. What really mattered was that Miguel loved his little town and I loved mine and both towns were part of something bigger—the United States.

The temperature had climbed into the high eighties by the time we arrived at Trenton, New Jersey, on the opposite bank of the Delaware River. The city was deserted. We parked the car and went for a walk along Assunpink Creek, a quiet strand of gurgling water with which Washington had grown quite familiar. It was in Trenton that he defeated the Hessians on the morning after Christmas in 1776; about a week later he returned to Trenton and repulsed a large British army on a small stone bridge across this creek, ultimately staging a brilliant nighttime escape that made possible his victory at the Battle of

Princeton. Washington had a history in Trenton, and it was here, on his way to his inauguration in New York, that he encountered what one historian has called "one of the most remarkable female rites of the late eighteenth century."

In terms of suffrage and political access, New Jersey was different from any other state in the Union. Since 1776, the state's constitution had given voting rights to any adult—male, female, white, or African American—who had lived in New Jersey for a year and was worth at least fifty pounds. (This would remain the case until 1807, when the Anti-Federalist state legislature restricted the right to vote to white males in an effort to prevent women, who tended to vote Federalist, from participating in the 1808 presidential election, ultimately won by the Anti-Federalist Thomas Jefferson's heir apparent, James Madison.) Whether or not New Jersey's liberal voting laws in 1789 had anything to do with it, the women of Trenton took the leading role in celebrating Washington's return. Under their direction, a twenty-foot arch supported by thirteen pillars was constructed over the bridge across the Assunpink. Just as had been done in Philadelphia, the arch was entwined with branches of evergreen, laurel, and flowers. Emblazoned across the arch's top in large gold letters was the phrase "The Defender of the Mothers Will Be the Protector of the Daughters." Above the inscription was a cupola of flowers encircling the dates of Washington's twin victories, December 26, 1776, and January 3, 1777, topped by a large sunflower.

When given the choice, Washington seems to have preferred the company of women over men. He loved to dance, and after a dinner party he could often be found in conversation with Martha and her lady friends rather than his male peers. He particularly enjoyed speaking with sharp-witted, articulate women. We will be talking later about his relationship with Nathanael Greene's widow, Caty Greene, but there was also the English writer Catharine Macaulay. Macaulay was the author of a multivolume history of England, making her one of the few published female historians in the world in the eighteenth century. She was obsessed with the notion of personal liberty. Her radical political beliefs annoyed more than a few English intellectuals, including Edmund Burke and Samuel Johnson. Her second marriage to William Graham, a man less than half her age, led to her virtual banishment by London society. None of this deterred George and Martha from hosting Macaulay and her husband at Mount Vernon for a ten-day visit. Washington was so taken with Macaulay that he offered her access to his papers for a history of the American Revolution. The matrons of Trenton were a long way from the fiery, intellectually courageous Macaulay, but for Washington on April 21, 1789, after several days of parades, dinners, toasts, cannonades, and speeches, the all-female gathering must have promised a welcome respite.

They were "dressed in white, and crowned with wreaths and chaplets of flowers," and when Washington began to pass by, the mothers and their daughters started scattering flowers across his path as they broke into song:

> *Virgins fair, and matrons grave*
> *Those thy conquering arms did save*
> *Build for thee triumphal bowers.*
> *Strew, ye fair, his way with flowers.*

Whether it was the arch, the flowers, the white dresses, or the song, the women of Trenton succeeded in doing something remarkable. They moved Washington to reflect on the past—something he almost never seems to have done. Nowhere in his diary of his presidential travels does he mention the past, even though many of his stops must have been full of memories and associations for him. In Trenton, however, Washington finally allowed himself to look back, if only briefly. In his letter of appreciation to the town's citizens he admitted to "the exquisite sensations he experienced in that affecting moment. The astonishing contrast between his former and actual situation at the same spot—the elegant taste with which it was adorned . . . the innocent appearance of the white-robed choir, who met him with the gratulatory song, have made such an impression . . . as will never be effaced."

By the time Washington had returned to his carriage and headed to Princeton, the spell had been broken. Up ahead, in New York City, his future was waiting.

Following a maddening series of traffic-clogged roads roughly paralleling Route 1, we made our way through New Jersey in the withering heat. Like Washington, we just wanted to get it over with. Later, I would return under completely different circumstances to New Brunswick. While speaking in the area, I had been approached by Bob Slivka, a member of the New Brunswick Historical Association. Bob had heard I was working on a book about Washington's travels as president and explained that the city would like to host me for a day of immersion in New Brunswick's history. Because Washington spent only the briefest amount of time in New Brunswick in 1789, stopping for an afternoon meal at Egbert's Tavern before crossing the nearby Raritan River at 5:00 p.m., I was skeptical at first. But Bob's enthusiasm was hard to resist, especially when he said they'd put together a team of local historians to assist in my research. And so, on a chilly day at the end of April, I arrived at New Brunswick City Hall for a 10:00 a.m. meeting with Mayor James Cahill and his staff.

One of the highlights of the day was the tour of Washington's inaugural path through town with Bob at the wheel and two fellow members of the historical association: Susan Mollica, the association's chair, and yet another Bob, Bob Belvin, the longtime director of the New Brunswick Free Public Library. Whenever I had a question, Library Bob would pass the query along to the researcher on his staff, who would text him the answer. Because Library Bob's ringtone was a recording from *The Princess Bride* of Wallace Shawn shouting, "Inconceivable!" this made for a delightfully raucous historical tour of New Brunswick.

At one point, we stopped at the provost's office at Rutgers University to look at a painting of Alexander Hamilton's artillery company postponing the British army's advance across the Raritan River in 1776. Someone explained that to further delay the British army, Washington had burned the bridge. "Had the bridge been rebuilt by the time Washington came through here in 1789?" I asked.

Library Bob: "Let me check."

We had just returned to the car when "Inconceivable!" erupted from Library Bob's phone. "No, the bridge had not yet been rebuilt," he reported.

Even though it wasn't on Washington's inaugural route, we stopped for a tour of the Indian Queen Tavern, just across the Raritan River. Washington had attended a celebratory dinner there soon after the evacuation of the British army from New York in November 1783. Of even more interest was that Washington's future vice president, John Adams, and Benjamin Franklin shared not only a room but a bed at the tavern while traveling through New Jersey in the early years of the Revolutionary War.

According to Adams, who recorded the incident in his diary, the room "was little larger than the bed, without a chimney and with only one small window." When Adams started to close the open window before climbing into bed, Franklin objected, "Oh! Don't shut the window. We shall suffocate." Adams, however, believed along with many people of the time that the night air contained an unhealthy "miasma" replete with diseases such as tuberculosis and cholera. For the good of a person's health it was best to seal out the noxious air. But Franklin disagreed. "The air within this chamber will soon be, and indeed is now worse than without doors. Come! Open the window and come to bed, and I will convince you." Franklin then proceeded to lecture Adams on his "theory of colds." Before long, Adams was fast asleep.

This anecdote speaks to the inadequacy of public accommodations in the eighteenth century as well as an important metaphysical question that persists to this day. Do we, like Adams, close the meta-phoric window and shut out the unseen dangers of the dark? Or do we, like Franklin, throw open that window and breathe in the cool night air? Is nature out to get us or save us? I suspect Washington was somewhere in between. He had slept beneath the open stars enough to know that there was nothing intrinsically lethal about the world out there. And yet he had suffered from more than his share of diseases—from smallpox to malaria. I bet he opened the window, if only a crack.

The temperature was in the mid-nineties when we stopped to walk Dora at Rahway River Park. By that time I was getting worried, not about Dora, but about Washington's state of mind. Each one of these towns and its microburst of adoration had been just one more twist of the knife. *He was not worthy! All these people's hopes were about to be dashed by the underwhelming reality of his presidency.* As his diary entries make clear, Washington was miserable as he approached Elizabeth (then known as Elizabethtown), New Jersey, and the specially built barge that was to take him to New York.

I let Dora off the leash so she could run in the relatively cool shade of the woods. Every now and then, she'd poke her head out just to make sure no squirrels had escaped her attention on the surround-ing meadow. Melissa and I could see a gray-haired couple, maybe ten years older than us, approaching with what looked to me like slightly outraged determination. "Is that dog under your control?" the hus-band demanded to know.

"Are you kidding?" I wanted to respond but actually said, "Yes, of course. Come here, Dora." I was preparing for a humiliating couple of minutes attempting to waylay Dora when she miraculously stepped out of the shadows and waited for me to clip on the leash. I smiled at the couple. So there!

We were on our way back to the car when an eleven-year-old girl with a purse over her shoulder started walking toward us just as purposefully as the elderly couple had done a few minutes before. Behind her on the sidewalk, her mother shouted at her to leave the dog alone. "Can I pet your dog?" the girl asked. "Sure, her name is Dora." "Does she shed much?" "Has your mother told you that you can't have a dog that sheds?" I asked. "Yes." "Well, I'm afraid Dora sheds." "Thanks," she said glumly and stormed back toward her mother.

Our journey ended at Veteran's Memorial Waterfront Park in Elizabeth, right across the street from the Lava Lounge. A sign on the black iron fence surrounding the park informed us that there was an "ongoing environmental investigation" at the site. Sixteen American flags waved in the sea breeze as jets from Newark Airport roared overhead. At the edge of Staten Island, no more than a quarter mile across the chocolate-colored waters of Arthur Kill, huge steel cranes rose up into the air like long-legged robots from a sci-fi movie. To our right, a drawbridge, cocked at a forty-five-degree angle over the Elizabeth River, lay frozen in its rust.

Near here Washington had climbed into a "Federal Barge" commissioned by a committee of prominent New Yorkers. I tried to imagine this plushly appointed vessel sliding past us toward the city in the distance, but I couldn't do it. Modern-day New Jersey was just too real, and Melissa and I were just too hot and tired. We needed to get out there, on the wide, sun-glinting water, and see New York Harbor for ourselves.

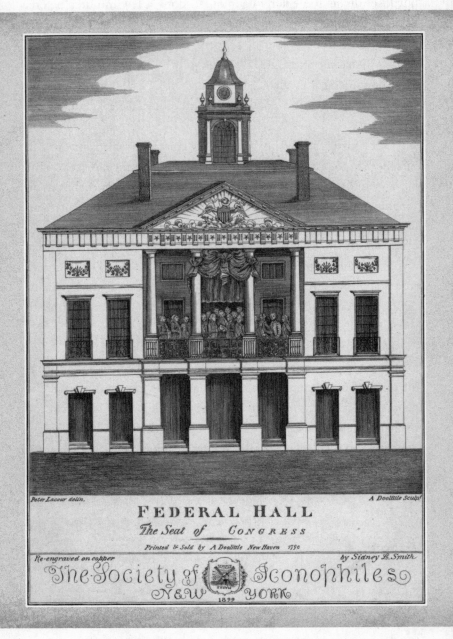

Washington's inauguration at Federal Hall in New York City.

CHAPTER 4

New York

When we finally boarded a boat for a tour of New York Harbor several months later, it was without Dora. Dora loves boats, but she also loves to leap into the water from the boat's gunwale, so we'd made arrangements for her to remain back home on Nantucket as a boarder at the island's animal hospital. At the end of every stay, Dora gets a report card. Much to my amazement, she has so far proven to be an exemplary inmate: eating and relieving herself with regularity and playing happily with the other dogs.

Unfortunately, Dora's good behavior is not enough to erase the dread I feel every time the animal technician hands me her report card. Suddenly I am twelve again and about to learn my teachers' dark verdict on my soul. Short of opening a newspaper with a review of one of my books, it's about as close as I'll probably get to the sense of impending doom Washington felt throughout his preinaugural crawl to New York.

Washington had established his reputation by somehow winning a war against one of the most powerful nations on earth. Now, in the spring of 1789, he was embarking on a far less glorious endeavor. It was time to translate the pronouncements of the Declaration of Independence into a functional government. A constitution had been written, but a deliberate vagueness had been built into the document to accommodate the unforeseen demands of the future. For all intents and purposes, it was up to Washington to create a new government.

Of all the challenges he saw ahead—and he saw plenty—picking appointees was one of the most onerous. Already he had been inundated with appeals from people wanting to serve in his administration. For every person he appointed, there would be an angry cluster of disappointed applicants who would inevitably accuse him of favoritism and possibly worse. At the outset, he wanted everyone to know that he was doing this not because he wanted to—quite the opposite!—but for the good of his country.

Back in January, even before the election had been completed, he had asked his secretary David Humphreys to help draft an inaugural address. The first version went on for seventy-three pages and cataloged, in embarrassing detail, all his reservations and fears. Over and over again he felt compelled to address the skeptics he kept hearing in his head, "the adversaries to this Constitution" and "my personal enemies," who would claim that he had "accepted this office, from a desire of enriching myself or aggrandizing my posterity." It was a rambling mess of a speech, and luckily, after finishing the draft, he sent it to James Madison.

Madison had played an instrumental role at the Constitutional Convention. He, along with Alexander Hamilton, had written the lion's share of *The Federalist Papers*—the brilliant series of newspaper articles defending the Constitution. After leading the pro-Constitution forces at Virginia's ratifying convention, Madison had been elected to the House of Representatives and had emerged as one of the few Virginians Washington could trust for political advice. Madison persuaded Washington not to bare his tortured soul on the occasion of his inauguration and even provided him with a shorter, far less introspective speech. But before it came time for Washington to deliver that address, he still had to endure one last round of adulation.

Washington's presidential barge departed from Elizabeth, New Jersey, under overcast skies. This forty-five-foot open boat featured an awning and cushions and was rowed by thirteen oarsmen dressed in white. Washington was accompanied in the barge by a group of dignitaries that included Elias Boudinot, a congressman from New Jersey. Even before the barge had ventured out of Arthur Kill, Boudinot was surprised by how quickly "a number of boats with various flags came up with us and dropped in our wake."

But the New Yorkers were just getting started. First Henry Knox appeared in "a large barge . . . with splendid colors . . . [as] boat after boat and sloop after sloop added to our train gaily dressed in all their naval ornaments." Then a large sloop approached under a press of sail. Standing on its deck were about twenty men and women singing "an elegant ode prepared for the purpose to the tune of 'God Save the King,' welcoming the great chief." Soon yet another vessel was headed their way with yet another group of singers. "Our worthy president was greatly affected with these tokens of profound respect," Boudinot wrote. "As we approached the harbor our train increased and the huzzaing and shouts of joy seemed to add life to this lively scene."

Suddenly the waters surrounding the barge erupted into foam. "At this moment a number of porpoises came playing amongst us, as if they had risen up to know what was the cause of all this joy." But the most impressive sight was still to come as the barge continued its advance toward the New York City waterfront. "We now discovered the shores crowded with thousands of people. Men, women, children. Nay I may venture to say tens of thousands; from the fort to the place of landing although near half a mile, you could see little else along the shores in the streets and on board every vessel but heads standing as thick as ears of corn before the harvest." At one point the crowd along the waterfront saluted Washington's barge as it passed by and in the process might have invented "the wave" seen at any modern-day sporting event. "The successive motion of the hats from the Battery to the Coffee House," Dr. James Cogswell wrote, "was like the rolling motion of the sea, or a field of grain waving with the wind when the sun is frequently intercepted with cloud."

As Boudinot had noted, Washington "was greatly affected" by this incredible scene, but not in the way Boudinot assumed. "The display of boats which attended and joined us on this occasion," Washington recorded in his diary, "some with vocal and some with instrumental music onboard; the decoration of the ships . . . , and the loud acclamations of the people which rent the skies . . . filled my mind with sensations as painful (considering the reverse of this scene, which may be the case after all my labors to do good) as they are pleasing." Not even amid the uproar of the biggest party New York had ever seen could Washington let go of his anxieties. And as it turned out, the man who would do as much as anyone to stoke the fires of future political discord was there that day.

One of the vessels secured to the waterfront was the schooner *Columbia*, recently arrived from Charleston with an unusual cargo: a male and a female orangutan. Although the orangutans were, according to *The Pennsylvania Packet*, "remarkable for [their] striking similarity to the human species" and were about to be featured in an upcoming exhibit, the captain of the vessel that had transported the exotic primates to New York was also worthy of comment. His name was Philip Freneau, and in addition to being an experienced mariner, he was a widely published poet who had graduated from Princeton with Washington's current political confidant, James Madison. In a few years, Washington's worst fears would be realized when his secretary of state, Thomas Jefferson, secretly enlisted Freneau, on Madison's recommendation, to begin attacking the Washington administration in the press.

It's highly unlikely, however, that Washington or anyone else that day took much notice of the *Columbia* and Captain Freneau, despite the presence of the two orangutans. Instead, it was the Spanish warship *Galveston*, with the colors of twenty-eight different countries fluttering from its rigging, that demanded the crowd's attention when Don Adrian Troncoso began to fire a thirteen-gun salute. "The first shot being so powerful in its detonation," the Spanish envoy proudly reported, "that it surprised the immense pageant by land and sea, meriting not only the general applause and hand-clapping of all, but five more cheers."

Despite aching with dread on that festive day in New York, Washington succeeded in projecting the image of trusting, compassionate authority everyone had come to expect. "He has the soul, look, and figure of a hero united in him," gushed the French envoy Comte de Moustier. "Born to command, he never seems embarrassed at the homage rendered him, and he has the advantage of uniting great dignity with great simplicity of manner." Washington wasn't much of a conversationalist and had absolutely no talent for small talk, but he had a genius for the seemingly spontaneous gesture or remark that could win over even the most stalwart skeptic.

Washington had just stepped from his barge onto the carpeted steps of Murray's Wharf at the base of Wall Street. A huge, eager crowd surrounded the landing. He was about to be introduced to the next group of dignitaries when he was approached by the officer of the guard appointed to escort him through the city. The officer said that "he had the honor to command his guard and . . . was ready to obey his orders." Elias Boudinot witnessed Washington's response. "The President answered that as to the present arrangement, he should proceed as was directed, but . . . after that, [the officer should] give himself no farther trouble, as"—here Washington turned to the crowd—"the affections of his fellow citizens was all the guard he wanted."

Melissa and I saw no cheering crowds along the shore or porpoises leaping into the air as our tour boat departed from Battery Park and headed out into the harbor. And yet what we did see was quite enough: the Statue of Liberty looming above the water, her oxidized copper skin darkened with verdigris. I had always thought the statue depicted the goddess of liberty standing proudly with her gilded torch held high—a welcoming beacon of hope for the millions of immigrants bound for nearby Ellis Island throughout much of the twentieth century. But once our boat, appropriately named *Liberty*, had taken us to the landing place on the south side of the island, I could see that, no, the goddess was not standing still; she was *striding* forward, the broken shackles of a chain at her feet.

The Statue of Liberty, I soon learned, had been inspired by the abolition of slavery during the Civil War. A gift from the people of France, it had been left to the Americans to raise the money for the statue's 150-foot-high pedestal. Fund-raising had lagged until the newspaper publisher Joseph Pulitzer appealed to the readers of the New York *World* and raised a significant portion of the required funds. The Statue of Liberty was finally dedicated in 1886.

Earlier in our journey from Mount Vernon to New York we'd made a point of seeking out Wyman Park Dell in Baltimore, where just the year before the conjoined statues of the Confederate generals Robert E. Lee and Stonewall Jackson had been removed in the dead of night on orders from the city's mayor. At the edge of a park we found the statue-less granite plinth. When the monument had been erected in 1948, it had been America's first double equestrian statue and depicted the two generals on the eve of Chancellorsville, a dramatic Confederate victory during which Jackson fell victim to fire from his own army. The Union general William Tecumseh Sherman had famously claimed, "War is hell." This memorial portrayed the conflict as a distant, romanticized tale of knights and squires. Still etched into the steps leading up to the pedestal was the sentence "They were great generals and Christian soldiers and waged war like gentlemen." Given the preposterousness of those words, it seemed only appropriate that the granite platform was empty.

Now, eight months later, as I stood on the deck of our bobbing tour boat in New York Harbor, I realized that the Statue of Liberty— a green colossus inspired by the abolition of slavery—was the ultimate Civil War monument.

It took Washington more than half an hour to make the half-mile journey from Murray's Wharf to his new presidential residence in the vicinity of what is today the on-ramp to the Brooklyn Bridge. Because of the large number of people spilling onto the street, he had no choice but to make the journey on foot. "It was with difficulty a passage could be made by the troops through the pressing crowds," Boudinot remembered. "[The people] seemed . . . incapable of being satisfied by gazing at this man. . . . The streets were lined with the inhabitants as thick as the people could stand, and it required all the exertions of a numerous train of city officers with their staves to make a passage for the company." At one point, Washington and his fellow dignitaries "were so wedged in . . . that they could not move for some time. The general was obliged to wipe his eyes several times before he got into Queen Street." Imagine it! Washington, so hemmed in by the crush of people that he was forced to stand there for minutes on end, feeling all those eyes, all that yearning, washing over him like waves on a beach.

Fifteen-year-old Eliza Morton was looking out a shopwindow when Washington passed by. "He frequently bowed to the multitude and took off his hat to the ladies at the windows," she remembered. The French envoy Moustier noticed that the crowd had forced Washington to abandon his usual habit of shaking hands. "Now he only shakes hands with those who offer theirs," Moustier observed, "instead of advancing his as he has always done before."

Finally, Washington arrived at his quarters, a large three-story brick house at the corner of Cherry and Pearl streets, where he was greeted by his secretary Tobias Lear. After dinner at the New York governor George Clinton's home, followed by a dazzling fireworks display, Washington returned to his residence and talked long into the night with Lear and David Humphreys. He was not in a buoyant mood. "The evening was spent by the president, Humphries, and myself in a most serious manner," Lear recorded in his diary, "reflecting upon the proceedings of the day and making many moral observations thereon."

A little over a week before, Washington had been sleeping beside Martha at Mount Vernon. Now, after a 250-mile journey of seeming nonstop bedlam, climaxed by as over the top a celebration as one could imagine, Washington was in his new quarters in New York City, exhausted and overwhelmed. What, he must have asked himself, had he gotten himself into?

Washington's inauguration was scheduled for the following week at Federal Hall on the corner of Wall and Broad streets. The building had recently been reconfigured to accommodate both houses of the legislature as well as offices for the executive and judiciary branches by the French architect Pierre Charles L'Enfant, who'd served on Washington's staff during the Revolutionary War and now headed up a successful civil engineering firm in New York. There is a wonderful hand-colored engraving of the building etched at the time of the inauguration. It has a red roof, a cupola, and a second-story balcony topped by a pediment. On the pediment is the seal of the United States, an eagle (with the head of what looks to me like a turkey) clutching thirteen arrows in its left talons and an olive branch in the right.

The first Federalist-style building in America, the original Federal Hall was demolished in 1812 and eventually replaced by a Greek Revival customhouse. That structure now serves as the Federal Hall National Memorial, a museum operated by the National Park Service. Every year, at noon on April 30, the park service sponsors a reenactment of Washington's inauguration at Federal Hall. This I had to see.

On the morning of the reenactment, Melissa volunteered to babysit our three young grandchildren in Brooklyn Heights. I walked across the Brooklyn Bridge alone, turned left near the site of Washington's long-since-obliterated presidential residence, and headed down Nassau Street for Federal Hall.

Today, a larger-than-life statue of Washington—his right hand outstretched as if resting on an unseen Bible—looms over the entrance of Federal Hall. High on its pedestal, the statue has been positioned at the approximate place of the original building's balcony, where Washington stood during his inauguration. Before I started up the steps, I paused to study the statue from the sidewalk and found myself remembering the time my father took me to my first political rally.

Before we moved to Pittsburgh, my father, an English professor, taught at the University of Vermont in Burlington. I was just three or four years old, and I remember sitting on my father's shoulders amid an enthusiastic throng on the city's green, looking up at someone—my father thinks it was John F. Kennedy—waving to us from a balcony. I can still remember the excitement, the pressing crowd, and a sense of something momentous as we all looked up at the waving man. This happened almost sixty years ago, and the memory still makes me feel a warm glow of, dare I say, *patriotism*? I can only imagine if it had been George Washington up there on that balcony being sworn in as the first president of the United States.

I proceeded up the steps and soon discovered about a hundred folding chairs set up beneath the rotunda of Federal Hall. Someone was speaking at the lectern on a small stage, but the main event had clearly not yet begun. A man dressed as Benjamin Franklin, with a small kite in his hand, was flitting about the edges of the hall with the disappointed look of a party crasher who'd just realized the hosts weren't serving any food or drink. I took a seat just as a fife and drum corps erupted to our left and began to march around the perimeter of the hall, followed by several well-dressed men (one in a top hat) with Masonic aprons around their waists.

Once they'd assembled around the stage and we'd all recited the Pledge of Allegiance and sung the national anthem, our bearded master of ceremonies took over at the lectern. "Thank you to all the tenors in the audience," he said before launching into his prepared remarks. After talking about the difficulties encountered at the Constitutional Convention during the summer of 1787 and refuting the charge that George Washington was an "indifferent" Mason ("Masons don't select indifferent Masons to be their grand master, and Washington was a grand master"), he began to describe Washington's inauguration "on that cool clear Thursday" in April 1789.

He told of how Washington dispensed with his military uniform for the inauguration, opting instead for a dark brown suit made from cloth manufactured at a woolen mill in Hartford, Connecticut. For the crowd gathered outside Federal Hall that afternoon, it must have made for an arresting contrast as Washington stepped out of his carriage and bowed to his right and left. The week before he had been dressed as a general. Now, wearing a relatively rustic, American-made suit, he was a leader shorn of pageantry, a man of the people who would be known not as Your Highness or Your Majesty but simply as Mr. President.

Our emcee told of how at the last minute someone realized something was missing. "The stage was set," he said, "but no Bible!" According to our host, Washington "seized on the opportunity to insist that a Bible be found." A member of the nearby St. John's Masonic Lodge provided the big reddish-brown King James Bible that was ultimately used and is now known as the George Washington Inaugural Bible and on display at the inaugural exhibit in Federal Hall. When Washington laid his hand on that holy book, it was opened to Genesis 49–50, in which Jacob tells his sons that their descendants, the twelve tribes of Israel, will create a great nation.

There were thirty-three thousand people living in New York at that time, but many more had flooded into the city for the inauguration. The crowd was facing south on Wall Street. "You are the cheering multitude!" our host proclaimed. "Huzzah! Here he comes now!" We all looked to our left, and there, emerging from the shadows, was an actor playing George Washington. He was dressed in a suitably brown suit with a white wig atop his head. (In 1789, Washington did not wear a wig; his long gray hair was powdered, with his ponytail gathered in a silk bag.) Accompanying Washington for the reenactment that afternoon beneath the rotunda were two men portraying chancellor of New York Robert Livingston and secretary of the U.S. Senate Samuel Otis, both wearing their own slightly askew wigs.

Initially, I must admit to being reminded of the scene from *Blazing Saddles* in which the town dignitaries are assembled around a stage to welcome the new sheriff with "a Laurel and Hardy handshake." But when the three actors began to reenact the inaugural ceremony, all potential absurdity vanished. I was with them in 1789 as Washington became our first president.

Eliza Morton, the same fifteen-year-old girl who had seen Washington as he walked toward his residence the week before, was on the roof of a house on Broad Street, right across from the balcony of Federal Hall. In her account, not published until the middle of the following century, she remembered seeing Washington when he first appeared at the balcony. "He laid his hand on his heart and bowed several times, and then retreated to an arm chair near the table." This was not apparently a scripted move. Washington had been so affected by what he saw that he collapsed into a chair. "The populace appeared to understand that the scene had overcome him," Eliza remembered, "and were at once hushed into a profound silence." Washington was barely holding it together. "After a few moments," Eliza continued, "the general arose and came forward," and Chancellor Livingston read the oath, which Washington dutifully repeated. He then stooped to kiss the Bible on its red cushion as Chancellor Livingston proclaimed, "Long live George Washington, President of the United States." "At this moment," Eliza remembered, "a signal was given, raising a flag upon the steeple of the hall for a general discharge of artillery of the battery. All the bells in the city rang out a peal of joy and the crowd shouted." After waving to the people gathered in the streets and in the windows and balconies of the surrounding buildings, Washington retired inside to deliver his inaugural address before Congress.

That afternoon in 2019, as we sat in our folding chairs beneath the rotunda of Federal Hall, our twenty-first-century George Washington stepped up to the lectern. By that point my mind was swimming in a weird netherworld of then and now. I was here, in the financial center of a city of more than eight million people, watching a man in a wig deliver the speech with which Washington's presidency had begun 230 years ago. The actor that day gazed at us with solemn determination, much as contemporary presidents affect at *their* Washington inaugurations. Washington in real life had looked more like a man on the edge of a nervous breakdown. "This great man was agitated and embarrassed more than ever he was by the leveled cannon or pointed musket," William Maclay, a senator from Pennsylvania, recorded in his diary. "He trembled, and several times could scarce make out to read [his speech], though it must be supposed he had often read it before." Maclay claimed to have "felt hurt" that Washington hadn't done a better job delivering his speech, for "I sincerely . . . wished . . . that this first of men [was] first in everything."

Maclay isn't the only person to have been disappointed by Washington's performance that day. A number of historians have faulted him for not doing then what he would do at his death: free his slaves. The argument goes something like this: if Washington had announced at his inauguration that he could not in good conscience hold other people in bondage while serving as the leader of a republic based on the principle "all men are created equal," he might have hastened the end of slavery and prevented the Civil War.

Other historians dismiss such speculation as historically naive. If Washington had freed his slaves during his presidency, Philip Morgan maintains, "white southerners would have responded with resounding silence; they would have assigned the act the aura of taboo."

Slavery would have continued to grow unabated. "Nothing and no one—not even George Washington—could halt the trends."

For my part, I think there is a tendency to believe Washington was more in control of himself and his circumstances than he actually was. Washington did his best to look like a leader in command, but if Eliza Morton and William Maclay are to be believed, he was anything but; Washington was *terrified* of what lay ahead, both for himself and for his country.

America in 1789 was still a tentative endeavor. And slavery wasn't the only issue. There was the question of how the new federal government was going to pay off its huge war debts. Would the American people—who had launched a revolution over the issue of taxation—allow their new federal government to tax them directly? And what about America's status in the world as a new and vulnerable nation? Britain and Spain, which both had colonial outposts contiguous to the United States, were eyeing America like predatory birds, eager to pounce if the new government should prove unequal to the task of holding together thirteen states with a history of rebellion.

"We are in a wilderness without a single footstep to guide us," James Madison despaired. Washington had fought a war to create a new country, and now he wanted to do everything he could to preserve this uncertain union of states. To broach the issue of slavery now, at the outset of his administration, would have potentially jeopardized his future attempts to create a lasting government. But how could he justify a government that sanctioned slavery? Would it have been better to face the demon at the start, even if it destroyed the Union before it had properly begun?

In the end, it's all speculation. Nothing we say or do now can change how the country began. We are left with Washington making the judgment call that he needed all the political goodwill he could get—particularly from the largely Anti-Federalist South—before the forces of factionalism began to pull the nation apart. Because he knew the trying times were coming. That was why he shook like a leaf while reading his inaugural address. What he couldn't have anticipated, and refused to believe until well after the initial damage had been done, was that someone from his own administration would take the lead in attempting to undermine his best efforts to create an enduring union.

On May 27, 1789—almost a month after his inauguration—Washington climbed back into the Federal Barge and set out across New York Harbor to meet Martha and their grandchildren, Nelly and Washy, who were waiting for him at the ferry landing in Elizabeth, New Jersey. Martha and the kids had not been happy about leaving Mount Vernon ("our family will be deranged," Martha had written to her nephew), but unlike Washington they seem to have enjoyed the journey north. Eight-year-old Washy, Martha had written to her niece, "seemed to be lost in a maze at the great parade that was made for us all the way we come."

His grandfather, of course, had taken little joy in the glitz and gaiety of the preinaugural tour. But now that he was president, things were different. He had his family with him once again. The mansion on Cherry Street was soon crowded with family members and about twenty servants, at least seven of them enslaved. Washington had already hired Samuel Fraunces, the owner of the nearby Fraunces Tavern, where Washington had bidden a moving farewell to his officers at the end of the Revolutionary War in 1783, to manage the household staff and serve as chef. The New Englander Tobias Lear was particularly taken with Fraunces's way with oysters and lobsters, which "made a very conspicuous display upon the table."

Even now that Martha and the children had joined him, Washington could feel the pressures of his new position tightening around him like a vise. Every decision he made in these early days was likely to have a lasting impact not only on his own presidency but on presidencies to come. "Many things which appear of little importance in themselves," he wrote to Vice President John Adams, "may have great and durable consequences, from their having been established at the commencement of a new general government." To be burdened by the past is bad enough, but to be *the first* is to feel the full, potentially unbearable weight of the future.

Already it was clear that if he indulged the many people who wanted to see him, he would be "unable to attend to any business *whatsoever.*" But to cut himself off completely from the public was also not an option. In early May, he'd sent a list of nine questions about what he should do to Adams and several others. Most of the questions dealt with managing his weekly schedule by establishing a series of dinners, teas, and levees, but there was also question 8:

> Whether, during the recess of Congress, it would not be advantageous to the interests of the Union for the President to make the tour of the United States, in order to become better acquainted with their principal characters and internal circumstances, as well as to be more accessible to numbers of well-informed persons, who might give him useful information and advice on political subjects?

Adams responded that "a tour might, no doubt be made, with great advantage to the public, if the time can be spared."

But the tour almost didn't happen. Not even a month later, Washington almost died. In early June what he later described as "a very large and painful tumor" sprouted on his left thigh, and he was overcome with fever. The doctors—a father-and-son team—decided to operate. The son plunged a scalpel into the tumor ("Deeper," his father urged, "you see how well he bears it"), and the infected mass was cut and scraped away. Soon after the operation, Washington asked the doctors about their prognosis. "Do not flatter me with vain hopes," he said. "I am not afraid to die, and therefore can bear the worst." The doctors acknowledged that Washington's life still hung in the balance. In an age before antibiotics the likelihood of his surviving the surgery in his already weakened condition was very low. "Whether [I die] tonight, or twenty years hence, makes no difference," he replied. "I know that I am in the hands of a good Providence."

For the next six weeks Washington lay immobilized on his right side. To prevent the sounds of passing traffic from disturbing him, chains were extended across Cherry Street. By July, Washington was still unable to walk or sit, but he was "able to take exercise in my coach, by having it so contrived, as to extend myself the full length of it." By early September, the remnants of the tumor—probably a cluster of subcutaneous boils known as a carbuncle—had shrunk to the "size of a barley corn." He was out of the woods physically, but he had learned a disturbing lesson. The presidency just might kill him. "The want of regular exercise, with the cares of office, will, I have no doubt, hasten my departure for that country from whence no traveler returns."

And then, in September, just as he finally began to recover from his own malady, he learned that his mother, Mary Ball Washington, had succumbed to breast cancer at the age of eighty. The loss of a parent, particularly the last living parent, is a shock to anyone, and for the next five months Washington wore a black cockade and ribbon in her memory. Washington's sister Betty had tended to their mother in the final stages of her illness. In October, Washington wrote to Betty about their mother and his own illness, reporting that the wound in his left thigh had not fully healed until only a few weeks before. He also reported that "a sort of epidemical cold" had arrived in New York, but so far "I have escaped." Neither grief nor the threat of widespread illness was enough, however, to deter his plans "to set out for Boston by way of relaxation from business."

The following day, October 13, he wrote to his good friend the staunch Federalist Gouverneur Morris, who had recently arrived in Paris. Despite Washington's personal travails, much had been accomplished during the first six months of his presidency. Henry Knox and Alexander Hamilton had just been confirmed as secretary of war and secretary of the Treasury, respectively. John Jay would soon be confirmed as the first chief justice of the U.S. Supreme Court. Even though Washington could barely walk throughout that summer of 1789, he'd insisted on making several, sometimes contentious, appearances in the Senate chamber of Federal Hall, where he'd established the precedent that the executive branch could negotiate treaties and nominate appointees without first consulting the legislature. The Constitution might have been hazy on the issue, but Washington insisted that the president have the ability to conduct the country's foreign policy without the Senate second-guessing his every move.

He'd also acted decisively when it came to supporting James Madison's efforts to add the Bill of Rights to the Constitution, a move designed to placate the Anti-Federalists. North Carolina and Rhode Island had not yet ratified the Constitution, but Washington was now hopeful they would soon see the light. In this spirit of confidence and optimism, with the prospect of an impending road trip brightening his spirits, he confided to Morris, "It may not . . . be unpleasing to you to hear in one word that the national government is organized, and as far as my information goes, to the satisfaction of all parties—that opposition to it is either no more, or hides its head."

Washington still had one major appointment to make: secretary of state. The same day he wrote to Gouverneur Morris, he penned a short letter to Thomas Jefferson, who was returning to America after more than four years as ambassador to France. Might Jefferson be interested in serving as the head of the State Department, "which under its present organization, involves many of the most interesting objects of the Executive Authority"?

Knowing that it would be several months before he received Jefferson's reply, Washington prepared for his upcoming trip. Accompanying him would be Tobias Lear and a new member of Washington's staff, Major William Jackson. A thirty-year-old South Carolinian, Jackson had served as the secretary of the Constitutional Convention. He was also a battle-tested veteran of the Revolutionary War. If Washington should require any kind of security detail during his upcoming travels, Jackson would be his man.

On October 15, two days after writing to Morris and Jefferson, at around nine o'clock in the morning, Washington departed for New England.

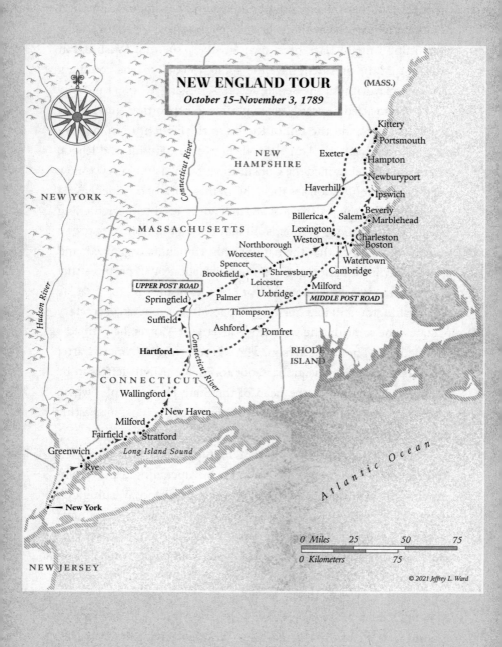

NEW ENGLAND TOUR
October 15–November 3, 1789

(MASS.)

Kittery
Portsmouth
Exeter
Hampton
Newburyport
Haverhill
Ipswich
Beverly
Billerica
Salem
Marblehead
Lexington
Charleston
Weston
Boston
Northborough
Watertown
Worcester
Cambridge
Spencer
Shrewsbury
Brookfield
Milford
UPPER POST ROAD
Leicester
Uxbridge
Springfield
Palmer
MIDDLE POST ROAD
Suffield
Thompson
Ashford
Pomfret
Hartford
RHODE
ISLAND

NEW
HAMPSHIRE

Connecticut River

NEW YORK

MASSACHUSETTS

CONNECTICUT

Connecticut River

Wallingford
New Haven
Milford
Fairfield
Stratford
Greenwich
Long Island Sound
Rye

New York

Hudson River

Atlantic Ocean

0 Miles   25   50   75
0 Kilometers   75

NEW JERSEY

© 2021 Jeffrey L. Ward

Part II

◇

NEW ENGLAND

In a Dream I Meet General Washington by N. C. Wyeth.

CHAPTER 5

Dreaming of George Washington

On a Monday morning in late October, I lay on the floor of Penn Station, dreaming of George Washington. Before I get into the details of my dream, let me tell you how I ended up with my cheek on the sticky tiles of a train station in New York City.

The night before, Melissa and I had both been stricken by an undetermined disease in our hotel room in Brooklyn. Whether it was food poisoning or the highly contagious intestinal bug we afterward learned was sweeping across the city, we awoke the next morning feeling spent and exhausted. In retrospect, we should have stayed in bed, but I was scheduled to speak that evening in Philadelphia, and we had a train to catch.

All went according to plan until our train was called and I struggled to stand with a knapsack full of books strapped to my back. The next thing I remember, Melissa was speaking into my ear. "Nat, you passed out. You okay?"

I sat up, blinking and disoriented. A policeman was walking briskly in our direction.

"I'm okay, I think." With Melissa's help, I stood up once again.

Soon both the policeman and an Amtrak employee were talking to us. By that point I was worried about making our train, but the policeman wanted to know my medical history. Suddenly the books in my backpack became extraordinarily heavy and all was blackness once again.

Lying there the second time, I began to dream—something I've since learned happens surprisingly often when someone faints. I was in the carriage with George Washington as we wended our way through New York City toward New England. Suddenly the carriage leaped into the air just like the magical car in *Chitty Chitty Bang Bang*, which I'd watched that weekend with my four-year-old granddaughter, and we were soaring over Manhattan. As we looked down on the island below, the rivers on either side whitened with sails, Washington smiled, his weirdly discolored dentures glowing in his mouth like a bug-spattered headlight. Soon we were swooping downward, landing with hardly a thud beside the gambrel-roof tavern kept by Mrs. Haviland in Rye, New York. And there were Melissa and Dora, waiting for us in the Honda Pilot at the edge of the town green.

"Nat. *Nat!*" I was back on the floor of Penn Station, and Melissa was rousing me into consciousness. In the ambulance on the way to Lenox Hill Hospital, I thought of Washington lying in his carriage during his recovery from the carbuncle operation. I decided that this is what happened when you followed a man who was constantly battling illness; you got sick. I didn't know how Washington might have taken it, but I felt as if all volition, all enthusiasm and hope, had been sucked from my body. I was an empty husk animated only by the expectations of others. *I must get to Philadelphia!* Was that how Washington got through eight years as president? *I must not let the American people down!*

I later learned I wasn't the only one to dream about Washington. In 1930, N. C. Wyeth, the renowned illustrator of Robert Louis Stevenson's *Treasure Island* and a host of other books, was atop a scaffolding in a bank lobby in Trenton, New Jersey, installing a mural. (The subject? Washington's all-female reception during his preinaugural tour!) At one point, Wyeth slipped and came close to falling thirty feet to the marble floor. The frightening experience haunted him all day, and that night he dreamed, a reverie that eventually resulted in the painting *In a Dream I Meet General Washington.*

It's now my favorite N. C. Wyeth painting: a bizarrely modernist portrayal of the artist standing on the wobbly boards of a scaffolding, his brushes in one hand, his paint-splattered palette in the other, as he talks to George Washington on a big white horse. Wyeth lived in Chadds Ford, Pennsylvania, where the Battle of Brandywine was fought in September 1777. In his dream, Wyeth watched the battle unfold while Washington narrated each turn of events. The battle did not go well for the Americans, but in the painting Washington doesn't seem particularly worried, looking down from his horse with a casual familiarity. Behind him a column of American soldiers marches past and Lafayette waves his hat from a distant hilltop. In the foreground several dead British soldiers lie on the grass in unsettling proximity to Wyeth's thirteen-year-old son, Andrew, who huddles over his sketch pad with a dog at his side. It's all there: intimacy, death, George Washington, family, and a dog.

The doctor at Lenox Hill soon established that I was severely dehydrated and nothing more serious. As I lay in the hospital bed with a bag of IV fluid beginning to drain into my depleted veins, I decided to keep the dream to myself. I knew Melissa felt as poorly as I did, even if she hadn't fainted, and the last thing she wanted to hear about was me flying in George Washington's carriage to Westchester County.

We began our New England tour at 6:30 in the morning of Memorial Day. Lower Manhattan was deserted. We were stopped at a red light when a car drove up behind us, waited for a few seconds, and honked. Apparently, traffic signals did not apply when there was no traffic, and I was supposed to drive through the red light. To show that I was nothing to be trifled with, I lowered Dora's window and she stuck out her head. Maybe if she had been a mastiff or a Doberman pinscher, the driver behind us would have been more impressed. The furry face of a Nova Scotia duck-tolling retriever definitely didn't have the intended effect, and he honked once again.

On Nantucket a driver has no choice but to be on his or her best behavior, because the person who just cut you off is likely to be someone you know—like your daughter's math teacher or your dental hygienist. After decades of containing my emotions while behind the wheel, I was suddenly gripped by an overpowering case of road rage. I raised my right hand in a defiant gesture. "*Nat*," Melissa said with uncharacteristic vehemence, "I'm not going to spend the next five days with you flipping people off. Stop it!" She was right, of course, and I apologized. Eventually, the light changed and we were on our way, both of us breathing easier when the car behind us turned down a side street.

The old road out of New York followed the Bowery to Union Square and then worked its way north through the length of the island. It was amazing to be in the city, virtually alone on a Memorial Day, driving down this empty furrow amid the high-rises. We plunged into the dark tunnel that took us beneath Grand Central Terminal and, after negotiating a series of quick turns, popped out onto Park Avenue. Once again we were gliding through the city with all of the unimpeded ease of the flying carriage in my dream. After crossing to the west side of Central Park on Ninety-seventh Street, we walked Dora in the park's North Woods, which had been a rocky forest in Washington's day. Then it was on to the Morris-Jumel Mansion at 160th Street, perched on the edge of Coogan's Bluff overlooking the Harlem River.

This Georgian gem of a house was built in 1765 by Roger Morris, a British army officer who married one of Washington's former girl-friends. In September 1776, Washington used the mansion as his headquarters in the hectic days after his retreat across the East River to Manhattan. Before it became hemmed in by block after block of brick row houses, the mansion stood alone and offered unimpeded views of the Bronx, Westchester County, Long Island Sound, and the Harlem River. Decades after Washington occupied the house, this was where Eliza Bowen Jumel, the wealthiest widow in New York City, married Aaron Burr, the former vice president who had shot Alexander Hamilton in a duel. Writers including Gore Vidal and Lin-Manuel Miranda have sought inspiration in this house. The place was closed for Memorial Day, and after looking longingly at the mansion and its gardens from the surrounding wrought-iron fence, we climbed back into the car and headed across the Harlem River to the Bronx.

Washington began his New England tour much as we had done: in relative solitude. There were no jubilant crowds, no military escort kicking up annoying clouds of dust; just the three men who would be holding down the fort in his absence—Henry Knox, Alexander Hamilton, and John Jay—who accompanied him for a few miles before turning back to the city. From then on it was just Washington and what he called his retinue.

His secretaries Tobias Lear and William Jackson rode horses on either side of the carriage. Washington's six servants, at least two of them enslaved, were dressed in blanket cloaks, liveries, jockey caps, buckskins, and boots. The Hessian Jacob Jacobus drove the carriage, pulled by four bay horses, with the assistance of two postilions. George Beard followed at the reins of the baggage wagon, while one of the enslaved men, either Paris or Giles, rode behind, leading Washington's white charger Prescott. Given that Washington was the highest-ranking political figure in the United States, this was not a particularly prepossessing retinue, and that was exactly the way he wanted it.

The first six months of his presidency had gone remarkably well, but already there'd been some naysayers. The great fear among the Anti-Federalists was that Washington's presidency would become a virtual monarchy. Vice President John Adams hadn't helped matters by proposing that the president have a title similar to that given to the crowned heads of state in Europe, something like "His Elective

Majesty" or "His Mightiness" or "His Highness, Protector of Our Liberties." (Senator William Maclay, an Anti-Federalist, proposed that the short and squat Adams assume the title of "His Rotundity.") Washington was greatly relieved when Congress ultimately decided to refer to him simply as the president of the United States.

No sooner had that controversy been laid to rest than the press seized on the issue of Washington's weekly levees—the hour-long open houses during which he interacted with the public. Because he was not the most outgoing person in the world, these affairs were predictably formal and stiff. Before the guests began to arrive, Washington, resplendent in a black velvet suit with a cocked hat in his gloved hand, a dress sword at his side, and silver buckles on his highly polished shoes, positioned himself at the fireplace. When presented with a guest, Washington bowed perfunctorily. Then it was on to the next guest.

The levees were on Tuesday afternoons and reserved for men. On Friday evenings, Martha held her own receptions that included both men and women and lasted for as long as three hours. Martha received guests from a settee, while Washington, having dispensed with his hat and sword, did his best to work the room. Compared with the courts of Great Britain and France, these receptions were downright democratic, but not according to the Anti-Federalists, who dismissed these overly formal gatherings as "court-like levees" and "queenly drawing-rooms."

Washington was deeply frustrated by the criticism. Given the limits on his time and the inherent dignity of the office, there was little else he and Martha could do. During his upcoming tour of New England he would make a point of proving to the American people that he was anything but a king.

George III traveled in what was called the Gold State Coach. Decorated on the outside with gilded carvings and colorful panels painted by Giovanni Cipriani and with a satin and velvet interior, this lumbering monstrosity of a carriage weighed four tons and was pulled by eight horses. Washington, on the other hand, elected to travel in the humblest of vehicles during his New England tour: an open carriage that did nothing to protect him from the rain showers that began to fall that morning around ten o'clock.

When a British monarch ventured into the countryside, it was known as a royal progress. Dozens, if not hundreds, of advisers and servants followed in the potentate's wake in a cavalcade that might stretch for a mile before descending on the elegant estate of a nobleman for the night. Washington had made it known he was staying only at public taverns and traveling with a bare minimum of staff.

And yet, when it came to his white horse Prescott, Washington, the former general, refused to compromise. Nothing was too good when it came to that pampered charger. At night, a pasty white substance was painted on his fur; come morning, Prescott's coat shone with the snowy elegance of Herman Melville's white whale. The horse's teeth were cleaned and his mouth rinsed. His hooves were painted black and polished until they gleamed like obsidian. But most impressive of all was Washington's gold-fringed, leopard-skin saddle pad, modeled on what the dying general Braddock had given him in 1755. Washington was the leader of a republic, but he was also a proud soldier, and when he mounted Prescott, who stood sixteen hands high, and settled into his gold-fringed saddle, he was a general once again. No wonder the Anti-Federalists were worried. As Abigail Adams observed about Washington, "If he was really not one of the best-intentioned men in the world, he might be a very dangerous one."

We arrived at Rye around 11:00 a.m. A Memorial Day celebration was under way at the town green, where a veteran from the war in Afghanistan spoke to the crowd about one of the lessons he'd learned on the battlefield: "Keep moving even if you don't know where the rounds are coming from." Awards were presented to an Eagle Scout and three Girl Scouts, plus the winner of an essay contest who'd answered the question "What does Memorial Day mean to me?"

Just across the street was the Square House Museum and the

home of the Rye Historical Society. Washington had spent a night here at both the beginning and the end of his New England tour. A docent was standing at the Dutch door overlooking the green. I asked if the building was open today. "Sure is," she said, "and feel free to bring your dog. She can't hurt anything. It's an old house!" Wow, our first (and, as it turned out, only) dog-friendly historic tavern.

Upstairs there was a bedroom where you were encouraged to lie down on a mattress that had been spread out in the middle of the floor. Washington would have slept in an actual bed; his servants—both free and enslaved—would have been relegated to more basic bedding like this. If it was good enough for Washington's retinue, it was good enough for Dora and me. Soon we were tussling on the coverlet spread over the mattress, with Dora rolling over and scratching her back on the redolent wool.

It was between here and Fairfield, almost thirty miles up the coast, that Washington encountered some of the most challenging terrain of the trip—a series of rocky gorges that had impressed the French writer Jacques Pierre Brissot just the year before as virtually impassable. Greenwich (then known as Horseneck) was the worst—"nothing but a steep slope of boulders," according to Brissot. "I cannot conceive how [the driver] succeeded . . . in preventing the carriage from being shattered . . . ; if the horses slipped, the coach would tumble 200 or 300 feet down into the valley below."

Modern giant bridges allow cars to pass over these chasms without a second thought. That became no longer possible when on June 28, 1983, at 1:30 a.m., a hundred-foot span of one of those bridges collapsed, and two tractor trailers and two cars plummeted into the blackness, killing three persons. I was working at a sailing magazine in Darien, Connecticut, at the time, and I remember hearing the surely apocryphal story of the northbound driver who succeeded in screeching to a halt at the edge of the precipice. He got out of his car and began waving frantically at the approaching traffic behind him. The next driver slowed down and, perhaps thinking the waving man was a hitchhiker, hit the gas and disappeared over the edge.

Once Washington's carriage emerged from the rocky abyss in Greenwich (which he described as "immensely stony and trying to wheels and carriages"), he began to appreciate the beauty of the surrounding countryside. It was a sunny autumn day, and the local farmers were "busily employed in gathering, grinding, and expressing the juice of their apples." The fields of Indian corn and pumpkins offered what Washington described as "a rich regalia." The road passed over rivers and streams, many of them dammed to accommodate grist and saw mills. Each dam created its own "handsome cascade," but the one in Stamford was particularly beautiful. "[The dam] is near 100 yards in width and the water now being of a proper height and the rays of the sun striking upon it as we passed, had a pretty effect upon the foaming water as it fell."

Washington spent the night in Fairfield, a town ravaged by the British army in 1779. "The destructive evidences of British cruelty are yet visible," he commented, "as are the chimneys of many burnt houses standing in them yet." One of the first new structures to rise above the devastation was Fairfield's Sun Tavern, where Washington probably stayed on the night of October 16. The tavern is now part of the Fairfield Museum and History Center, an organization run by an old friend of mine, Mike Jehle, who'd begun his career at the Nantucket Historical Association when I was writing my first work of history, *Away Off Shore*. Melissa and I arrived at the end of a Memorial Day picnic, and we found Mike outside the museum's interpretive center putting away some folding chairs.

Mike showed us the Sun Tavern, explaining that Washington would probably have stayed on the second floor, with the liveried servants in the attic. Taverns like this were not just places to sleep and eat; they were what a panel on the first floor called communication hubs. Post riders and stagecoaches stopped regularly with letters and newspapers that were read and discussed over drinks, which included my eighteenth-century favorite, flip—a mixture of beer, rum, and sugar heated to a foaming boil with a red-hot poker drawn from the fire. Small posters called broadsides were routinely plastered to the tavern's walls, informing people about upcoming events ("President Washington is coming to town!") and offering services and products for sale. In the years prior to Lexington and Concord, taverns like this served as the chat rooms that spawned a revolution. Now, in 1789, Washington hoped these same taverns would be where people talked approvingly about his new government.

In Stratford, Washington's entourage saw something strange. In the middle of a field, with no water in sight, a group of workmen under the direction of Captain Alison Benjamin were putting the finishing touches on a forty-five-ton sloop named the *Hunter of Berkshire*. Years later, Benjamin's daughter recalled how Washington's carriage came to an abrupt halt, and the president himself stepped down to ask how they planned to get the vessel to the sea. Benjamin explained that they were about to begin building a sled underneath the hull. "When winter came it would glide down hill to the creek, a branch of Yellow Mill stream, fully a quarter of a mile away, and in the spring would settle through the ice into the water." Today the Yellow Mill Channel runs into the highly industrialized stretch of water between Stratford and Bridgeport, a city Melissa and I lived in for a summer when I was working at the sailing magazine and Melissa was a summer clerk at a law firm in Stamford. In fact it was at a harborside park in Bridgeport, where signs in both English and Spanish warned us not to swim in the highly polluted water, that our daughter, Jennie, took her first steps. Little did we know that she began walking within a few miles of where George Washington stopped to admire a ship in the middle of a field.

Washington arrived in New Haven on a Saturday afternoon. By then word of his impending appearance had spread across the countryside. The nineteenth-century historian Jared Sparks wrote of how "men, women, and children, people of all ranks, ages, and occupations, assembled from far and near, at the crossings of the roads and other public places where it was known he would pass." The Connecticut state legislature was in session in New Haven at that time and had prepared an elaborate reception for Washington. However, by taking what he called the lower road in West Haven, Washington managed to elude the committee sent out to escort him into the city. That did not prevent him from being subjected to the usual round of dinners and addresses later that evening.

Travel on the Sabbath was frowned upon in the formerly Puritan colonies of Connecticut and Massachusetts, so Washington had no choice but to spend the next day, a Sunday, in New Haven. He dutifully attended both morning and afternoon services and had time to fine-tune his upcoming itinerary. One way to get to Boston from New Haven was the Lower Post Road, which followed the coast, much as I-95 does today. But this would have required him to pass through Rhode Island, which had not yet ratified the Constitution. Instead, he opted to head inland on the Upper Post Road, passing through Hartford and Springfield before following the southern edge of Massachusetts toward Boston. By giving Rhode Island such a wide berth, Washington was sending an unmistakable message.

Fourteen years earlier, in June 1775, Washington had followed essentially the same path through New England to take command of the provincial army in Cambridge, Massachusetts. It was during this journey that he was first addressed by the title he would use throughout the war—"His Excellency George Washington," a suitably royal-sounding title for thirteen colonies looking for a surrogate king to lead them in a war against the monarch of Great Britain. It was a tribute to how far both Washington and the country had traveled over the intervening years that His Excellency was now known as Mr. President as he retraced his steps through New England.

While in New Haven, Washington stayed at the Leverett Hubbard House at the corner of George and Meadow streets. Sadly, the tavern was demolished in 1913 to make way for a new hotel. Because Washington had slept there (memorialized by a marble tablet preserved at the New Haven Museum), diligent efforts were made to document the building, the first stone house in New Haven, before the wrecking ball hit.

Looking at the elevations, photographs, and written accounts in the archives of the museum's Whitney Library, it's possible to get a sense of what Washington would have seen when he entered the front door. Graceful stone arches once soared over the hallway. When Washington turned to go up the stairs, he would have noticed that the wooden railing had been hacked by the swords and bayonets of British soldiers during the Revolution. The building had a hip roof supported by a two-foot-square pillar of oak that ran from the cellar all the way to the apex of the roof, where supporting beams branched out like the ribs of an umbrella. In addition to the usual gardens, a stone terrace extended along the side of the building.

We stopped in the vicinity of where the Leverett Hubbard House once stood on George Street. Urban redevelopment had turned the block into a functional but soulless space of asphalt and concrete, just another street corner in just another American city. And yet, thanks to the documentary record at the New Haven Museum, a vestige of the vanished past had been preserved. When Washington slept here, he was literally *making* history.

In the little town of Wallingford, about fourteen miles beyond New Haven, we stumbled upon the High Meadow Bed and Breakfast. It turned out to be a place so historically and thematically appropriate that I began to wonder whether the powers that be were messing with us. The building was an eighteenth-century tavern that had been moved in the 1970s from Branford, Connecticut, on the Lower Post Road to Wallingford on the Upper Post Road. The house was surrounded by fields of high grass, with mowed paths that led down the hill to a small pond. Best and most miraculous of all, the proprietors had a dog. And not just any dog. They had a brown standard poodle named Charley, identical, as far as I could tell, to Steinbeck's poodle of the same name.

Dora and Charley got along like fast friends, loping through the fields and swimming together in the pond. Melissa took a picture of the two of them trotting side by side down the mowed path. Dora, who usually insists on taking the lead, remains a deferential half step behind. Although they proved to be perfectly compatible, they were very different dogs. Dora was most interested not in Charley but in the chipmunks that inhabited the nooks and crannies of the old house's foundation. Charley, his head held high and impeccably groomed, clearly thought the chipmunks were beneath him. Much like the dog in Steinbeck's book, his obsession was with marking the edges of his territory, his right rear leg swinging up and down with the regularity of a metronome.

If George Washington had been a dog, I decided, he wouldn't have been a toller or even one of his beloved foxhounds. He would have been a standard poodle like Charley: a noble dog ever mindful of his boundaries.

Charley and Dora in Wallingford, Connecticut.

The printer at Sturbridge Village.

CHAPTER 6

"Only a Man"

One of the reasons Melissa and I moved to Nantucket was so that Melissa wouldn't have to devote so much of her day to commuting to and from work. On Nantucket we would all be together in the same figurative boat. Then, with the publication of *In the Heart of the Sea* in 2000, when both our kids were in high school, I embarked on my first book tour. Since then a book tour has become an almost annual ritual. We had originally moved to Nantucket so that Melissa's job would not divide us as a family. Now it was my job that was keeping us apart for weeks at a time every year. So it came as no surprise when Melissa wondered aloud on our way to Hartford, "So what was Martha doing while George toured New England?" Melissa knew what it was like to be at home when her husband was on the road.

At the time I didn't have a good answer to her question. I've since come to realize just how unhappy Martha Washington was back in New York. In late October, as her husband made his way across Connecticut and Massachusetts, she wrote to her niece Fanny, "I live a very dull life here, and know nothing that passes in the town. . . .

Indeed I think I am more like a state prisoner than anything else. There [are] certain bounds set for me which I must not depart from, and as I cannot do as I like, I am obstinate and stay at home a great deal."

In a letter to her friend Mercy Otis Warren in Boston, Martha explained that her most fervent wish—a wish shared by her husband— had been "to grow old in solitude and tranquility together" back in Mount Vernon. That said, she could not blame Washington "for having acted according to his ideas of duty in obeying the voice of his country." She knew that many women, particularly younger women, would be "prodigiously pleased [with] the splendid scenes of public life" that went with being married to the president. She also knew that Washington and his staff were doing everything they could "to make me as contented as possible." Despite all her misgivings and regrets, she was "determined to be cheerful and to be happy in whatever situation I may be, for I have . . . learnt from experience that the greater part of our happiness or misery depends upon our dispositions, and not upon our circumstances; we carry the seeds of the one or the other about with us, in our minds, wherever we go."

Later, when I read Martha's words to Melissa, she issued another one of her trademark sighs, then smiled broadly. "I like her," she said.

Washington loved gadgets. In 1787, during the Constitutional Convention in Philadelphia, he purchased a fan chair—a Windsor armchair with foot pedals that caused a decorated cardboard panel to fan the air above the sitter's head. He later built the most sophisticated flour mill in the country as well as a highly engineered octagonal barn for threshing grain. He was fascinated by experimental plows and intricate timepieces and knew that the only way America was going to end its dependence on British imports was by creating its own technological revolution. Former colonies of farmers would have to become a nation of mills and factories.

In Hartford, Washington saw where his inaugural suit had come from: the Hartford Woolen Manufactory, founded the year before by

Jeremiah Wadsworth, former commissary of the Continental army and one of the wealthiest men in Hartford. "This place . . . seems to be going on with spirit," Washington wrote optimistically even as he admitted the mill's broadcloths "were not of the first quality." This was just one of half a dozen textile mills he visited during his New England tour. Already he'd seen a water-driven linen manufactory in New Haven and samples of "very fine" cloth spun from silkworm cocoons cultivated by hopeful entrepreneurs in Wallingford. Still to come were sailcloth (known as duck) manufactories in Boston and Haverhill and a cotton manufactory in Beverly.

Most promising of them all was the windmill-driven factory in Boston producing card combs—the wire hand brushes used to prepare wool or cotton for spinning into yarn. The factory employed nine hundred people and produced sixty-three thousand card combs a year. "There are machines for executing every part of the work in a new and expeditious manner," Washington noted approvingly, "especially in cutting and bending the teeth, which is done at one stroke."

Washington recognized that these new enterprises were essential to the country's economic future, vowing earlier in the year that "the promotion of domestic manufactures will . . . be among the first consequences . . . to flow from an energetic government." What he didn't say was how difficult a challenge America faced. Prior to the Revolution, almost all manufactured goods, particularly anything related to textiles, had come from Britain, where recent technological breakthroughs such as the flying shuttle, the spinning jenny, and the water-powered loom had given that country what has been described as "an insuperable competitive advantage." Not surprisingly, Britain jealously guarded that advantage by outlawing the export of textile machinery; it was even illegal to make drawings of the new inventions because the diagrams might be secreted abroad. According to the historian John Steele Gordon, "If the United States were to develop a textile industry of its own . . . , it had only two choices. It could reinvent what was then high technology on its own, or it could steal it."

With the exception of the card factory (which was still thriving well into the next century), the mills Washington visited during his New England tour represented farsighted but ultimately unsuccessful attempts to create homegrown versions of British technology; within the decade most of these embryonic factories were defunct.

That left stealing the technology. On November 11, 1789, only a few weeks after Washington visited the Hartford Woolen Manufactory, a packet from England arrived in New York with a twenty-one-year-old passenger from Britain named Samuel Slater. Slater had just completed his apprenticeship at a textile mill in Belper, Derbyshire. Ambitious and intelligent, Slater had come to realize that the chances of his ever acquiring a mill of his own in England were highly remote. Such was not the case on the other side of the Atlantic, assuming, of course, he could reproduce British technology in America. Slater had carefully studied all aspects of textile mill design and painstakingly committed each detail to memory. In a little over a year, with the financial backing of the Quaker Moses Brown, he opened America's first cotton-spinning mill in Pawtucket, Rhode Island.

In the fall of 1789 this was yet to come, but Washington had already seen evidence of what was in store. At the sailcloth manufactory in Boston there were twenty-eight looms with fourteen young women "spinning with both hands (the flax being fastened around their waist) [while others] turn the wheels for them." Working from 8:00 in the morning until 6:00 in the evening, the spinners, who tended to be, Washington noted, "the daughters of decayed families and are girls of character," turned out fourteen pounds of thread per day—an unimaginably high figure in the days when most spinning was done at home. To Washington's mind, factories such as this were "of public utility and private advantage."

There were others, particularly in the agrarian South, who were not so sure. From Thomas Jefferson's perspective, American farmers were "the chosen people of God." (Left out of Jefferson's exaltation of the southern farmer was the region's reliance on slavery.) Manufacturing, on the other hand, "begets subservience and venality, suffocates the germ of virtue, and prepares fit tools for the designs of ambition." In short, the factories of New England were bad for the Republic. "While we have land to labor then," Jefferson wrote in *Notes on the State of Virginia*, "let us never wish to see our citizens occupied at a work-bench, or twirling a distaff . . . for the general operations of manufacture, let our workshops remain in Europe. . . . The mobs of great cities add just so much to the support of pure government as sores do to the strength of the human body." Given that Washington's financial secretary, Alexander Hamilton, was an even bigger booster of domestic manufacturing than Washington, this would make for a potentially antagonistic dynamic within his administration if Jefferson should become his secretary of state.

Melissa and I decided to see for ourselves the realities of textile manufacturing in the late eighteenth century by visiting Old Sturbridge Village, a living museum that re-creates life in New England through the 1830s and is just twelve miles south of Spencer, Massachusetts, where Washington spent the night on October 22, 1789. Melissa and I know Old Sturbridge well. In fact, it was at the Publick House Historic Inn at Sturbridge that we spent the first night of our honeymoon in May 1980. (Even then we were history nerds.) Almost exactly thirty-eight years later, we were headed back to Sturbridge.

There are fifty-nine antique buildings, three water-powered mills, and a working farm on the two hundred acres of Sturbridge Village. Our first stop was the textile exhibit at the Fenno House. A hand loom and spinning wheel competed for space on the first floor, the very technology the Slater Mill was designed to replace. Then it was on to the carding mill, the water-powered wheel of revolving cylinders that eventually superseded the hand cards Washington had seen so efficiently produced in Boston. It took ten hours for a person using two hand cards to work a pound of wool; a carding mill run by the miller and an assistant processed the same amount of wool in ten minutes. We studied the cylinders, each studded with wire bristles, as a group of eleven-year-old boys gabbed in the corner. "You heard that kid?" one of them said incredulously. "He said he didn't know they had chairs back then!"

Walking the lanes of Old Sturbridge as excited schoolchildren flowed in and out of the open doors of each house and shop, I was struck by how different a place this was from Mount Vernon, where the mansion loomed over the clay-daubed hovels of the enslaved workforce. Washington was well aware of the contrast between the two regions. As he traveled up the west bank of the Connecticut River from Hartford, he observed, "There is a great equality in the people. . . . Few or no opulent men and no poor—great similaritude in their building— the general fashion of which is a chimney (always of stone or brick) and door in the middle with a staircase fronting the latter."

Fourteen years earlier, when Washington had arrived in Cambridge to take command of the provincial army in the weeks after the Battle of Bunker Hill, he had been aghast by the men this egalitarian culture had produced, calling them "an exceeding dirty and nasty people." Now, in 1789, he saw things differently. These villages of unadorned houses, each with, Washington noted, a small farm "not averaging more than 100 acres . . . worked chiefly by oxen . . . with a horse and sometimes two before them both in plow and cart," might look like Jefferson's ideal of republican virtue, but they were already the breeding ground of a generation of tinkerers and inventors who were about to change the face of America. Like it or not, the factories of New Haven, Hartford, Boston, Beverly, and Haverhill were the country's future, and Washington was all for it.

Before spending the night at the Jenks Tavern in Spencer, Washington received an express from the Massachusetts governor, John Hancock. In the early days of the Revolution no patriot leader had a bigger reputation, nor a bigger fortune, than John Hancock. Known throughout Massachusetts as King Hancock, he was, not surprisingly, chosen as president of the Second Continental Congress. According to John

Adams, who in 1775 nominated Washington to be commander of the Continental army, Hancock had expected that he, not Washington, would get the nod. Whether or not there was any lingering resentment, Hancock, once he became governor of Massachusetts in the later years of the war, proved frustratingly unresponsive to Washington's repeated requests for supplies and soldiers.

Hancock lived in a magnificent mansion on Boston's Beacon Hill. Knowing that Washington was due to reach the city in a day or two, Hancock requested that the president stay with him. Washington, of course, declined, but tried to do it tactfully: "I beg your excellency to be persuaded of the grateful sense which I entertain of the honor you intended to confer on me." It remained to be seen what kind of reception Governor Hancock was going to give President Washington.

Washington decided to dial down the wow factor when it came to his visit to Worcester, exchanging his military uniform for the brown suit he'd donned for the inauguration. The press loved it. Isaiah Thomas's *Massachusetts Spy* commented approvingly on the subdued suit and called him "the political savior of [our] country." As his entourage rode into Worcester, the local artillery company fired five times for the states of New England: "three for the three in the union—one for Vermont, which will speedily be admitted—and one as a call for Rhode Island to be ready before it be too late." This was exactly the message Washington hoped to deliver.

Melissa and I also had something to deliver in Worcester: an old, taped-over Dewar's scotch carton full of manuscripts. My father is a retired English professor with an expertise in the nineteenth-century novelist James Fenimore Cooper, author of *The Last of the Mohicans* and many other books. My dad and mother spent much of their retirement producing the definitive editions of several of Cooper's novels, traveling to archives across the country and laboriously copying many original manuscripts. Thanks to the efforts of Isaiah Thomas, the premier newspaperman of the eighteenth and early nineteenth centuries, Worcester is home to the American Antiquarian Society (AAS), which has the finest collection of early American newspapers in the world. They also have a treasure trove of letters, journals, and other documents relating to the history of New England and America, and my father had arranged to donate this boxful of Cooper materials to the AAS.

I've visited the AAS many times for research and to give talks underneath its lovely rotunda. But I'd never had the chance to explore its vast, largely subterranean vault of newspapers. After delivering my father's box, which was gratefully received, we were taken by Vince Golden, the head of periodicals, down into a wonderfully musty warren of bound newspapers, the volumes stored in wide gray document boxes. Vince showed us three different accounts of Washington's visit to Worcester as well as the run of Benjamin Franklin's *Pennsylvania Gazette* that Isaiah Thomas bought for a couple of hundred dollars—a big sum in the early nineteenth century. There was also a Confederate newspaper from Louisiana, which because of the scarcity of paper during the final years of the Civil War had been printed on wallpaper. What bothers Vince are the papers that have been permanently lost, but he remains ever hopeful that more of these vanished periodicals will someday come to light.

When we were at Sturbridge earlier that day, we visited the Isaiah Thomas Printing Office, where they demonstrate the printing techniques of the early nineteenth century. At one point the printer, a bearded man with a gray ponytail, said, "Because the technology is simple, it lasts. If the power goes out, we keep running." Looking at what seemed like miles of metal shelving full of old newspapers, I wondered where all the words currently being written and read on computer screens will go—and how will the historians of the future find them?

Much of Washington's time in Worcester was spent planning his entrance into Boston the next day. Representatives from the city's selectmen as well as the Middlesex militia had traveled to Worcester to iron out the details. First he would be met by the militia in Cambridge; then it was on to Boston and a big parade. "Finding this ceremony was not to be avoided though I had made every effort to do it," Washington recorded in his diary, "I named the hour of 10 to pass the militia . . . and the hour of 12 for my entrance into Boston." With that settled, he climbed into his carriage and headed for the town of Shrewsbury, the road along the way lined with citizens, all of them eager "to hail him welcome."

The road through Shrewsbury passed right by the house of Artemas Ward, the general who had been in command of the provincial army when Washington arrived in 1775. Washington's criticisms of the New Englanders did not sit well with Ward, and the two generals appear to have become increasingly estranged. It did not help matters that Ward was the first officer to propose the strategy that ultimately allowed the Americans to prevail: the fortification of Dorchester Heights, a move Washington initially rejected in favor of attacking British-occupied Boston directly. Only after Washington's plan to take Boston by storm had been unanimously voted down by his council of war did he begrudgingly agree to fortify Dorchester Heights. Washington would get the credit for expelling the British, but it was Ward's plan that had won the day. Artemas Ward had witnessed Washington at his arrogant worst, and there is no record of Washington's making any attempt to see him when his carriage passed by Ward's house.

We do know, however, that Washington stopped in Shrewsbury. In the nineteenth century, the local historian Elizabeth Ward (a descendant of Artemas Ward's who lived in the general's house) told how the town's children lined the street, the boys on one side "making their bows and the girls sweeping their graceful curtsies on the other," as the presidential entourage passed by. "The outriders in their uniforms bright with scarlet cloth and gold lace, were so splendid that the children hardly noticed the stopping of the carriage, until a gentleman in plain brown dress alighted and George Washington himself stood before them, speaking to every child and shaking hands with the older ones." One girl, the daughter of John Farrar, was especially excited to meet Washington, "her imagination picturing him as some superior being." But when the president stood before her, "dressed more plainly than his guard and postilions . . . , this spirited young woman of ten . . . refused her curtsy and turning her back upon Washington exclaimed, 'He is nothing but a man!'" According to Ward, Washington was much amused by the girl's response and "presented her with a silver quarter [subsequently] preserved in the family as a great treasure."

Whenever I hear the phrase "tradition has it . . . ," my antennae start quivering. Making this particular anecdote all the more suspicious is that this is not the only instance during the New England tour when some variant of the words "nothing but a man" was attributed either to Washington himself or to a child who had just seen him for the first time. In Salem there is the boy who after walking thirty miles to see the president says in wonder, "You are a man, you are nothing but a man." Then there is the unruly boy in Haverhill who bursts into Harrod's Tavern insisting that he see the president. Washington, it turns out, has already retired to his room, but when he hears the disruption outside, he opens the door, and the boy stands there dumbfounded. "Calling the lad to his side," the story goes, "Washington gently patted his head, saying, 'I am George Washington, my little lad, but I am only a *man*.'"

It certainly sounds like balderdash to me. And yet, as Samuel Francis Batchelder wrote in an essay examining the dubious tradition of the Washington elm in Cambridge (under which the general supposedly took command of the provincial army), "A tradition may grow and flower surprisingly; but it doesn't grow like a kind of historical orchid. It must have its root in something definite. Very few traditions associated with a given location spring from nothing at all." In other words, these traditions may be 90 percent hooey, but there is probably some historical seed of truth lurking there somewhere. For my part, I think it's significant that one of the first recorded instances of the Washington "only a man" tradition springs from Shrewsbury, the home of Artemas Ward, the person who knew better than anyone that America's first president was indeed "only a man."

Soon after passing through Shrewsbury, we decided to stop for lunch in Northborough, the next town on the old road to Boston. Not far from Washington's route we found an Italian restaurant called Linguine's.

We sat one booth over from a man and woman having a leisurely lunch. The man was, we later learned, sixty-eight. He had trembling hands and did almost all the talking. He was in the middle of a well-told story when we sat down—something about a trip full of hair-breadth escapes and adventure. He was such a good raconteur that it was impossible not to eavesdrop, and both Melissa and I sat silently sharing our veal parmesan as we listened to every word.

He began to talk about his experiences in Vietnam when he was eighteen. He was in a tank at the turret gun when they hit a mine. He was knocked unconscious by the explosion, his head thrown back against the tank. The three men below him were much more seriously injured. They were all his good friends, particularly one of them, and were taken away by the medics. "I had a bad concussion," he said, "and probably should have had some kind of medical attention, but I stayed on active duty, and as it turned out, I never saw that good friend of mine again. I heard that he had survived, but I never did see him. I was almost always in combat for the rest of the tour."

Just recently he attended the fiftieth reunion of his unit, and there was his old friend, the one he hadn't seen since he was badly wounded in Vietnam. "The years were written across his face," he remembered, "but as soon as he began to talk, it was as if the two of us were eighteen again. It turned out he lived in Portland, Maine, only a few hours away. I'd even been in Portland a couple of times over the years but never thought to look him up. He asked how my mother was doing. Apparently, I'd talked a lot about my mother. She'd died decades ago, but suddenly it was as if she were still here with us, and we were kids in Vietnam again. Later, when he went to get us some more drinks, his wife said that he talked about me all the time, retelling some of the stories I used to regale him with. I began to look around at the men in the room, and it's funny, but I had this feeling of immense pride. We had been through an awful experience over there in Vietnam, but here we were fifty years later, and we had lived good, productive lives. We had achieved something; held it together."

He was an unassuming guy but a born storyteller with the ability to capture the attention of anyone close enough to overhear him. I could imagine him in a tavern in 1789, talking about his experiences in the Revolution or his sighting of George Washington as he rode through Northborough in his carriage. An experience retold by someone like this Vietnam vet would have had a power on the order of Paul to the Galatians: the vehicle through which the New Word of the American Gospel was shared from person to person across a town, a state, and, ultimately, a nation.

Washington stopped for the night at Weston, where he stayed at John Flagg's tavern. He had covered forty-two miles, the longest day's travel of his New England tour. He had a strict schedule to meet the following day, a Saturday, and Weston placed him close enough to get to Cambridge by ten the next morning. In Weston he received another express from John Hancock. Although the governor was not happy that Washington had refused his invitation to stay with him ("it would have given me pleasure had a residence at my house met with your approbation," he groused), Hancock did hope the president might be able to have dinner with him. This time Washington accepted the invitation.

The parade flag of the Boston Cordwainers.

CHAPTER 7

Turf Wars

We couldn't find a place to stay in Weston, but we did find a hotel just nine miles away in Lexington, where, in Washington's words, "the first blood in the dispute with Great Britain was drawn." I had hoped to walk Dora on the town green but realized it was too crowded with people sunning themselves to let her off the leash. A few blocks away Melissa and I found a park with a trail and some woods and let Dora go. What we didn't realize was that there was a pond in the middle of the park. We soon found Dora churning up the surface of a stagnant, cattail-fringed mud puddle covered with green slime. By the time she returned to shore, the sludge had already started to congeal. Once back at the car we attacked her with an old beach towel and some bottled water, but the muck was caked on like brown cement. We needed a shower and some soap. But how were we going to get her into our hotel room in this condition?

The place turned out to be much classier than we'd expected—a hipster hotel with a lot of modern art and stainless steel and not a stick of wooden furniture. A concierge guarded the front door. The hotel advertised as pet friendly, but Melissa thought our best option was for me to take Dora around to the back of the building, where a glass door opened onto the hallway near the elevators. Once Melissa had delivered our bags to the room, she came down in the elevator and waved us in.

The room, of course, proved to be so unrelentingly white that you needed sunglasses. The coverlet on the king-sized bed looked like an untouched field of snow. Melissa immediately walked into the bathroom and started the shower, which wasn't easy given the inscrutable collection of knobs and dials. I had crouched down to pick up our filthy pet when Dora decided to bolt for the door. Soon she was out of the bathroom and on the bed, all jazzed up by my unsuccessful efforts to contain her. Ignoring our anguished cries, she danced back and forth across the coverlet, her bushy tail flinging scales of dried muck. Then she rolled over and started wiggling with a manic glee. I finally grabbed her by the collar and pulled her back into the bathroom. I ended up joining her in the shower (by then my clothes were so dirty that it was for the best), and after a couple of minutes we emerged, dripping but clean.

I found Melissa staring at the bed. The field of snow now looked like a used diaper. We left the next morning with our heads hanging low and a significant tip on the dresser.

Being on time was important to Washington, a preoccupation that had grown into an obsession during his eight years as commander of the Continental army. When his secretary Tobias Lear first started at Mount Vernon, he was "involved [in] tardiness on two occasions." The second time, Lear blamed his watch. Washington told him "to get a new one or he would have to get a new secretary." When the Middlesex militia said they would be ready at 10:00 a.m. on the Cambridge Green, they better be ready, especially because Washington was due in Boston just two hours later.

But, of course, they were late. "Most of the militia having a distance to come," Washington noted, "they were not in line till after eleven." This meant that Washington, who was now wearing his general's uniform with its gold epaulets, had to wait for more than an hour. Making the delay all the more annoying was the realization that Governor Hancock was not going to be attending the festivities. Lieutenant Governor Samuel Adams and the executive council of the legislature gave their apologies, but apparently the governor, who suffered from gout, was not feeling well. Because Hancock had not deigned to inform Washington beforehand (and had been well enough just the day before to invite the president to dinner), it was hard not to see the governor's absence as a snub.

This wasn't the first time Washington had been treated with apparent disdain by a governor of Massachusetts. Back in 1756, during the Seven Years' War, Washington, at twenty-four already a seasoned colonel in the provincial army of Virginia, journeyed to Boston in hopes of receiving a royal commission in the British army from Governor William Shirley. Shirley had recently become the commander in chief of the British forces in North America after the death of General Edward Braddock in western Pennsylvania. Much to Washington's disappointment, Shirley refused to grant the commission Braddock had promised him—a slight that inevitably contributed to Washington's willingness to lead the Continental army against the British king during the American Revolution. Now, thirty-three years after that first visit to Boston, Washington was once again encountering some unexpected animus from a Massachusetts governor.

The morning was gray and cold, and once Washington had reviewed the thousand or so militia assembled on the Cambridge green, he and his entourage, which now included His Rotundity, Vice President John Adams, crossed the Charles River to Roxbury. Before embarking on the tour of New England, Washington had invited Adams to join him. Adams and Washington were about as different as two people could be. Adams later admitted to Mercy Otis Warren (to whom

Martha had confided the difficulties of being the first lady) that he was "a morose philosopher and a surly politician" who had no interests beyond work and the pleasures of family and socializing with a few friends. He hated large public gatherings, dances, horse races—virtually anything the rest of the world judged as fun. I have nothing but sympathy for John Adams. I, for one, can't stand sitting on a beach—an activity (if you can call it that) to which many people devote their entire vacations. Adams, who kept his bedroom windows shut tight, took it a step further and would have been miserable spending a month touring New England with Washington. So he declined the president's invitation, a decision that might have had an enduring impact on the vice presidency, which Adams later described as "the most insignificant office that ever the invention of man contrived or his imagination conceived."

Boston at that time was an island of just over one square mile, connected to Roxbury by a thin sliver of land known as the Neck. Today Washington Street follows what was once the Neck. Because the waters that surrounded the city in 1789 have long since been filled in, it's difficult to envision what Washington would have seen as he approached Boston. On his left would have been the Back Bay—not a neighborhood, but an inlet dotted with sails and lined with small manufactories; on his right would have been the South Bay, now a T stop but then a wide body of water that opened into Boston Harbor, where the many ships were dressed with signal flags for the big day.

On our way into Boston on Washington Street, Melissa and I stopped at Peters Park, near the end of what would have been the Neck. Dora wasn't especially impressed. Instead of wood chips or dirt, their dog run was covered in pea stone, which apparently hurt Dora's tender, countrified paws. As a bevy of pit-bull mixes and French bulldogs cavorted around her on their calloused feet, Dora picked her way across the dog run as if the stones were burning coals. At one point, she stopped and looked at us with pleading eyes, and soon we were back in the car and headed into downtown Boston.

It was near here that Washington was once again forced to cool his heels. Several carriages had stopped ahead of him as officials representing the city and the state argued over protocol. Even though Hancock hadn't shown up, the governor insisted that it was his representatives' prerogative to formally welcome Washington to the city. The Boston selectmen thought otherwise, claiming that the governor should have met the president at the Massachusetts-Connecticut border and left it to the city's dignitaries to welcome Washington to Boston. Until the two sides figured it out, Washington, who was already an hour behind schedule, would have to wait.

The newspaper editor Benjamin Russell, who as a thirteen-year-old boy had watched the Battle of Bunker Hill from high ground nearby, was a member of one of the committees. "Both authorities remained in their carriages while the aides and marshals were rapidly posting between them," Russell remembered. "The president and his secretary had been mounted for a considerable time on the Neck, waiting to enter the town." Washington asked what the matter was. When informed of the contretemps, he "expressed impatience." Then he asked his secretary William Jackson, "Is there no other avenue to the town?" By that time Washington had begun to turn his horse around and start back to Roxbury. This seems to have persuaded the contending parties to settle the dispute. Washington was informed that "the controversy was over, and that he would be received by the municipal authorities." The selectmen (and Washington) had won.

The road into Boston from the Neck had been renamed Washington Street just the year before the president's arrival. The route would take him past the site of the famed Liberty Tree (chopped up for firewood by the British during the Siege of Boston); the Old South Meeting House, where a reputed five thousand people gathered in the hours before the Boston Tea Party back in 1773 (and which still stands today); and finally to the State House (known now as the Old State House), where the young architect Charles Bulfinch had designed a kind of presidential welcome center that included a triumphal arch and an elevated gallery from which Washington was to review the festivities once he'd marched into the city.

An extra six thousand people had jammed into Boston to see Washington, swelling the crowd to an estimated twenty-four thousand. While the men tended to congregate on the streets, the women, many of whom wore white sashes with "GW" emblazoned across them, enjoyed the view from above. According to Isaiah Thomas's *Massachusetts Spy*, "The windows of the houses from the entrance of Boston at the Neck to the State House . . . were filled with ladies; on some houses temporary galleries were erected and covered with carpeting, all filled . . . as were the tops of houses, balconies, etc.; in some houses opposite the State House, windows were let for a very good price. Hundreds of ladies took their seats in open air before 11 a.m. and never quitted them until after 4 p.m."

It was the biggest crowd Boston had seen since the days of the Great Awakening, when in 1740 the evangelist George Whitefield preached before an equally mammoth crowd on Boston Common— probably the largest gathering of people until that point in all of colonial North America. Whitefield, a charismatic Calvinist minister who routinely brought his listeners to tears, had launched a new era of spirituality throughout the colonies. Now it was George Washington's turn to travel the country, inciting by his mere presence, if not his words, a new political era in the history of the American people.

As church bells rang and cannons fired from Dorchester Heights and other fortified places around the city, Washington marched through a gauntlet of local dignitaries and tradesmen toward the State House. Closest to Washington were the city's schoolchildren, all with quill pens in their left hands. Ten-year-old William Sumner was there that day, and he, along with his classmates from the West Boston Writing School, "stood in the gutters in front of the long rows of men whose strength was required and exerted to protect them from the crowd on the sidewalks as the procession passed." Sumner remembered that "the general rode on a noble charger . . . , and as he rode, his head uncovered, he inclined his body first on one side and then on the other, without distinctly bowing, but so as to observe the multitude in the streets and the ladies in the windows and on the tops of the houses, who saluted him as he passed." Isaac Harris, the son of a mast maker, was also standing in the gutter at the edge of Washington Street. The boys had been instructed to wave their quill pens and doff their caps just as the president passed by. Harris and the boy next to him agreed to "stroke their pens across the president's boot" at the critical moment. "They did it successfully," he remembered, "and kept the pens as mementos."

Once Washington had marched through Bulfinch's arch at the State House, on which was written "To the man who unites all hearts" on one side and "To Columbia's favorite son" on the other, he made his way to the gallery. With his appearance on this richly carpeted balcony, what Washington described as "a vast concourse of people" erupted into three cheers. After that, a choir leaped from their seats and began singing a patriotic ode and the procession began. Over the course of the next hour, fifty different guilds, each with its silk flag flying, marched past Washington on the balcony beside the State House.

Today a museum is housed within the Old State House. I had an appointment with the curator, and as I mounted the steps of this ancient brick building, Melissa and Dora headed over to the nearby Boston Common. Up in the attic of the Old State House, which felt like a child's playhouse flanked by the office towers of downtown Boston, the museum's curator Sira Dooley Fairchild showed me their collection of flags from the 1789 parade. There were the flags held by the mast makers and tailors, but my favorite belonged to the cordwainers (or shoemakers). This old silk banner still had a pocket sewn into it for the flagpole and was decorated with three goats' heads. Why goats' heads? It turns out the word "cordwainer" is derived from the town of Córdoba, where Spanish Moors produced cordovan leather from the skin of the Musoli goat—hence the heads.

Sira told me about the costume historian associated with the museum who had researched the clothing worn by the founding fathers.

Sira said that it's evident from Washington's clothes that he not only was tall but had gigantic thighs from all the horse riding. Benjamin Franklin was surprisingly tall with broad shoulders from working the printing press in his youth. John Hancock was also tall, but with narrow shoulders and a very big butt, what you might expect from a deskbound merchant who suffered from gout. Speaking of gout, according to a local newspaper, Hancock spent the afternoon of Washington's joyful reception "cast upon a painful couch" in his mansion. I think Washington wasn't so sure.

After the celebration, once he'd retired to his quarters just a few blocks from the State House, Washington notified the governor that he would *not* be attending dinner at his house that afternoon. It was only "under a full persuasion that [Hancock] would have waited upon me so soon as I should have arrived" that Washington had accepted the invitation in the first place. With Hancock a no-show, he was not about to honor the governor with his presence. Only after Hancock had made the effort to visit him at his own quarters would Washington consider accepting a dinner invitation.

Hancock had taken a leading role in making sure Massachusetts ratified the Constitution. But it was one thing to be all for the Constitution and the creation of a strong executive branch and quite another to have to publicly acknowledge the preeminence of that executive, especially after he'd just spurned an invitation to stay at the governor's mansion on Beacon Hill. Under the previous system of government, the states had been where all the political power and prestige resided, and Hancock seems to have been reluctant to defer to the new president of the United States on his home turf of Boston. Washington resolved to make it unmistakably clear that a governor waited on the president no matter what the circumstances.

By that evening, Hancock realized he had badly miscalculated. Until then, no politician in Massachusetts had done a better job of connecting with the people. Whether it was hosting rum-fueled political rallies on Boston Common or pardoning the leaders of Shays's Rebellion (which had been led by poor farmers who couldn't pay their taxes), Hancock had the common touch. But Washington's popularity was beyond anything the Massachusetts governor could have imagined. The president, *The Salem Mercury* reported, "unites all hearts and all voices in his favor. . . . At his approach, party disappears—and everyone runs a race in endeavoring who shall be foremost in paying him the tribute of grateful respect." Even noted Anti-Federalists were now falling over themselves to honor the president. Another story told of the gentleman, "notorious for his opposition to the Federal Constitution," who was now "forward to show [his] respect to the first officer under it." When someone expressed amazement that an "Anti of his stamp" could suddenly undergo such a transformation, a local Federalist replied that "he conceived it to be a fulfillment of that text of scripture, *I came not to call the righteous, but sinners, to repentance*." By touring New England, Washington wasn't just learning from the American citizenry about what was happening in their towns and states; he was also instructing them in the reality of the new federal government. Washington greeted the people with a smile and a bow, but he was also asserting the authority of his office.

That evening, Hancock sent Lieutenant Governor Samuel Adams and several others to Washington's quarters "to express the governor's concern that he had not been in a condition to call upon me so soon as I came to town." Washington informed them "in explicit terms that I should not see the governor unless it was at my lodgings." The next day, a Sunday, Washington attended church in the morning. When he returned to his quarters, there was a letter waiting for him from Hancock: "The governor's best respects to the president if at home and at leisure, the governor will do himself the honor to pay his respects, in half an hour. This would have been done much sooner, had his health in any degree permitted. He now hazards everything as it respects his health, for the desirable purpose." An hour or so later, Hancock's carriage pulled up to Washington's door. "Two stalwart servants" carried in the governor, "his legs sheathed in red flannel." Hancock, Washington noted in his diary, "assured me that indisposition alone had prevented his doing it yesterday, and that he was still indisposed; but as it had been suggested that he expected to *receive* the visit from the President, which he knew was improper, he was resolved at all hazards to pay his compliments today." It was a humbling encounter for the governor, who had learned (as had several noteworthy British officers during the Revolution) that it didn't pay to mess with George Washington.

The next day, Washington, along with hundreds if not thousands of Bostonians, got sick. The same illness that had been working its way up the coast when Washington departed from New York (and had struck both Washy and Nelly, who Martha reported had "very bad colds") had followed him to Boston, where it became known as the Washington influenza. As I could testify from my experience at Penn Station, following Washington came with a physical cost.

Washington had hoped to visit Lexington Green but decided to stay home for most of the day. He did, however, find the strength to have tea with the properly chastened governor Hancock at his mansion on Beacon Hill. On Tuesday morning, Washington was feeling better and began the usual rounds. In addition to the factory visits, dinners, toasts, and speechifying, he attended a concert at the Stone Chapel (known today as King's Chapel). Because so many of the performers had come down with the Washington flu, the concert was considerably shorter than it might otherwise have been. At one point, Washington, seated in a pew near the pulpit, glanced back and saw a young Danish artist named Christian Gullager sketching him. Gullager later completed a painting based on his first glimpse of Washington, who looks at us probingly from the corners of his eyes. This is a very different Washington from the general of the Revolution. The presidency has already taken its toll. Instead of the tanned, round-cheeked dynamo of not even a decade earlier, this is an old man: withered and gaunt, or, as Senator William Maclay will describe him in a year's time, "pale, nay, almost cadaverous . . . his frame would seem to want filling up." And yet Washington's inner vitality is undeniable in the

Gullager portrait, boring into us from piercing, appraising eyes. This is *President* Washington—grumpily intent on seeing the thing through, even if it kills him.

He was scheduled to depart from Boston on Thursday, October 29, at 8:00 a.m., and sure enough the Old South clock was striking the hour as he stepped into his carriage. A company of cavalry, led by Major Caleb Gibbs, the former head of Washington's elite Life Guards during the war, had volunteered to escort him from Boston to Charlestown on the other side of the Charles River, but they were nowhere in sight. Seeing a chance to escape Boston without the usual cloud of dust, Washington ordered his entourage to head for the city's North End and the new bridge connecting Boston to Charlestown.

Ten minutes later, Major Gibbs and his men arrived at Washington's quarters to discover that he was gone. Off they charged in pursuit, and it was only because Washington stopped to inspect the new bridge that they finally caught up with him before he had left the city. "Major Gibbs," Washington said "with perfect good humor," "I thought you had been too long in my family not to know when it was eight o'clock."

It was while driving from Boston to Salem that I finally figured it out. Until this trip, I had always taken the highway, I-95, up the coast. To get to a town, I took the appropriate exit, then turned down a series of side streets to the town center. It was kind of like parachuting into the town—suddenly finding myself on Main Street without any sense of how the town was connected geographically to the communities around it.

By taking the old road up the coast—Route 1 or 1A, depending on where we were—we began to see how the towns fit together. These were not autonomous settlements; they were part of an organic whole as Route 1/1A invariably became each town's Main Street. The highway had turned these once proud little communities, each with its own company of militia, into commuting suburbs. But there was more to these towns than their ease of access to I-95 or the train line into Boston. By following Washington, we were retracing the ancient umbilical cord of colonial New England.

Even though it took him four miles out of his way, Washington made sure to visit Marblehead. He owed the town a lot. At the beginning of the war, during the Siege of Boston, Washington had chartered a schooner owned by Marblehead's John Glover and turned it into a privateer, marking, some have claimed, the beginning of the American navy. Soon after, Glover formed the Fourteenth Continental Regiment, comprising largely cod fishermen from Marblehead, six hundred of whom served in the war. These were the men who manned the vessels during Washington's nighttime retreat across the East River after the defeat at the Battle of Long Island. They were also the ones who had made possible the December 26 victory at Trenton by transporting Washington's small army across the icy Delaware River.

The war and the lagging cod fishery had been tough on Marblehead. "The houses are old—the streets dirty—and the common people not very clean," Washington observed. In a town of 5,000, there were 459 widows and 865 orphans. The written address Washington received from the selectmen of Marblehead, who apologized for not giving him a better welcome, was unusually somber. "The return of peace did not restore us the former advantages of the fishery," the selectmen wrote, "and we have yet patiently to expect that attention of the general government which may remedy these evils."

The finest home in Marblehead was owned by Martha Swett Lee, the widow of the shipowner Jeremiah Lee, who had caught his literal death of cold while hiding from British soldiers in a field in the early morning hours before Lexington and Concord. On the day of Washington's visit, Mrs. Lee, who could no longer afford the servants required to staff the mansion, did her best to show a brave face, pasting paper cutouts of eagles on the panes of the front windows, "silhouetted against the flames of welcoming candles." She even served the first of several "cold collations" Washington enjoyed during the tour—a light meal of cold meats, perhaps a salad, and some sweets.

In Salem, just two miles to the north, Washington received yet another enthusiastic welcome. But after the sadness and despair of Marblehead, he simply wasn't in the mood. "His appearance as he passed through Court Street in Salem was far from gay," a young woman recorded in a letter to a friend. "He looked oppressed by the attention that was paid him, and as he cast his eye around, I thought it seemed to sink at the notice he attracted. When he had got to the courthouse, and had patiently listened to the ditty they sung at him, and heard the shouts of the multitude, he bowed very low, and as if he could bear no more, turned hastily around and went in the house."

This young woman, known to us as only N. Fisher, makes the first recorded mention of the "you are nothing but a man" anecdote, then adds, "But he is a man and we feel proud of it. I for one should be sorry if he were another, unless indeed it were a woman." Assuming this letter isn't a nineteenth-century forgery, N. Fisher was one of America's first feminists.

In Ipswich, we had lunch at a fried clam shack called the Clam Box. I was sitting at a picnic table with Dora waiting for Melissa to get our order. Beside us was an elderly man, whose retiree-age daughter was also up at the counter. He looked longingly at Dora and said, "It's nice to have a dog waiting for you when you come home."

Instead of fried clams, Washington had yet another cold collation in Ipswich, a town then known for its pillow lace. The pillow refers to how the lace is made: needles are stuck into a small pillow according to a predetermined design while bobbins of thread are worked around the needles to create an intricately patterned lace. Before lace became mass-produced in the 1820s, pillow lace represented the pinnacle of fashion, with a yard of lace equal in value to a cord of wood or sixteen pounds of wool. When the men and boys of Ipswich were away fighting the Revolution, the town's women supported their families by making lace. At the time of Washington's visit, there were 600 lace makers in Ipswich, an incredible number in a town of only 601 households. Before leaving town, Washington purchased some black silk pillow lace for Martha, which she used to trim a cape that is still a part of the collections at Mount Vernon.

In our younger days, Melissa, the lawyer, was the breadwinner, and I, the struggling writer, stayed at home with the kids. I had become a father assuming there would be plenty of househusbands just like me, but such was not the case. As far as I could tell, I was the only guy on Nantucket in the late 1980s and the 1990s at home with his kids. I tried hanging out with the moms at the playground, but to be honest, it just felt weird. Then I began taking the kids to the island's library, the Nantucket Atheneum. In those days, before the building underwent an extensive renovation, the children's library was in the heavily mildewed basement, where my kids and I were typically the only patrons on a weekday afternoon in winter. The collection wasn't great—the librarian refused to purchase any books by Roald Dahl, judging them impious—but that smelly basement was, for me at least, a parental sanctuary in the bewitching hours before dinner.

I have, therefore, a special fondness for small-town libraries, and in Newburyport on the Merrimack River our pursuit of George Washington took us to the equivalent of Nantucket's Atheneum—the Newburyport Public Library. In 1789, the president lodged in a big brick building that in 1865 was turned into the town's library. ("Washington Slept Here—in the periodical section!") Giselle Stevens, the head librarian, showed me the Director's Room, where their most treasured possession is a Gilbert Stuart portrait of Washington that was actually painted, like many copies of the famous painting, by Stuart's daughter Jane, who was a talented artist in her own right. "It's our Jane portrait of Washington," Giselle said proudly.

The research center was down in the basement, where the archivist Sharon Spieldenner told me that John Adams's son John Quincy was in Newburyport at the time of Washington's visit, reading law under the famed local attorney Theophilus Parsons. Some people think Parsons penned the town's address to the president, but others attribute the letter to John Quincy; in any event, the son of the vice president was the one who read the address to Washington. Washington apparently liked what he heard and during his second term as president named the then twenty-seven-year-old Adams as his ambassador to the Netherlands.

During the half an hour I spent getting a tour of the Newburyport Library, I kept looking for someone such as I once was—a young father with his kids amid a pile of books. But, no, there wasn't a single male over fifteen years old in the entire place. Then, after I'd said my goodbyes to the staff at the circulation desk, I saw him coming through the front door: a grown-up Harry Potter look-alike with two daughters and a bag of books. On my way out I tried to catch his eye, but he was too busy helping his kids through the swinging glass door to notice the old guy in a baseball cap with the notebook in his hand, smiling at him.

As Melissa repeatedly pointed out, we had no legitimate reason to stop at Hampton, New Hampshire. When Washington passed through on his way to Portsmouth accompanied by seven hundred mounted militiamen and dignitaries, a small crowd was gathered at what is now the intersection of Winnacunnet Road and Route 1, but Washington just kept going. Melissa insisted that we should do the same—especially because it was already 3:00 p.m. and we needed to get to Portsmouth. But Hampton was where my nine-times-great-grandfather Thomas Philbrick had lived in the seventeenth century. It would be just a quick detour and we'd be back on our way to Portsmouth in no time.

We had been through this before. While researching my book *Mayflower* in England, I had insisted that we visit the village in East

Anglia where Thomas Philbrick had been born: Bures on the Essex-Suffolk border near the Stour River, the region made famous by the painter John Constable. It had happened to be a Sunday, and we even attended a service at St. Mary, the church where Thomas had been christened in 1584. (When I asked the minister if there were any Philbricks still around, he said, "A few, but they don't say much.") Even though I'd managed to drag Melissa to Bures, neither one of us had ever visited Hampton. We were always on the highway, going somewhere else. Washington, however, had gotten me closer to the town of my ancestors than I'd ever been, and I put on the blinker and turned right down Winnacunnet Road.

Even before we turned, I could see a wide tidal marsh on our right, which excited me. It looked very much like the landscape Thomas Philbrick had left behind in England. It also looked just like the Creeks on Nantucket—the tidal marsh a quarter mile from our house to which I've been drawn ever since we moved to the island. Was it some kind of ancestral memory? The original structure, a garrison house that Thomas Philbrick purchased from William Sanborn in 1647, had long since been replaced by a modest Victorian home. The original property had extended all the way down to the marsh behind it. After taking a few turns, we discovered that the town dump was now located between the house and the marsh and that on the far shore of the wetland was the dome of the Seabrook Nuclear Power Plant. A drive to the ocean introduced us to Hampton Beach, a boardwalk that was just beginning to gear up for the crowds of summer.

Having grown up a frustrated sailor in Pittsburgh, I used to listen longingly to stories of our family's nautical past. The first Thomas Philbrick had been a shipmaster, and according to the old genealogy on the bookshelf, "A natural affection for the sea appeared among his descendants for generations. The young men took to the water as young ducks take to the stream, and seemed never more happy than in their 'Home on the rolling wave.'" Inevitably, I began to assume that the seaside New Hampshire town where Thomas and his children settled must be a salty version of Brigadoon—a place where time stood still.

But, of course, no such place exists. Not even Sturbridge Village remains the same from year to year. But a landfill in the backyard and a nuclear power plant across the way? As we drove past the arcades, gift shops, and fried-food joints of Hampton Beach, I said to Melissa, "I guess my forefathers weren't exactly preservationists."

Advertisement.

ABSCONDED from the houshold of the President of the United States, ONEY JUDGE.
a light mulatto girl, much freckled, with very black
eyes and bushy black hair. She is of middle stature,
slender, and delicately formed, about 20 years of
age.

She has many changes of good clothes, of all sorts,
but they are not sufficiently recollected to be described—As there was no suspicion of her going off, nor
no provocation to do so, it is not easy to conjectu-
whither she has gone, or fully, what her design is;—
but as she may attempt to escape by water, all masters of vessels are cautioned against admitting her
into them, although it is probable she will attempt
to pass for a free woman, and has, it is said, where-
withal to pay her passage.

Ten dollars will be paid to any person who will
bring her home, if taken in the city, or on board any
vessel in the harbour;—and a reasonable additional
sum if apprehended at, and brought from a greater
distance, and in proportion to the distance.

FREDERICK KITT, Steward.

May 23   a1t

Advertisement for runaway Ona Judge.

CHAPTER 8

"A Child of God"

Even before Washington left Boston, his secretary Tobias Lear
had sprinted ahead to Portsmouth. According to the set itinerary, this town of five thousand on the south bank of the
Piscataqua River would mark the northernmost point of Washington's New England tour. Portsmouth was also the twenty-seven-year-
old secretary's birthplace. Of even more importance, it was the home
of Lear's childhood sweetheart and fiancée, Polly Long. Lear was
now a local celebrity, and it's easy to imagine him—chubby-cheeked,
with reddish-blond hair—dashing about town with cheerful self-
importance as he arranged the details of the presidential visit with
Governor John Sullivan (who had served with Washington in the war)
and Senator John Langdon (who had officially informed Washington
by letter of his having been elected president) and catching up with
his family, friends, and, of course, Polly.

Lear rejoined Washington's entourage just before it reached
Portsmouth, taking Washington's seat in the carriage as the president
mounted his white charger for the entrance into town. What followed
over the course of the next four days closely resembled what had

occurred in Boston: a parade (with the guilds arranged in almost the same alphabetical order), dinners, toasts, musical paeans, speeches, and balls (Washington noted that the women had "much blacker hair than are usually seen in the Southern States"), but without the drama of Washington's standoff with John Hancock.

At one point, Washington honored Lear's widowed mother with a visit. Lear had grown up in a humble house on Hunking Street. A huge crowd gathered outside the Lear home and watched through the windows of the front parlor as Washington chatted with Lear's mother and his sisters while bouncing Lear's three-year-old niece on his knee. A six-month-old nephew named George Washington Storer was also presented to the president. When told the little boy had been named for him, Washington is said to have placed his hand on the child's head and intoned, "May he be a better man than the one whose name he bears." (The sheer number of these "only a man" traditions, no matter how dubious, makes you think that Washington really was telling anybody who would listen that despite all the adulation he was by no means perfect. That did not prevent him, however, from making sure anyone with political power knew *he* was the boss.) Polly might have also attended the family gathering on Hunking Street. In less than a year the couple would be married, with Polly becoming a virtual lady-in-waiting to Martha as her husband went about his duties as Washington's private secretary.

On Monday, November 2, Washington went on a boat trip "to view the harbor of Portsmouth." According to *The Salem Mercury*, the morning was wonderfully serene, the water's surface ruffled only by the tide. Because the Piscataqua is one of the fastest-flowing rivers in North America (second only to the Columbia in the Pacific Northwest), with currents recorded as high as ten knots, the organizers must have coordinated the tour with the changing tide. Washington and Senator Langdon were in one barge, manned by oarsmen in white suits, while Lear and Jackson followed in another barge with oarsmen in blue suits. A third barge, filled with the same singers who had greeted Washington when he first arrived in town, provided a musical accompaniment. In addition to examining the rocky convolutions of this island-riddled harbor, they ventured out as far as today's 2-KR buoy and fished for cod. When Washington failed to get a nibble, a fisherman in a nearby boat handed him a line with a cod already on it. According to the tale, the grateful Washington thanked the fisherman with a silver dollar. (As one spoilsport historian has pointed out, the silver dollar wasn't minted until 1794.) In any event, Washington got his fish, and we can only assume the fisherman was compensated for his diplomatic gesture.

Earlier in the harbor tour, Washington landed briefly on the opposite shore from Portsmouth at Kittery Point. There he tied up to "the old stone dock" originally built by the wealthy merchant William Pepperrell. In 1745 during King George's War, Pepperrell financed and led the expedition that captured the French Fortress of Louisbourg on Cape Breton. In appreciation for this impressive feat, the British king awarded Pepperrell a baronetcy, making him the first colonial to gain such a distinction. By 1789, Pepperrell had died, his loyalist son had fled to England, and most of the family property had been confiscated by the American government. Only Pepperrell's eighty-one-year-old widow, Mary, remained in Kittery, where she lived in poverty in her Georgian house across from the Congregational church. Although Washington didn't visit Lady Pepperrell (who is supposed to have refused to see the president), he did meet with the church's minister, Benjamin Stevens.

So it was Kittery in what is now Maine—not Portsmouth—that marked the northernmost point of Washington's tour. Melissa and I had visited Portsmouth plenty of times, but we had never been to this little town on the other side of the river and decided to see if we could find a place to stay in Kittery Point.

Melissa started investigating, and there it was on the screen of her phone: "the Red Cottage," circa 1740, on a knoll overlooking Portsmouth Harbor and listed on Vrbo. It was almost too good to be true, especially when I started reading paragraph 5 of the property description: "On November 2nd, 1789, George Washington came ashore on the stone pier in front of the cottage to attend the Congregational church at the head of the lane." Melissa contacted the owner, Jim Austin, by email, letting him know we were following George Washington and were especially interested in his stop at Kittery Point. Jim emailed us right back. The cottage wasn't available, but he would be delighted to meet with us. And get this: his four-times-great-uncle was Tobias Lear.

Jim lived in a house on the same three-and-a-half-acre property as the Red Cottage. The oversized windows of Jim's living room had 180-degree views of the harbor, with Portsmouth seemingly just a stone's throw away. It was around lunchtime, and we'd offered to take Jim to a restaurant, but he said he'd prefer to talk with us at his place. "We can eat my fish chowder and whelks." It sounded good to us.

Jim explained that he lives in a "genealogical vortex." In addition to Tobias Lear, he is related to the American naval hero Stephen Decatur, who fought in various engagements against the Barbary pirates before the War of 1812. In the 1920s, Jim's grandfather Stephen Decatur Jr. was rummaging through a chest of family papers kept in an old drafty barn just behind the current location of the Red Cottage. "The chest had not been opened for nearly eighty years," Decatur recounted, "and the existence of these extraordinarily interesting records had been forgotten." What he found was the ledger kept by Tobias Lear when he served as Washington's private secretary. The large red-leather book, filled with daily transactions, from the purchase of theater tickets to that leopard-skin saddle pad, provided a remarkably detailed window into Washington's household during his first term as president. Drawing upon this and other Washington-related documents that had come into Lear's possession after the president's death and had never before seen the light of day, Decatur compiled *Private Affairs of George Washington: From the Records and Accounts of Tobias Lear, Esquire, His Secretary*. The book had been a huge help to me, and now to be talking to Jim in sight of the same structure where these documents had been discovered was truly amazing.

Jim told of the time in the 1950s when his grandmother and her two brothers took the chest from the barn and spread its contents across the porch of the family house. Jim was just ten years old. "There was all this amazing stuff," he remembered, "and they divided it among the three of them." Included in the trove were letters written by George and Martha and what seems to have been Washington's personal map of the Siege of Yorktown.

But how had these documents ended up in the possession of Tobias Lear? Lear wasn't descended from Washington, but by the time of the president's death he had become a member of the family. After the death of Lear's Portsmouth-born wife, Polly, in the yellow fever epidemic of 1793, Lear married Frances "Fanny" Bassett Washington, the widow of the president's nephew and Martha's niece. When Fanny died a year later of tuberculosis (the same disease that killed her first husband), Lear married Frances Dandridge Henley, yet another niece of Martha's. It is not surprising, then, that Lear, who was tasked with assembling Washington's papers after his death, ended up with a portion of the correspondence. Somehow this made George and Martha more *human* to me. They were people whose words had been read and treasured by their loved ones and eventually stuffed into a trunk, only to be discovered years later in a barn in Maine.

Once we'd finished our bowls of chowder and eaten our fill of whelks (a variety of sea snail) dipped in mayonnaise, Jim took us outside to see the stone dock onto which Washington stepped in November 1789. The horizontal slabs of granite were now contained within the pilings of a modern pier with a ramp leading down to a floating dock that could accommodate the nine-foot rise and fall of the tide. And there, up on the hill to the left, was the Red Cottage, modernized and expanded to accommodate as many as fourteen people.

Jim followed us to our car, where we introduced him to Dora. He reached through the open window and scratched the top of Dora's head and told of how as a child he used to spend summers on this point with his grandmother. She'd been born in 1890 and was steeped in family lore. She spoke of the time when the Civil War hero Admiral

Farragut slipped on a rock and broke his nose during a visit to the Red Cottage. When Jim, a smart-alecky teenager, claimed that Farragut must have been drunk, she was outraged. He smiled and looked out at the harbor. "She and her friends used to talk for hours about the old days," he said, "and I drank it in like osmosis."

In the evening in Portsmouth we had a drink on the sun-drenched porch of Jeff and Molly Bolster. Jeff was a history professor and the author of *Black Jacks: African American Seamen in the Age of Sail*, a book that had a big impact on me when I was researching maritime life on Nantucket; he'd also written a review of *In the Heart of the Sea* in *The New York Times* that meant a great deal to me given Jeff's immense knowledge both as a sailor and as a historian. Molly was the director of the Gundalow Company, a nonprofit that built and now operates a sixty-five-foot reproduction of a gundalow—big, barge-like vessels indigenous to the Portsmouth region that had transported freight up and down the Piscataqua River. I desperately wanted to get out on the gundalow; not only was it equipped with a sail, but it had the same lateen rig as my old Sunfish. Unfortunately, the gundalow was booked the next morning, and as usual we needed to move on.

We soon learned that like Melissa both Jeff and Molly had just retired. Jeff had even gone to the lengths of throwing out the notes and drafts of *Black Jacks*. (I couldn't imagine it just yet, tossing all that typed and scribbled-over paper, which represented years of work, into a dumpster.) For the Bolsters, an era had ended and a new era lay ahead. They owned an oceangoing sloop called *Chanticleer* and planned to sail to the Caribbean and take it from there. As I'm writing this, they've ventured through the Panama Canal and just arrived in New Zealand, inciting, I must admit, a considerable amount of envy on my part.

That evening in Portsmouth, Jeff took me on a tour of his yard, which happened to abut that of Tobias Lear's boyhood home. I was talking about Washington's visit to the house when Jeff pointed to a small hump of land in the corner of the Lear property. "Doesn't that look like the perfect place for an outhouse?" he asked. "Sure does," I said. Jeff smiled. "George Washington pissed there!"

Once we'd returned to the porch, Jeff talked of Portsmouth's connection to a very different kind of Washington legacy. In the spring of 1796, six and a half years after Washington's triumphant visit to the city, a twenty-year-old escaped enslaved woman named Ona Judge arrived in Portsmouth. By that time the country's capital had moved from New York to Philadelphia, and Ona had just arrived on the sloop *Nancy* from that city.

Ona, it turned out, had been First Lady Martha Washington's personal servant. Martha was planning to present Ona to her temperamental granddaughter Eliza as a wedding present, and Ona, who knew Eliza all too well, wanted no part of it. With help from the free Black community in Philadelphia, she made her escape. Martha was angered and hurt, and Washington, who was nearing the end of his second term as president, took up his wife's cause with a vengeance.

Almost immediately, ads were placed in the Philadelphia papers, describing the runaway as "a light mulatto girl, much freckled, with very black eyes, and bushy black hair . . . of middle stature, but slender, and delicately made." The Washingtons were convinced that "a Frenchman" had lured Ona away from them. But such was not the case. Ona simply wanted to be free.

Even though Washington had long been contemplating the emancipation of his enslaved workers at Mount Vernon, he resolved to do everything possible to get Ona back. Ona was the property not of Washington but of the estate of Martha's deceased husband and was therefore known as a dower slave, meaning that technically he couldn't free her even if he wanted to. Upon Martha's death, Ona and the other dower slaves would go to Martha's grandchildren. As Washy's and Nelly's guardian, Washington was legally bound to look after their financial interests, and he went after Ona with all of the remorseless zeal that had characterized his pursuit of Lord Cornwallis at Yorktown.

He was first alerted of Ona's whereabouts by Senator John Langdon, whose daughter, a frequent guest of the Washingtons' at the presidential mansion in Philadelphia, recognized her on the streets of Portsmouth. Although Langdon was not willing to help hunt down a woman who had successfully escaped to freedom, that did not stop him from notifying Washington of Ona's presence in the city.

What Washington did next not only is morally repugnant but involved a heinous abuse of presidential power. He requested that the Treasury Department contact the Portsmouth collector of customs, Joseph Whipple, and ask for his assistance in retrieving Ona Judge. But instead of seizing Ona, Whipple chose to interview her. He learned that "she had not been decoyed away . . . but that a thirst for complete freedom . . . had been her motive for absconding." According to Whipple, she was willing to return to Mount Vernon if she was guaranteed her freedom on Washington's and Martha's decease. Washington rejected the offer, insisting that "it would neither be politic or just to reward unfaithfulness with a premature preference." What mattered most to Washington was not that Ona was the victim of a brutal and inhuman system of bondage but that she had been disloyal to his wife. "For however well-disposed I might be to a gradual abolition or even to an entire emancipation [of the enslaved]," Washington explained to Whipple, he could not extend the promise of freedom to Ona without being unfair to his other enslaved house servants "who by their steady attachments are far more deserving than herself of favor."

We have come to the cold pocket of horror within George Washington. This is the Washington who was capable of punishing an enslaved worker who repeatedly attempted to escape by selling him to the sugar plantations of the Caribbean. This is the Washington who in the days before leaving for the Constitutional Convention had an enslaved house servant whipped for repeatedly walking across the freshly planted lawn in front of Mount Vernon. This is the horror that must temper any acknowledgment of George Washington's central role in the formation of the United States.

A few months later, Ona married an African American seaman named Jack Staines. When they were refused a marriage certificate in Portsmouth, I am happy to report that they were granted one by the county clerk in the nearby town of Greenland, New Hampshire, named Thomas Philbrook (a variant of Philbrick).

Three years after the failed negotiation with Whipple, Washington sent Martha's nephew Burwell Bassett, a state senator from Virginia, to Portsmouth to try to reclaim Ona a second time. Bassett stayed at the home of Senator Langdon, and when Langdon learned that after an unsuccessful attempt to persuade Ona to return to Mount Vernon voluntarily Bassett planned to use force, someone in the Langdon household (possibly one of his African American servants) alerted Ona, who fled to a friend's house before Bassett returned a second time. "You've got to hand it to the citizens of Portsmouth," Jeff told me. "No one was willing to do Washington's dirty work."

Two months after Ona successfully eluded Bassett, on December 14, 1799, Washington died after a brief illness. As stipulated by his will, all his slaves (but not Martha's dower slaves) were eventually freed. How to reconcile this final act of emancipation with Washington's pursuit of Ona until the day he died? Washington knew that slavery was wrong and immoral and wished to communicate that message through his will. And yet his intimate connections to the institution—through his marriage, his grandchildren, his position in Virginia society, and his financial bottom line—prevented him from recognizing the cruelty and injustice of pursuing a twenty-year-old woman who had dared to pursue her own freedom rather than wait around to see if the president and his family would someday grant it to her.

Ona had a difficult life. Her husband, Jack, died less than seven years after their marriage, leaving her with three children to raise. Ona was forced to move in with another family, while her two daughters,

Eliza and Nancy, were hired out as indentured servants and her son, Will, was apprenticed as a sailor. Ona outlived both her daughters; what happened to Will is unknown. In 1845, by which time Ona was approaching eighty, she was interviewed by an abolitionist minister. Was she sorry, he asked, that she had left the Washingtons "as she has labored so much harder since"? "No," Ona replied, "I am free, and have, I trust, been made a child of God by the means."

Site of the Amos Wyman House, Billerica, Massachusetts.

CHAPTER 9

The Middle Road Home

Washington had thought about continuing his tour into Vermont, but early snow in the north and pressing business back in New York (a hoped-for treaty with the Creek Indians in Georgia had not gone as planned) required that he return as soon as possible. He took a different route back, avoiding Boston altogether and taking the Middle Post Road through northeastern Connecticut to Hartford. It was a shorter, more direct route than the one he had taken north, but that didn't prevent him from getting lost. "The roads . . . are amazingly crooked to suit the convenience of every man's field," Washington complained, "and the directions you receive from the people equally blind and ignorant."

Now that he was attempting to cover as much distance as possible each day, Washington reverted to the travel regime he'd established even before the Revolutionary War. Every morning he was on the road bright and early—sometimes before dawn—traveling as many as ten miles before stopping for breakfast at a tavern. Two more stops followed—the first to feed or "bait" the horses, the second to feed the humans before the final push to a tavern around nightfall. By the end of the day, he'd covered between forty and forty-five miles without unnecessarily tiring the horses.

There seems to have been no attempt to publicize Washington's return route, and many towns were caught almost completely unawares by the sudden appearance of the president. In Milford, Massachusetts, the Congregational minister was in his barnyard, "getting out the manure," when one of the men working beside him cried out, "There is General Washington!" The minister's seven-year-old son, Elias, looked up and "saw two Black servants on horseback—one behind the carriage," cruising past the common before coming to a halt at the town's tavern. The minister dropped his shovel and hightailed it to his house, where he shaved and changed his clothes "in a hurry" before heading to the tavern "to see General Washington." To Elias's everlasting regret, his father "did not think to take me with him, and I never saw Washington."

Melissa, Dora, and I didn't begin retracing Washington's return route through New England until the following winter, heading out from Portsmouth on the morning of February 14, Valentine's Day. After stops at Exeter, New Hampshire (where Washington enjoyed yet another cold collation); Haverhill, Massachusetts (now an old mill town, but in 1789 the most "beautiful" place Washington had so far seen); and Andover (where, like Washington, we toured Phillips Academy, founded in 1778), we pulled into a Homewood Suites in Billerica.

Billerica was where we first encountered the "Washington elm" phenomenon. Yes, there was the Washington elm in Cambridge, but that had to do with the Revolution. Beginning in Billerica, just about every town on the way to Hartford had a marker memorializing the huge elm tree under which Washington stopped to rest and refresh himself beneath the welcoming shade. There are several problems with these traditions. The first is that it was November when Washington passed through these towns. All the deciduous trees, elms included, had lost their leaves by then, and besides it was *cold*; who needed shade? The second problem is that Washington was in a hurry. Unless he had some kind of elm fetish, there's no way he paused at each one of these trees to wipe his brow and ponder the beauty of the surrounding town. The third problem is that the trees, which were large and leafy in the late nineteenth century, were mere seedlings back in 1789. Washington probably didn't even notice these spindly little saplings as he roared past in a cloud of dust. So please, Billerica, Wellesley, Holliston, and any other towns I've missed, please reconsider all your claims about the Washington elm.

As I said before, it was Valentine's Day when Melissa and I arrived in Billerica. I tried as best I could to find a nice romantic restaurant for that special evening, but they were all booked. That left a nearby industrial-sized beer pub, the Tilted Kilt—think Hooters but in plaid. So there we were amid the television screens and throbbing rock music, trying to stare dreamily into each other's eyes as women in short, tight-fitting kilts served us burgers and beer. We have George Washington to thank for a Valentine's Day neither one of us will ever forget.

It was bitterly cold the next morning when we headed out to walk Dora in a snow-covered patch of forest behind the hotel. It was probably the most unspectacular section of woods we'd ever ventured into, but it contained something special: a cellar hole beside a rock with a polished marble plaque. This was where the Amos Wyman House had once stood. Here, between two parking lots, was where Samuel Adams and John Hancock hid from British soldiers during the day and night of the Lexington and Concord battles before they headed to Philadelphia for the Second Continental Congress. It just goes to show that history lurks in the most unlikely places.

Although we'd visited Lexington before, we hadn't made it to the Munroe Tavern, where Washington stopped to have his mid-afternoon meal after starting his day in Haverhill on the Merrimack River. Everything the president touched, sat on, or even looked at while at the Munroe Tavern (including the metal loop to which he hitched his horse) has been saved like pieces of the true cross. There is also a letter written by the young Sarah Munroe describing the president's visit. It's an absolutely terrific document—full of sharp observations and very well written. Unfortunately, it's a fake. In 1889, during a centennial celebration of Washington's visit, James Phinney Munroe, great-grandson of the owner of the tavern, read this letter before a large gathering in Lexington. What he failed to reveal was that *he*, not Sarah, had penned the letter. Munroe later claimed that it "seemed then so innocent a deception." But that did not prevent several Boston newspapers from reprinting the letter as fact. In response to the resulting confusion, Phinney published a retraction of sorts, and yet the letter continues to deceive unwitting researchers to this day. As we shall see, this is by no means the only time Washington's tour of America has inspired someone in the nineteenth century to create his or her own version of what it must have been like when the president came to town.

Just as the maps app on Melissa's phone announced, "Welcome to Connecticut," we saw them: four men in a nondescript car parked along the side of the road. Even before we pulled up behind the car, they were walking toward us: Joe Iamartino, Mark Snay, Tom Chase, and Stan Swanson, all members of the Thompson Historical Society. They were here to show us the cellar hole of the Golden Ball Tavern and the remains of the old tollgate. As we walked down the narrow road without a car in sight, Melissa and I marveled at how *rural* this section of southern New England was. We were only an hour or so from Boston, Providence, and Worcester but were surrounded by a forest so dense that it was worthy of the northern reaches of Maine. Joe explained that we had just entered the sparsely settled Quiet Corner of Connecticut, otherwise known as the Last Green Valley, and that the road we were now walking down had only recently been paved.

When Washington passed through here, a twelve-year-old boy named Independence Whipple was standing on the side of the road near his family's house. Independence lived to ninety-six, and the vision of Washington's entourage clattering down the road had been permanently imprinted in his brain. First to pass by was "a gentleman in uniform on a beautiful dapple horse," followed by two aides, also on dapple gray horses. Four bay horses "with two negro boys as riders" pulled the carriage, followed by the baggage wagon. When the carriage came opposite him, Whipple "saw a military gentleman" looking toward him. Assuming the man in the carriage was someone special, the boy took off his hat and bowed. Later he learned that it had been President Washington "on his return home from his northern trip."

Soon we were back in the car and following the members of the Thompson Historical Society into town. On our way we passed a cemetery overflowing with Harley-Davidson motorcycles and pickup trucks. Tattooed men in their fifties and sixties with bandannas around their necks stood on each side of the road directing traffic. We could see a crowd of similarly dressed mourners gathered around a grave. Mark later explained this was the funeral of a local biker: the brotherhood of the Harley was burying one of its own.

As a Mason and a member of the Society of the Cincinnati, Washington knew about brotherhood. By the time of the New England tour, he had stopped shaking people's hands, but he made an exception for Revolutionary War veterans. In Haverhill, a former member of his Life Guards named Bart Pecker forced his way through the crowd and cried out, "General, how do you do?" Washington instantly recognized the voice and responded, "Bart, is that you?" and grabbed Pecker's hand. Washington could tell the years had not been kind to the old soldier and handed him a gold piece. In Newburyport, it had been a down-on-his-luck veteran of the Seven Years' War known as Colonel Cotton who seized Washington's hand. The two hadn't seen each other in thirty years, and in this instance Washington gave the veteran a guinea. Cotton subsequently "made a hole through the guinea and wore it round his neck till poverty obliged him to part with it."

In 1974, when Melissa and I first met as sailing instructors on Cape Cod (Melissa was a townie, and I was a summer kid), the radio was full of ads for Sunday stock car races—"Sunday! Sunday!" If memory serves me right, the ad was for a track in Epping, New Hampshire, but it could have just as easily been for the Thompson Speedway, the first asphalt-paved oval racetrack in North America. Now known as the Thompson Speedway Motorsports Park, the racetrack happens to be right across the street from where Washington stopped to get breakfast at the Jacobs tavern.

Mark had determined that the tavern burned down in 1918 at what is now the third tee of a golf course. (I can see the plaque now: "Washington teed off here.") Once Washington had finished his meal, he was walking back to the carriage when the coachman began to drive away without him. Instead of telling the coachman to stop, Washington started running. The president was "so fleet of foot that he . . . overtook the fast-flying horses, and when on the step of the coach waved his hand in farewell to his host." Washington was enjoying this dash through the wilds of Connecticut.

And then it all came to a depressing halt when he pulled into Ashford, Connecticut, on a Saturday evening. "It being contrary to law and disagreeable to the people of this state . . . to travel on the Sabbath day," Washington was forced to spend two nights at the Perkins tavern—"not a good one," he recorded in his diary. With nothing else to do, he attended both the morning and the evening services at the Congregational Meetinghouse and "heard very lame discourses from a Mr. Pond."

Two days later, at a tavern in Milford, Connecticut, Washington reached the point that he couldn't take it anymore. As Tobias Lear wrote to Senator Langdon, the accommodations during their return trip—particularly as they worked their way from Boston to Hartford—had been "very indifferent." The beds had been lumpy and the food unappealing. In two cases—in Brookfield on their way north and in Uxbridge on their way south—they had even suffered the indignity of being denied accommodations, forcing them to search for an alternative with darkness coming on. Washington was trying to do the right symbolic thing by staying in these small-town taverns, but that didn't mean he was enjoying it. When you consider that Washington had been on the road now for almost a month in an open carriage in late October and early November, perhaps we can begin to understand why he had a tantrum worthy of a pampered rock star when he stopped for breakfast at the tavern in Milford.

The only food available were some crackers and a bowl of milk. Even worse, Washington was given a broken pewter spoon with which to eat. This seems to have been the proverbial last straw. He asked the proprietor if he might have a functioning *silver* spoon. The proprietor said he couldn't afford anything as fancy as a silver spoon. Right next to the tavern was a church, and Washington asked the young serving girl if she could go to the parsonage to see if they might have a silver spoon he could borrow. Sure enough, the girl returned with the desired utensil, and Washington tipped her a guinea.

On Friday, November 13, after almost exactly a month on the road, Washington's carriage arrived at his presidential residence in New York, "where," he reported with satisfaction, "I found Mrs. Washington and the rest of the family all well." He had visited sixty cities and villages. He was in excellent health. And as Martha reported to her friend Mercy Otis Warren, "All his sensibility has been awakened in receiving such repeated and unequivocal proofs of sincere regards from all his countrymen."

Washington had to be feeling good about the prospects ahead. While he'd been touring New England, his secretary of the Treasury, Alexander Hamilton, had been busy preparing a taxation plan designed to put the country on solid economic footing for the first time since the outbreak of the Revolution. Washington soon learned that Thomas Jefferson had agreed to serve as his secretary of state, meaning that he now had two of the brightest political minds of the age serving in his administration. It remained to be seen, however, whether Hamilton and Jefferson were capable of working together.

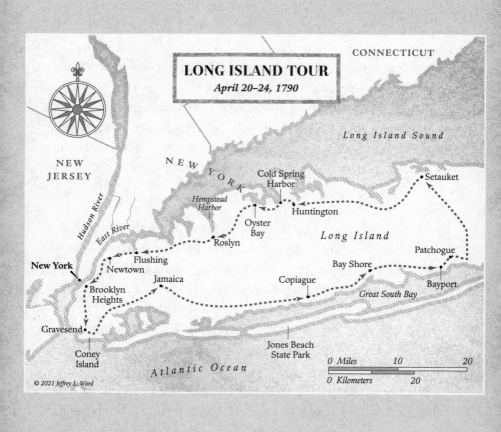

Part III

◇

INTO THE STORM

Espionage during the Revolutionary War.

CHAPTER 10

The Spies of Long Island

It's hard to remain anonymous when you're the president. Just ask Harry and Bess Truman. No matter how under the radar they tried to keep it during their drive across the country in 1953, someone always seemed to alert the press and blow their cover. And yet, for four days in April 1790, during a tour of western Long Island, George Washington somehow succeeded in keeping a remarkably low profile. There is absolutely no mention of this particular presidential tour in the newspapers of the day. And that might have been just the way Washington intended it. Because this excursion wasn't about generating support for his administration and its policies. This trip was about a debt Washington owed to a handful of people who had made it possible to win the Revolutionary War.

The British army occupied New York City and all of Long Island for most of the conflict. Washington, stationed about fifty miles up the Hudson River in the vicinity of West Point, was desperate for information about the enemy's intentions. With the help of Benjamin Tallmadge, a young officer with ties to a little town on the north shore of Long Island called Setauket, Washington created what historians have come to call the Culper (a code name derived from Culpeper County, Virginia, where Washington worked as a surveyor in his youth) Spy Ring. Through a series of couriers and informants (with code names like Samuel Culper and Culper junior), messages written in invisible ink or in code were carried from Manhattan to Setauket (a trip of about sixty miles), where they were taken by boat across Long Island Sound to Fairfield, Connecticut, and ultimately to Washington's headquarters on the Hudson.

Other than his spy chief, Benjamin Tallmadge, Washington was probably the only person in the United States who knew the identities of everyone involved in the Culper Spy Ring. In the spring of 1790, these unheralded saviors of the Republic continued to live in obscurity in this remote portion of Long Island; not even their own families knew about their activities during the war. And that's how it would remain for the spies' lifetimes. If this experiment in republican government known as the United States should fail and America once again became a possession of Great Britain, it would be extremely dangerous if a person's role as a spy came to light. It was therefore imperative that the spies' identities remain a secret. (Not until 1939, with the publication of Morton Pennypacker's *General Washington's Spies on Long Island and in New York*, were the spies' identities revealed for the first time.) Washington couldn't thank them publicly, but that didn't prevent him from going out there and seeing for himself the people who had quietly and at great personal risk helped win the war.

And besides, he needed a change of scene. It was now five months since his return from his New England tour. The honeymoon he'd enjoyed during the first nine months of his presidency was over. In February, Alexander Hamilton had put forward his ambitious new economic plan. The cornerstone of his proposal was called assumption, a plan by which the federal government would assume each state's debt from the war—a necessary move if the country's purse strings were to be transferred from the states to the federal government. The New England states, which had huge outstanding debts, thought this was a great idea. Not so the South, particularly Virginia, which had already paid down a considerable portion of its debt. Southerners also objected to Hamilton's decision to redeem at full value the wartime promissory notes issued to army officers. Although Washington had urged his officers to hold on to these notes, most of the soldiers, desperate for cash, had sold the notes to speculators for only a fraction of their face value. Hamilton's plan would give these speculators, many of them from the North, a huge financial windfall while leaving the men for whom the money was originally intended with nothing. In the end, however, a debt was a debt, and the Treasury secretary had no choice but to fulfill the country's fiduciary obligations.

Hamilton had assumed that one of his collaborators on *The Federalist Papers*, James Madison, would support him on these controversial proposals. During the Constitutional Convention three years earlier, the two had even discussed the necessity of assumption. But now, as a congressman from Virginia, Madison decided to side with his state's interests rather than the economic needs of the federal government, and he denounced the plan. It was the beginning of the political divide that would soon consume the country as rancor and partisanship quickly rose to the fore in the House and the Senate.

Adding to the acrimony were attempts by the Quaker abolitionist Warner Mifflin and others to introduce legislation that would end the slave trade and initiate the gradual abolition of slavery, despite the Constitution's provision that no laws could be passed against the foreign slave trade for at least twenty years. On March 16, Washington met with Mifflin about the proposed legislation. This was Washington's opportunity to let his personal views on slavery be known, but he remained mum. Instead of using his office to champion a legislative proposal, as he had done with the Bill of Rights in the fall, he sidestepped the issue altogether. Once again Washington decided that to tackle slavery at this early stage in the Republic's development would foment the crisis that might break the Union apart. He might have been right in his assessment, but by ducking the Quaker call for abolition, Washington had made it easier for future generations of

Americans—both in the North and in the South—to turn a blind eye to the evils of slavery.

The divisiveness in Congress also applied to the question of where the country's permanent capital should be located. Northerners wanted it to remain in New York. Those in the Middle Atlantic region preferred Philadelphia, and southerners wanted it on the Potomac River. In this instance, Washington, who otherwise found himself in the northern political camp, sided with the South. Ever since his retirement from the Continental army in 1783, he'd been championing the Potomac as the waterway that should connect the nation to its future in the West. In 1785, he'd help form the Potomac Company—an enterprise dedicated to improving navigation on the river. He proceeded to broker a series of meetings—first between representatives from the states of Virginia and Maryland (which shared the Potomac as a border), then with representatives from additional states—that culminated in 1787 in the Constitutional Convention. It was perhaps inevitable that Washington's belief in the Potomac, along with his equally fervent support of Hamilton's economic policies, would lead to the legislative compromise that ultimately allowed the nation to move forward. But that was yet to come.

For now it was all contention and enmity, and into this increasingly polarized political scene stepped Thomas Jefferson, who began his duties as secretary of state on March 22. Compared with Hamilton—who was tightly wound with the brusque, purposeful manner of a former army officer—Jefferson, fresh from the salons of Paris, seemed in no particular hurry. "He sits in a lounging manner," William Maclay observed, "on one hip commonly, and with one of his shoulders elevated much above the other. . . . [H]is whole figure has a loose, shackling air." Jefferson was taking it all in.

Soon after Jefferson's arrival, Washington was hit by another bout of illness—"a slow fever" that left him even more emaciated than he'd been since the previous summer's health scare. Not until the middle of April had he begun to improve. There was much to do in

New York, but Washington needed to get his health back on track. What he needed was a road trip.

On Tuesday, April 20, 1790, after a day of rain, he crossed the East River to Brooklyn Heights, where his carriage and baggage wagon were waiting for him. Soon he was headed east along the southern edge of Long Island. "The road," he recorded in his diary, "kept within sight of the sea, but the weather was so dull and at times rainy that we lost much of the pleasures of the ride." Better times were ahead.

We crossed the East River on the Brooklyn Bridge, then took Flatbush Avenue to Gravesend. In 1790, Gravesend was a town on a dirt road with newly plowed fields of oats, corn, and wheat on either side. Washington noted that the farmers fertilized their crops with horse manure collected from the streets of New York City and that post-and-rail fences divided up the fields. Today, Gravesend is a neighborhood of Brooklyn, and instead of fields and fences, storefronts and apartment buildings lined each side of the street as above us the elevated subway tracks periodically thundered with passing trains.

We took a slight detour to Coney Island. Because it was a Monday morning in late January, parking wasn't an issue, and Dora exploded onto the empty beach, running at top speed until she was a distant speck on the gray horizon before turning around and joining us once again, her fur salty and wet, her tongue lolling, and her tail wagging. After a night in a Manhattan hotel and a morning in the car, she was so happy to be running on the edge of the sea that it made both of us smile just to be in her presence on this wind-whipped urban beach.

For the next hour and a half we slogged our way east and south through an unceasing snarl of traffic. We weren't having much fun, unlike Washington, who had awoken the next morning to a beautiful spring day. By the time he stopped at Zebulon Ketcham's tavern in Copiague for something to eat, he was feeling downright giddy. "As people collected around the inn and were desirous to have a sight of him," a local historian relates, "Washington good naturedly took two or three turns on the stoop with his hat off, and then went in." Imagine it: the president twirling like a fashion model on the stoop of a tavern on Long Island. Washington wanted to avoid all ceremony and military display during this tour, but that didn't prevent him from enjoying the attention his unexpected appearance inevitably drew.

Soon after leaving Ketcham's tavern, Washington stopped to watch the Quaker Jonah Willets plowing his field behind a team of oxen. A member of the presidential party, perhaps William Jackson, told the farmer that the man in the carriage was George Washington. The farmer was decidedly unimpressed. "George Washington, eh?" he said just as he came to the end of his furrow and turned his plow around. "Whoa, boy, gee up! G'long!" Willets shouted at the oxen and on he went.

For the rest of the day Washington traveled "in view of the sea . . . and as near it as the road could run for the small bays, marshes and guts, into which the tide flows." What Washington was seeing to his right wasn't actually the ocean; it was the Great South Bay—a giant estuary between the southwestern edge of Long Island and the Atlantic. Eventually, he stopped for the night at the home of Isaac Thompson in Bay Shore. Today the Thompson house is known as Sagtikos Manor, and we were due there for a 2:00 p.m. tour. Unfortunately, it was already 1:15, and we still had plenty of ground to cover. Time to quit pretending to be eighteenth-century tourists and get there as fast as possible.

We assumed the maps app would send us to the parkway to the north; instead, we were directed south to Jones Beach State Park for a circumnavigation of the westerly lobe of the Great South Bay. Almost immediately we'd extracted ourselves from the traffic-congested interior and were flying down an empty road with sand and marsh grass all around and a redbrick water tower looming ahead. Jones Beach attracts six million visitors a year, making it the most popular beach on the East Coast. On that bleak Monday afternoon there wasn't a car, let alone a person, in sight. We were all by ourselves on a highway built across the dunes by Robert Moses, the "power broker" of Robert Caro's book of the same name. Caro tells of how in the decades before and after World War II, Moses clear-cut entire city neighborhoods in his lust to build bridges and highways that reached even as far as here—a once-pristine stretch of beach more than forty miles from Manhattan. Caro also recounts how Moses constructed handsome arched overpasses across the roads that were purposely too low to accommodate the buses that would have otherwise brought "city dwellers" to Jones Beach. Soon we were on the Robert Moses Causeway and headed back to the main body of Long Island.

We were met at Sagtikos Manor by a delegation of four volunteers led by Christine Gottsch, a proud descendant of Caleb Brewster, the Setauket spy who sailed the coded messages across the Sound in a whaleboat. Back when Washington spent the second night of his tour at this big white house, the place was known as Apple Tree Neck farm. Christine explained that the house's owner, Isaac Thompson, had been born in Setauket and might have been among Washington's many informants on British-occupied Long Island. General Howe's replacement, Sir Henry Clinton, stopped at the Thompson house—a visit that would have provided Isaac with valuable information to pass along to the American high command. Christine told of how after being shown the bedroom in which Sir Henry had slept, Washington said he would be quite happy to stay in their "second-best room."

We'll never know whether Washington ever spoke directly to any members of the Culper Spy Ring during his Long Island tour. Did he find the opportunity to thank each one of them in some clandestine way; did he even pay them something for their efforts on the country's behalf? We do know that even though the Thompson house was not technically a tavern, Washington paid Isaac for his stay. Perhaps that was enough for the Culper spies—payment for room and board and a visit from the president of the United States.

That night we stayed in our first Airbnb, a bedroom in a ranch house in Bayport on a canal-like finger of the Great South Bay. We picked up the key from a designated drop box and never even saw the home's owner. We did, however, hear the owner's dog, which sniffed curiously at the edges of the locked door that separated us from the rest of the house.

It was simply too much for Dora to smell, hear, and not see another dog. She pawed at the door and mewled with frustrated excitement. In addition to barking like an ordinary dog, a Nova Scotia duck-tolling retriever has a unique howl: a plaintive, almost melodic ululation that I've come to associate with the Acadians' retreat into the backwoods of Nova Scotia in the early eighteenth century. As Dora let loose her mournful yowl, I couldn't help but picture a dispossessed Acadian family huddled around a fire in a dark wood as their toller sang sadly to the moon. Melissa quickly brought me back to the here and now.

"I think it's a good time to get some dinner," she suggested.

We piled Dora back into the car and headed to the nearest restaurant.

Washington stopped at Patchogue (where he downed a baked potato offered by some boys cooking on a fire beside the road) before heading north across the island to the nerve center of the Culper Spy Ring at Setauket. Setauket—virtually at the midpoint of Long Island's north shore, with Flushing about fifty miles to the west and Orient Point about fifty miles to the east—reminded both Melissa and me of Nantucket. Not only does the town have the same year-round population of about fifteen thousand and plenty of old captain's houses, there is a remoteness to it. You are out there in the middle of Long Island with the wide water of the Sound to the north. Despite this sense of isolation, we soon learned that Setauket is experiencing a tourist boom. The popularity of the series *Turn*, based on Alex Rose's *Washington's Spies*, as well as the book *George Washington's Secret Six* by Brian Kilmeade, has made this little hamlet a mecca for people who want to know more about the Culper Spy Ring.

At the Three Village Historical Society we met with Margo Arceri, who has the vanity license plate "Culper" and leads spy tours of the area, and Bev Tyler, a former air traffic controller who is now the town's leading historian. When the historical society's *Spies* exhibit opened on October 3, 2010, the average attendance on a Sunday was, according to Bev, "zero to three." By 2013, it had jumped to around 26, and then in 2014, with the premiere of *Turn*, attendance skyrocketed to 60, with Bev's walking tours regularly topping out at 120. Margo said that people from all across the country are making their way to Setauket; just a few days before she'd shown a German spy enthusiast and his son around town.

One of the central characters in the Culper Spy Ring was the tavern owner Austin Roe, who regularly rode in and out of New York for supplies as well as the coded messages he brought back to Long Island. Roe hosted Washington during his night in Setauket. According to tradition, Roe was so excited by the appearance of the president that he fell off his horse and broke his leg. Bev got into our Pilot and directed us to the Austin Roe tavern, which has been moved from its original location and is now a private residence on the side of a hill amid a grove of trees. The house had a wonderfully spooky, Charles Addams feel to it, but my favorite spot was the point of land where a woman named Anna Smith Strong used to hang a black petticoat from her clothesline to signal that Caleb Brewster had sailed in from Connecticut.

From Setauket, Washington turned west, following Long Island's north shore back toward New York. We did the same and spent the night in Huntington, about twenty-five miles from Setauket. By then what the meteorologists were calling the polar vortex had Long Island in its frozen grip, and Melissa and I were in need of heavier jackets. In downtown Huntington there was an Old Navy that had just what we needed. I found a coat worthy of an Arctic explorer with a fur-fringed hood on sale for twenty-seven dollars. You can't buy a T-shirt on Nantucket for twenty-seven dollars. Melissa also found a coat for around the same price. We loved Huntington.

So did George Washington. We have "a venerable lady, now passed away," to thank for a firsthand account of the dinner Washington enjoyed at Platt's Tavern in Huntington. According to Henry Clay Platt, who recounted her testimony during a centennial celebration of the signing of the Declaration of Independence, "men and veterans came in flocks for miles around to see the father of his country, who had a pleasant smile and good word for them all. . . . He said he wanted to have a quiet time and to see the people." Interestingly, the venerable lady provided Platt with yet another version of the "only a man" tradition: "One little boy, who had heard so much about George Washington and venerated his name, was unable to see him in the crowd that surrounded him," Platt related. "His mother took him in her arms and as he saw Washington for the first time exclaimed, 'Why, mother, he's only a man!'" As had occurred in Haverhill, Washington overheard the boy's remark and said, "Yes, my child, only a mere man."

At the Huntington Historical Society we saw the maple-and-oak chair on which Washington sat while enjoying dinner at Platt's Tavern. During the celebration of Huntington's 250th anniversary, President Teddy Roosevelt, who lived in the neighboring town of Oyster Bay, was encouraged to sit in this same chair. "It was deemed appropriate," a descriptive panel read, "that the 26th president of the United States would sit in the chair used by the 1st president."

Between Huntington and Roosevelt's hometown of Oyster Bay is the tiny hamlet of Cold Spring Harbor. Setauket might have reminded Melissa and me of Nantucket, but Cold Spring Harbor actually was once a whaling port. A portion of the settlement became known as Bungtown for all the bungs (wooden stoppers for whale-oil casks) that were once made there. While Melissa sat in the car on a conference call, Dora and I visited the dog-friendly Cold Spring Harbor Whaling Museum. It's a wonderful museum with a fully rigged whaleboat just like the one we have on Nantucket. Unfortunately, our tour had to be cut short when Dora seized a toy dolphin from the lower shelf of the gift shop display and made a run for it.

When Washington visited Cold Spring Harbor in April 1790, an eight-year-old girl named Sarah was standing at her father's gate.

Eighty-eight years later, in 1878, the now ninety-six-year-old Sarah Mead, then living in Greenwich Village, talked to a reporter about the time the president visited Cold Spring Village on Long Island. (Imagine it: not only had Sarah seen George Washington, but she had lived through the War of 1812, the gold rush, the Civil War, and the Battle of the Little Bighorn, not to mention the nation's centennial.) Sarah remembered seeing Washington coming up the road mounted on a large horse. Right next to Sarah's house, workers were in the midst of building a one-room schoolhouse. As Washington approached the construction site, he called on everyone in his entourage to give three cheers for the new school. "He then dismounted from his horse," Sarah recalled, "assisted in raising one of the rafters, and left a dollar wherewith to treat the men." Yes, Washington was enjoying himself during his tour of Long Island.

Oyster Bay was the home of Washington's most important informant during the Revolution: Robert Townsend, aka Culper junior, who posed as a loyalist merchant in New York City while sending Washington a regular stream of messages via the courier Austin Roe. Townsend grew up at Raynham Hall, now a historic house museum in Oyster Bay. The museum's historian, Claire Bellerjeau, showed us the family plot where Robert was buried. When he died in 1838 at the age of eighty-four, not even Townsend's family members knew of his spying activities.

Instead of staying with the Townsends at Raynham Hall, Washington spent his one night in Oyster Bay at the home of Daniel Youngs, a loyalist during the war who served as a forage captain for the British army. The question is, why, especially given Robert Townsend's pivotal role in the Culper Spy Ring? To help answer that question, I turned to Phil Roosevelt, the editorial director at *Barron's* magazine, whom I'd met several years before when he attended a *Moby-Dick* marathon read on Nantucket. Phil, it turned out, had grown up not just in Oyster Bay (also home to his kinsman President Theodore Roosevelt) but in the very same house in which Washington slept on April 23, 1790.

Phil said that his father always insisted the home's owner at the time of the president's visit had really been a spy during the war. That's also what Morton Pennypacker, the first researcher to identify the members of the Culper Spy Ring, claimed, pointing to Daniel Youngs's lackluster performance as a forager for the British army as indirect proof. Apparently, Youngs did such a terrible job of rounding up hay that he was regularly admonished by his superiors. But as Phil points out, there is no direct proof whatsoever that Youngs was a patriot informant. Phil's theory is that by staying at Youngs's house, Washington was making a point about forgiveness. Now that the war was over, it was time for all Americans—Federalists, Anti-Federalists, and even former loyalists—to stand united.

I asked Phil what it was like growing up in a house like this. He said people would sometimes knock on the front door and expect to be given a tour. Every now and then Phil would actually show them around. By that point, the room in which Washington had stayed had been turned into a bathroom. Phil was then in middle school, a time in life when anything associated with bodily functions is hilarious. Phil said he took "great delight" in showing his unsuspecting victims the bathroom and saying with great authority, "Washington slept here."

Washington was out of Youngs's house before six in the morning. He was on the homestretch and wanted to be in Manhattan before nightfall. A few hours after leaving Oyster Bay, he pulled into what is today the town of Roslyn at the head of Hempstead Harbor for breakfast at the home of Hendrick Onderdonk, who owned a paper mill.

Word of the president's impending arrival had gotten to the Onderdonk family just minutes before. They'd been in the midst of eating a breakfast of roasted clams when they learned that Washington would be there any minute. The women swept the clamshells into their aprons and quickly prepared the table for the honored guest.

The Onderdonk house where Washington once had breakfast is now Hendrick's Tavern, which despite the name is an upscale Italian restaurant featuring the George Bar, a kind of shrine to our first president with so many portraits of the founding fathers that the owners could someday open a museum of their own. As it is, the restaurant already has at least one docent. When Melissa and I were having lunch at Hendrick's, our server overheard us talking about Washington. That was all he needed to launch into the story of how George enjoyed a breakfast of roasted oysters with the Onderdonk family before visiting the paper mill behind the house, where the president even made his own sheet of paper. I asked the server how he knew all this. "Everybody knows about Washington's visit to Roslyn," he said.

After passing through Flushing, Newtown, and Brooklyn Heights, Washington took the ferry to Manhattan and was back in the presidential mansion before sundown. The tour of Long Island had done him an immense amount of good. "The president . . . has been riding on Long Island all last week," the Pennsylvania senator Robert Morris reported to his wife, "and he has regained his looks, his appetite and his health." It was a good thing, too, given the challenges awaiting his administration when it came to Hamilton's assumption plan and finding a new permanent location for the nation's capital.

And then, not even a week later, Washington caught the flu from, of all people, James Madison. The entire city, it seemed, was sick. By May 7, Washington had lost his hearing. He had trouble breathing and a terrible cough. Blood appeared in his spittle. Three different doctors were consulted. Fearing the worst, William Jackson contacted a doctor in Philadelphia, who quickly left for New York to be at Washington's side. On May 15, Senator Maclay stopped by the presidential mansion and found "every eye full of tears . . . his life despaired of." That same afternoon, around five o'clock, the doctors told Theodore Sedgwick, a congressman from Massachusetts, that "they had no hopes of his recovery." Washington had been seized by a fit of hiccups, creating a convulsive gurgling in his throat that Martha assumed was his death rattle.

Then, just an hour later, Washington became drenched in sweat. The fever had broken.

Rough weather off Nantucket.

CHAPTER 11

Newport

It wasn't until May 22 that Washington could sit upright in a chair. The next day, he succeeded in walking back and forth across the room a dozen times. By the end of the month he was back at work, but he was still not himself. "Within the last twelve months," he wrote to a friend in Alexandria, "I have undergone more and severer sickness than thirty preceding years afflicted me with . . . altogether." The next illness, he feared, would "put me to sleep with my fathers."

"For God's sake, my dear general," Lafayette wrote from France, "take care of your health, don't devote yourself so much to the cabinet, while your habits of life have from your young years accustomed you to a constant exercise. Your preservation is the life of your friends, the salvation of your country. It is for you a religious duty not to neglect anything that may concern your health." By the time Washington received Lafayette's letter, he'd established the routine that might have saved his life. For two hours every morning, between five and seven, he went riding on horseback. Never again during the next seven years of his presidency did he suffer the same near-fatal round of illnesses that gripped him during the first year in office.

As Washington struggled with his health in May and June, the contention over Hamilton's budget proposals, as well as the question of where to locate the nation's capital, reached a crisis point. Thomas Jefferson described it as "the most bitter and angry contest ever known in Congress before or since the union of the states." On June 8, the Senate adjourned "amid furious uproar." All that spring Alexander Hamilton had been leading the lobbying effort over assumption. But by the middle of June, the Treasury secretary had begun to fear his budget plan might never come to fruition.

In the meantime, Jefferson had been contending with his own health issues—a series of migraine headaches that flattened him for much of April and May. But by June, when he moved into his new quarters in New York, Jefferson had begun to feel better. A few weeks later, he ran into a despondent Hamilton in front of the presidential mansion. "[Hamilton] painted pathetically the temper into which the legislation had been wrought," Jefferson remembered; "the disgust of those who were called creditor states; the danger of the *secession* of their members and the separation of the states. He observed that the members of the administration ought to act in concert; that though this question was not of my department, yet a common duty should make it a common concern . . . ; that the question having been lost by a small majority only, it was probable that an appeal from me to the judgment and discretion of some of my friends might effect a change in votes."

On June 20, Jefferson, Hamilton, Madison, and some others sat down to dinner at Jefferson's new residence at 57 Maiden Lane. Today there is a plaque memorializing the compromise that arose from that dinner. On a hot day in September, Melissa, Dora, and I took a tour of "Hamilton's New York," and the guide—a fellow history nut named Kevin Draper—showed us the park bench from which Lin-Manuel Miranda channeled that historic scene while writing his famous musical. There's nothing left of Jefferson's former residence—just a wide sidewalk fronting some modern buildings—but such is the power of place.

As a result of the dinner, Hamilton got his budget proposal, and the southerners got the capital on a ten-mile square of land on the Potomac River. As a sop to the Middle Atlantic states, the temporary capital was to move from New York to Philadelphia in the coming fall. A compromise had been reached in which everyone gave up something for the greater good. "In general," Jefferson wrote to George Mason in Virginia, "I think it necessary to give as well as take in a government like ours." Although Washington had not taken an active role in the politicking leading up to the breakthrough, partly because his health precluded it, his secretary William Jackson, along with Alexander Hamilton, had been seemingly omnipresent in the halls of Congress in the weeks leading up to the critical vote.

What Jefferson hadn't yet realized were the full ramifications of Hamilton's budget proposal. By transferring ultimate taxing power from the states to the federal government, Hamilton had laid the economic groundwork for the nation we have today. The balance of power had been permanently shifted in a national direction, and the southerners, who were becoming increasingly distrustful of Hamilton's alignment with northern commercial interests, didn't like it. "I was duped into it by the secretary of the treasury," Jefferson later complained to Washington, "and made a tool for forwarding his schemes, not then sufficiently understood by me, and of all the errors of my political life this has occasioned me the deepest regret." In protest of what they considered an overabundance of federal power, Jefferson and Madison ultimately (and surreptitiously) took up the banner of the opposition. In the years ahead, Anti-Federalists assumed the name of Republicans (not to be confused with the present-day political party that claims the same name), a "standing rebuke" to what they perceived as the increasingly monarchical pretensions of Washington's presidency.

In the summer of 1790, however, the members of Washington's cabinet were still working in concert. "I feel myself supported by able co-adjutors, who harmonize extremely well together," Washington wrote to Lafayette. "I believe that these and other appointments generally have given perfect satisfaction to the public." With the tumult of the spring behind them, even Jefferson was hopeful: "It is not foreseen that anything so generative of dissension can arise again, and therefore the friends of the government hope that this difficulty once surmounted in the states, everything will work well."

In early June, Washington learned that Rhode Island had finally ratified the Constitution—the thirteenth and last of the original colonies to do so. Once he'd signed Hamilton's assumption bill as well as the legislation to create a permanent capital on the Potomac, Washington had one more important item on the agenda: a treaty with the Creek Indians in western Georgia. A delegation of twenty-six chiefs under the leadership of Alexander McGillivray, son of a Creek mother and a Scottish father, had arrived that summer for a lengthy round of negotiations. By the middle of August the treaty had been signed, and Congress had gone into recess. Washington was looking forward to returning to Mount Vernon after more than a year's absence.

On what seems to have been the spur of the moment, he decided that before he left for Virginia, he wanted to visit Rhode Island. It would be a good way to support the state's Federalists while providing the fresh air and exercise his body demanded. And if he traveled by water instead of land, he could get to Rhode Island and back in less than a week. On the morning of August 15, Washington and his entourage, which included Jefferson and New York's governor, George Clinton, boarded the packet *Hancock* and sailed for Newport.

Melissa and I decided to do the same thing—sail to Newport. But instead of departing from New York, we sailed from our home port of Nantucket. Both of us wanted to bring Dora. Our sailboat—a thirty-eight-foot centerboard yawl named *Phebe* (the old-fashioned spelling of Phoebe and the name of an early Nantucket whaleship)— is equipped with netting on the safety lines, making it a floating playpen perfect for both grandchildren and dogs. Dora is great on a

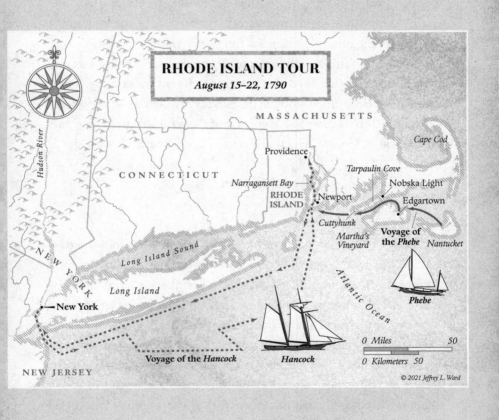

RHODE ISLAND TOUR
August 15–22, 1790

MASSACHUSETTS

Hudson River

CONNECTICUT

Providence

Narragansett Bay
RHODE
ISLAND

Newport

Cape Cod

Tarpaulin Cove

Nobska Light

Edgartown

Cuttyhunk

Martha's
Vineyard

Voyage of
the *Phebe*

Nantucket

NEW YORK

Long Island Sound

Long Island

New York

Atlantic Ocean

Phebe

Voyage of the *Hancock*

Hancock

0 Miles   50

0 Kilometers 50

NEW JERSEY

© 2021 Jeffrey L. Ward

sailboat. She's nimble and fearless and has even learned some commands. Before crossing through the wind (known as tacking), I say,
"Ready about," and Dora immediately springs to attention, staring at
me with an expression that seems to say, *Just tell me what you want me
to do and I will do it!* Then comes the next command, "Hard a lee," and
she crosses with Melissa and me to the other side of the boat as the
sails fill on the other tack. She's a fun dog to have on a boat.

But a sail of this length (a round trip of about 150 miles) was asking a lot of a dog that needed at least three decent walks a day. There
would be two overnight stops, at the islands of Martha's Vineyard and
Cuttyhunk, on our way to Newport, but that still left three long days
on the water. No, we reluctantly decided, we'd better leave Dora at
home.

It turned out to be a wise decision.

We were traveling by water in pursuit of Washington, but it felt, at
least to me, as though we were also following in the wake of John
Steinbeck. *Travels with Charley* begins at Steinbeck's home on Long
Island's Sag Harbor, another old whaling port. Before he embarks on
his road trip, a hurricane strikes. It very nearly kills him, but Steinbeck succeeds in moving his motorboat, the *Fayre Eleyne* (named for
his wife, Elaine), out of harm's way. Only then does he climb into the
pickup truck and head out to explore America. I had no way of knowing it as we motored past the stone jetties at the mouth of Nantucket
Harbor, but Melissa and I were about to have our own encounter with
a storm.

We spent the first night at Edgartown on Martha's Vineyard. We
awoke the next morning to overcast skies. Thunderstorms were predicted to the southwest, in the direction of Newport, but the weather
radar showed at least a three-hour gap between storm cells, giving us
enough time to get as far as Tarpaulin Cove on the east side of
Naushon Island, which extends off Cape Cod's southwest tip, before

the heavens unleashed. The plan was to get to Tarpaulin for lunch, ride out the storm at anchor if necessary, then continue.

We were about three miles from reaching Tarpaulin Cove, with half a dozen other boats in sight, when the sky suddenly started to darken behind us—the opposite direction from the thunderstorms to the southwest. Then our phones started bleating in unison. Melissa pulled hers out of the pocket of her raincoat. The screen read, "Extreme Alert. NWS Tornado Warning in the area till 11:45 AM. Take shelter." A tornado? We were on a sailboat in the middle of Vineyard Sound. Where were we supposed to take shelter?

We immediately donned our life jackets. I turned on the engine, and we prepared to take down the sails. Under normal conditions, the jib rolls up like a window shade on a roller furler on the bow. Before I could begin to pull the appropriate line, we heard something from behind: a frightening, no, *terrifying* roar that burst over us like an explosion. Suddenly everything had vanished behind a gray wall of wind and rain. It was just us in the middle of a storm. We were stunned and disoriented, unable to comprehend how the wind could be blowing this hard, pelting us with piercing needles of horizontal rain. What we didn't know was that the tornado was passing over Vineyard Sound, just to the north of us. We saw no funnel, just a smothering cloud of gray.

By then I had rounded the boat up into the new wind direction and resumed trying to furl the jib. With the help of a winch I managed to roll up the sail, only to watch in astonishment as the knotted furling line pulled through the drum and the jib unfurled. These were forces we had never encountered before. As the jib luffed hysterically, Melissa uncleated the halyard to the mainsail, which slid only partially down the mast. Normally, I would have gone forward and muscled down both the mainsail and the jib, but by that point the boat was teetering on the edge of a capsize. We had no choice but to stay where we were and hang on for dear life. It was blowing so hard there were no waves; the wind had flattened the water, as if smoothed by an invisible hand. I was still having trouble believing any of this was actually happening.

For the next half an hour (a seeming eternity), the storm raged on. All I could do was try to keep *Phebe* pointed into the wind, but the flogging sails kept threatening to pull us over. During one massive gust we both thought the end had come. Melissa clung to the lifelines and looked back at me with an expression I will never forget—the kind of look I imagine a couple exchanges as their airplane plummets to earth. It occurred to me that we'd become the panic-stricken characters from one of my books. It also occurred to me that if the boat capsized and we drowned, people would say, "Well, at least they died doing what they loved." Baloney. This was a horror show. Give me a hospital bed and a morphine drip any day.

It was difficult to see much of anything, but at some point we began to realize we were coming up on a shoreline. Twice I tried to tack, turning the wheel hard over and revving the engine, but the flogging sails made it impossible to drive the boat's bow through the eye of the wind. The rapidly approaching shore added a new element of tension to the ordeal. Just in time, the rain started to slacken and the wind eased dramatically. *Phebe* finally responded to the rudder and turned onto the other tack, away from the looming shoreline. Complicating the maneuver was the fact that the two jib sheets (the ropes used to pull in the sail) were, after half an hour of beating against each other, balled up into a rocklike fist of line. But no matter, the worst of the storm was over, and with the wind down to what felt like a gentle zephyr after what we'd just been through, there was reason for hope.

It was then that I glanced at the wind-speed indicator for the first time. It read forty-one knots. *Forty-one knots!* That was the most wind we'd ever sailed *Phebe* in until that morning. *How hard had it been blowing at the storm's height?* Strangely enough, as the wind decreased, the waves began to build (remember, it was still blowing hard), and giant green combers were now breaking over the bow.

Melissa took the helm while I clambered forward on the wildly pitching deck, gathering the mainsail into an ugly furl and lashing it to the boom before leaving the jib in an equally ugly heap on the wave-washed deck. Visibility had improved, but we were still cloaked in a gray mist that made it difficult to figure out exactly where we were. Was that Martha's Vineyard ahead of us or Naushon? Then we saw an unmistakable landmark: Nobska lighthouse, just to the east of Woods Hole on the Cape's southernmost tip. We were headed north, toward Cape Cod with Naushon a mile or two to our left and the Vineyard about the same distance behind us and to the right.

On our first date in the summer of 1974, Melissa and I went for a walk on the rocks surrounding Nobska light. Perhaps to stave off first-date jitters (not only was this our first date; it was my first date, *ever*), I began pretending I was the Abominable Snowman from the Claymation classic *Rudolph the Red-Nosed Reindeer*. All was going well until I tripped and cut open my big toe. (That was when I learned never to climb on rocks in bare feet nor, for that matter, impersonate a Claymation character.) The profuse bleeding required that we immediately find a drugstore in Woods Hole for a box of Band-Aids. Not the best way to begin a courtship, but here we were, forty-five years later, staring at the beacon where it all began, a hopeful augury.

We turned *Phebe* to the southwest and headed for Tarpaulin Cove, where we could see that another survivor of the storm was dropping anchor. Once we'd joined them in the anchorage (and exchanged a heartfelt greeting), we dropped our own anchor just a hundred yards from shore. We went below and changed into dry clothes and had lunch. Only then did the reality of what we'd been through begin to sink in—how while we were worrying about the thunderstorms ahead, an unpredicted tornado was racing toward us from behind. Melissa fought back tears. I was afraid to venture out of the emotional blank I'd entered in the midst of the storm and went back on deck to furl the sails.

The gnarl of jib sheets was the size of a football, a lump of rope so dense it seemed made of wood. Each of us took up the end of a jib sheet, and with the help of a marlin spike and a screwdriver we pried open the mass and began to untangle the lines. It proved to be a necessary and cathartic collaboration. Half an hour later, the jib was back on the headstay and neatly furled. *Phebe* was ready to sail again, but not us. We decided to spend the night with our compatriot at Tarpaulin Cove and venture out in the morning.

Our phones had been in our pockets throughout the storm and were dead. In an attempt to wick out the moisture and having no rice aboard, we buried them in a bowl of Rice Krispies. Astonishingly, both phones had come back to life by the end of the day. In the meantime, Melissa turned on her tablet and the emails flooded in. A rendezvous with some other Nantucket sailors had been planned for Newport, and many of them wanted to know whether we were still alive. So did our dads on Cape Cod; even our two children in Brooklyn (how had they heard about the tornado?) were desperate for information. Most of our sailing friends had wisely spent the day on Martha's Vineyard and reported that at the storm's height seventy knots had been clocked in nearby Vineyard Haven. We also learned that the tornado (technically known as a waterspout) had been spotted from the docks at Oak Bluffs. Fearing the cyclone was headed their way, authorities temporarily evacuated the waterfront. The tornado ended up veering to the north, back toward Cape Cod, prompting my ninety-year-old father to flee to his basement. It was a good thing, too. Winds of ninety miles per hour were recorded just a few miles from my dad's house in Hyannis, and a roof was torn off a hotel in Yarmouth.

Later that evening around sunset, as we sat in *Phebe*'s cockpit, still stunned by our brush with a tornado, a young, very thin coyote appeared on the beach beside us. Naushon is an island, but it's full of coyotes, the first of which swam across from Cape Cod around 1986. Watching the coyote, which sniffed at the clumps of eelgrass at the tide line, I thought of Dora. Thank God she was back home on Nantucket.

Unlike us, Washington and his entourage had "an agreeable passage" to Newport. They sailed into the harbor around ten in the morning. On Goat Island, a mile to the west of the city of Newport and just to the north of the harbor entrance, was Fort Washington, armed with twenty-eight cannons. The soldiers at the fort hoisted the state standard and fired a salute as cannons joined in from the city's wharves and the bells rang out from the church spires. Once Washington had disembarked at Long Wharf, the commercial heart of Newport, he was greeted by the usual group of dignitaries and clergymen, who formed a procession and escorted the president and his entourage through "a considerable concourse of citizens" to their lodgings.

Upon our arrival at Newport, Melissa and I met up with some friends who had heard about our adventures off Martha's Vineyard. They had something to share with us—a video from *The Boston Globe* website taken during the storm in Cape Cod's Chatham Harbor. I don't know about Melissa, but I could feel the sweat begin to ooze out of my palms as I watched those same near-hurricane-force conditions lash the moored boats in Chatham. How had we come through it in one piece? For the next few days, Melissa and I were like Coleridge's Ancient Mariner, ceaselessly repeating our tale to anyone who would listen. We both found it therapeutic, I think, but by the end of our two days in Newport we'd become thorough bores.

Today Newport is, in many respects, a lot like Nantucket—an old port that has become a popular tourist destination. But the histories of the two places are very different, even if both places embody disturbing yet quintessentially American contradictions. It's an oversimplification, but Nantucket is all about Quakerism and whaling. Newport, on the other hand, is all about religious toleration and slavery. Roger Williams founded the colony as a place where people from all religious backgrounds could worship as they pleased. (It's no accident that Rhode Island, the last original colony to join the Union, was the first to declare its independence from Great Britain.) Rhode Island's charter granted all "persons" religious freedom, which meant that there were cases in the eighteenth century when wives successfully sued their own husbands for the right to worship where *they* pleased, not where their husbands happened to worship.

A traditional New England town has a Congregational church on a central green. Not so Newport, where no single religion was supported by the state. Instead of a green, Newport had, and has, what was known as the Parade, a wide avenue bracketed by the two most important public structures in the city: the former statehouse, known today as the Colony House, at the top of the hill, and the Brick Market Building at the bottom, with Long Wharf reaching out into the harbor beyond. Rhode Island was all about government (preferably as little as possible) and money (preferably as much as possible), and in the eighteenth century there was no better way to get rich than the slave trade.

Walking the streets of Newport today, you can't help but marvel at the wonderful collection of historic homes. The truth is many if not most of these homes were built with profits associated with slavery. Some of Newport's wealthiest citizens were slave traders, sending their ships to Africa, loading them up with enslaved men, women, and children, and selling their human cargo to plantation owners in the South and the Caribbean. It's been estimated that 60 percent of the slave-trading voyages launched from North America originated in Rhode Island; in some years it was as high as 90 percent. When Washington visited Newport, the slave trade in Rhode Island had been outlawed for three years, but that appears to have had no effect on the city's slave traffickers; in fact, Newport's biggest year in slave trading was 1807, twenty years after the supposed ban.

Unlike the South, where the enslaved represented the majority of the population, slavery was largely invisible in Newport, although an estimated 30 percent of the city's population in the mid-eighteenth century was made up of free and enslaved African Americans. In many respects, Rhode Island, more than any other state in the Union, embodied the contradictions and subterfuges of the nation it had only reluctantly decided to join.

Melissa and I met with Ruth Taylor, the executive director of the Newport Historical Society, at the Colony House on Washington Square, where Washington attended a dinner during his stay in the city. The Colony House is a large, impressive building. The old pine floors are knotted and scoured like the flagstones of an ancient cathedral. During the Revolution, which economically devastated Newport, the British army occupied the city, and there is a section of the floor of the Colony House that is still dented with the parallel gouges made by the wheels of a British gun carriage. Once the British had left and the French army moved in, the building was used as a hospital. Newport never fully recovered from the war. By the time of Washington's presidential visit, Providence had begun to eclipse Newport as the commercial center of the state.

When Washington visited the Colony House, he was ushered into the council chamber, where a group of prominent citizens had been assembled. Then it was on to the representatives' chamber and an elaborate dinner. There were thirteen toasts. The best, a sly acknowledgment of Rhode Island's lack of enthusiasm for the Constitution, was number 8: "May the last be the first." That evening, Washington went for a ramble. "The president walked in several parts of the town," the *Newport Herald* recorded, "to the great satisfaction of the people, who looked with unceasing pleasure on THE MAN."

The next morning, before he boarded the packet and headed up Narragansett Bay to Providence, Washington received the usual sheaf of written addresses from various civic and religious groups. Most of them are entirely forgettable. One of the addresses, however, was different: a letter from Moses Seixas, the founder of the Bank of Rhode Island and a member of Newport's Jewish congregation.

The Jewish community in Newport dated back to 1658, when fifteen families arrived from the Caribbean—the end of a multigenerational odyssey that had begun more than 150 years earlier with the expulsion of the Jews from Spain. In 1759, construction began on what is now the Touro Synagogue, not far from the Colony House on a hill overlooking Newport Harbor. In his address to Washington, Moses Seixas wanted to know if he and his Jewish brethren were guaranteed religious freedom in the new republic. Washington's response is so good that you have to wonder who actually wrote it. Was it one of his secretaries, William Jackson or David Humphreys, both of whom were with him in Newport, or was it, just maybe, Thomas Jefferson?

Just to show you how much Jefferson valued the principle of the separation of church and state, we need only look to his gravestone. Leaving the fact that he'd been the president of the United States conspicuously absent, the gravestone lists his accomplishments as founder of the University of Virginia and the author of two works: the Declaration of Independence and the Virginia statute for religious freedom. The issue was that important to him. No matter what you might think of Thomas Jefferson, he wrote like an angel. Listen to Washington's reply to Moses Seixas:

> All possess alike liberty of conscience and immunities of citizenship. It is now no more that toleration is spoken of, as if it was by the indulgence of one class of people, that another enjoyed the exercise of their inherent natural rights. For happily the government of the United States, which gives to bigotry no sanction, to persecution no assistance, requires only that they who live under its protection should demean themselves as good citizens, in giving it on all occasions their effectual support.

In other words, in a country based on the principle that everyone is created equal, mere tolerance of others is not enough; we must honor their innate *right* to freedom. It is a message that is as important today as it was in August 1790, and if Washington's reply to Moses Seixas was, in fact, written by Thomas Jefferson, the letter stands as the high point of Jefferson's contribution to Washington's presidency.

I grew up in Squirrel Hill, an overwhelmingly Jewish neighborhood of Pittsburgh. During holidays like Yom Kippur, I and maybe two others were the only kids to show up for class in our grade at Linden Elementary School. Despite being raised as an Episcopalian, I played a menorah candle in our school's Chanukah pageant, my arms waving over my head in imitation of a burning candle. I attended I don't know how many bar mitzvahs, many of them at the Tree of Life synagogue, a couple of blocks from my house.

On October 27, 2018, less than a year before our visit to Newport, a forty-six-year-old man walked into the Tree of Life during a morning service with a Colt AR-15 semiautomatic rifle and three Glock semiautomatic pistols and opened fire. Eleven were killed and six wounded, making it the deadliest-ever attack on a Jewish community in the United States.

When I heard the dreadful news, I immediately got in touch with an old friend whose mother still worshipped at the Tree of Life. It turned out she had been running late the morning of the shootings and was stopped by the police before she could enter the synagogue. It had been that close.

I was therefore not surprised to find a guard and a security fence fronting the entrance to the Touro Synagogue as Melissa and I approached the building during our visit to Newport. Meryle Cawley, the site manager, explained that "the climate has changed recently," adding with evident sadness that in the eyes of some people "it's now okay to express anti-Semitism." Hence the security measures. But it was clear Meryle did not want to dwell on the negative. Before we entered the synagogue, she directed our attention to the view from the front steps. "Here we are on the hill," she said, "looking down on the town. Where else but in Rhode Island would a Jewish synagogue have the prime spot in a New England seaport?" She pointed out that the building is at an oblique angle to the street to make sure the congregation's holy ark faces directly east toward Jerusalem.

The synagogue, made of painted brick, was designed by the famed architect Peter Harrison, who in addition to designing the beautiful Redwood Library in Newport was responsible for the equally elegant King's Chapel in Boston, where the artist Christian Gullager had hastily sketched Washington's haggard but forceful face during the concert. Once Melissa and I stepped through the door, we found ourselves in one of the most captivating and *holy* historic spaces we had ever had the pleasure to visit. It's light and airy, with wainscoting around the walls and an upper gallery supported by twelve columns, each made from a solid tree trunk, representing the twelve tribes of Israel. Meryle pointed to a central chandelier and explained that the original candles were made out of spermaceti from a sperm whale. Not only did spermaceti candles burn brighter than wax candles, but they were dripless. "The new wax candles drip," Meryle said, "so we have to be careful." (Even though Nantucket was the whaling capital of the world, the secret formula for creating spermaceti candles was developed in Newport around 1748 by Jacob Rodriguez Rivera, a Spanish Sephardic Jew.)

Meryle also pointed out four decorative upward-projecting bells (known as *rimonim*) on the handles of the Torah scrolls. She explained that these were stand-ins for the highly valuable originals made by the silversmith Myer Myers, a contemporary of Paul Revere's. The original bells (kept under lock and key) are worth millions, but the real treasure from my point of view was the congregation's five-hundred-year-old deerskin Torah on display in the front of the synagogue behind a pane of protective glass. Meryle said the Torah (which reportedly came from a Jewish congregation in Amsterdam) was turned to the Song of the Sea, the poem sung by the Israelites after the Pharaoh's army was destroyed by the Red Sea.

It wasn't until we were back on *Phebe* that I had the chance to look up a translation of the Song of the Sea. It turned out to be a passage of the Bible with which I was already quite familiar. Melissa was at the helm steering us up beautiful Buzzards Bay, her home waters while growing up. On our right was West Falmouth Harbor, where the two of us first met as sailing instructors. Up ahead on the other side of Cleveland Ledge lighthouse was Sippican Harbor, near where our son's partner's family lived. We were due there that night for dinner. The Song of the Sea is in Exodus. Not only did the passage inspire the title of my book about the sinking of the whaleship *Essex*; it had a new and very personal relevance after our terrifying experience on Vineyard Sound. The passage also spoke to the resilience of not just the Touro congregation but any people who find their freedoms under attack, and I read it out loud to Melissa:

> In the greatness of your majesty
> you threw down those who opposed you.
> You unleashed your burning anger;
> it consumed them like stubble.
> By the blast of your nostrils the water piled up.
> The surging waters stood up like a wall;
> the deep waters congealed in the heart of the sea.

"Wow," Melissa said. "The Lord works in mysterious ways."

Quaker abolitionist and cotton mill investor Moses Brown.

CHAPTER 12

Providence

On a hot summer day in July we picked up my father at his house on Cape Cod and headed to Providence, a drive of about an hour and a half. My father was born in Providence and lived in a house that is now part of the Brown University campus. Both Melissa and I had been undergraduates at Brown, and for years we'd talked about getting my dad to show us his boyhood haunts. Washington had spent considerable time at Brown (which was then known as Rhode Island College) during his 1790 visit to Providence, so I figured there was no time like the present to visit the campus with my father.

My dad was riding shotgun, and Melissa and Dora were sharing the back seat. My dad was born in 1929, just before the stock-market crash. He was the youngest of four. Both of his older brothers, Charlie and Dick, served in World War II (Charlie was a P-51 pilot stationed in England; Dick was nearly killed during the Battle of the Bulge), as did his sister's husband, Bernie, who was in the Pacific theater. A little kid during the Great Depression and a teenager during World War II, my dad claims he was raised by his dog, Brownie, a big springer spaniel. So it's no surprise that he and Dora have a special relationship. When we stay at my father's house, the two of them end the evening with a friendly tussle on my dad's bed.

We exited from the highway and were soon on South Main Street, with the steep two-hundred-foot-high hill of the East Side on our right and downtown Providence on our left. In the eighteenth century, what is now a wide plain of asphalt between Main Street and the beginnings of downtown was a natural inlet deep enough that vessels of considerable size could sail along the west side of Main Street. It was fun to think of Washington's packet, the *Hancock*, ghosting along the foot of the hill until it came to the brick Market House, which still stands at the foot of College Street. Washington's sail from Newport had taken more than seven hours, so it must have been fairly late in the day by the time the packet turned into the wharf as the cannons roared and the bells rang. Even before the packet had been secured to the dock, Rhode Island's governor, Arthur Fenner, had leaped aboard so he could be the first to pay his respects to the president. Rhode Island might have been the last of the original thirteen states to join the Union, but its governor was no John Hancock.

Washington and his entourage joined a procession that marched through the streets of the city to the musical accompaniment of three African American fiddlers. Providence in the eighteenth century was much like San Francisco in the nineteenth century: a city on the side of a steep hill facing the water. It made for a natural amphitheater as the citizens jammed the steeply pitched side streets and crowded around the windows and roofs of the houses for the best possible view of the president. Part of what made it so exciting was that the visit was so unexpected. Why would Washington take the trouble to visit a state that had not even participated in his election? But, seizing the opportunity to welcome the reluctant Rhode Islanders into the fold, here he was.

By the time Washington's procession had climbed the hill to Benefit Street, evening was coming on. Just across from the brick statehouse were the president's quarters at Abner Daggett's Golden Ball

Inn. Washington stood at the door of the tavern to review the parade as it passed by, then retired for a quiet dinner and some tea before bed.

With my dad calling the shots, we turned right up College Street, then left on Benefit, a street of impeccably maintained historic buildings, many of them owned by either Brown University on the uphill side or the Rhode Island School of Design on the downhill side. "How small everything looks!" my father said. The Golden Ball Inn is long gone, but not, we discovered, the two buildings that once constituted St. Dunstan's School on the corner of Church Street, where my father and his brothers went to elementary school. My father said that in the depths of the Depression most of the houses along Benefit Street were in terrible disrepair. He remembered walking home from school on the day of the 1938 hurricane, which no one knew was coming. The wind was so strong that huge slate roof shingles, big enough to cut a nine-year-old boy in half, were flying through the air. Meanwhile, at the foot of the hill, a massive storm surge had inundated downtown Providence, trapping his father in his second-story office. The next day his father told of looking out his office window and seeing bodies floating down the flooded street. Only later did he realize the bodies were mannequins from a nearby department store.

We turned up the hill in search of Prospect Terrace. A series of unhelpful one-way streets made it harder than it should have been, but eventually we pulled in beside the park and its panoramic view of the city. Underneath a granite arch stood a statue of Roger Williams in the chunky, heroic style of the Art Deco figures of Rockefeller Center in New York, looking out upon the city. Prior to the statue's dedication in 1939, Williams's remains were moved to a tomb underneath the statue. During the disinterment it was discovered that the roots of an apple tree had enveloped Williams's body and taken on a human shape. It's wonderful to contemplate: an apple tree nourished by the remains of Roger Williams! His bones were eventually deposited in the new tomb, and today his statue gazes upon yet another statue—that of the eleven-foot-high, gold-covered figure known as the Independent Man atop the rotunda of the Rhode Island State House—highly appropriate for a leader who was interested not in keeping religion out of government but in keeping government out of religion.

Washington was preparing for bed at the Golden Ball Inn when there was a knock on the door. The students at Rhode Island College had a request. Back then the campus contained only a single massive four-story building, known, appropriately enough, as the College Edifice. The students had illuminated all 146 windows of the building with candles in the president's honor and wondered whether he might come take a look.

It was not a good night for a walk. A cold rain was coming down, and to get to the Edifice, they would have to walk up a steep, slippery hill in the dark. But Washington was all for it. Dragging his entourage along, the president set out up the hill toward the building that presided over eighteenth-century Providence much as the Parthenon does Athens.

The Edifice, now known as University Hall and to this day one of the largest buildings on Brown's central green, was built in 1770 after members of the Brown family succeeded in moving the college (founded by Baptists in the nearby seaport village of Warren) to Providence. There were four Brown brothers, and all of them were intimately connected with the college. Moses had been instrumental in moving the campus to Providence. Joseph had designed the Edifice, and Nicholas had built it, while John, the college's treasurer, had laid the cornerstone. The four brothers had once been very close, both personally and professionally. But in 1764, they put money into a slave-trading voyage to the west coast of Africa that went horribly wrong. By the time the slave ship *Sally*, captained by Esek Hopkins (future commander of the Continental navy), reached the Caribbean, 109 of 196 enslaved Africans had died. Three of the brothers, Nicholas,

Joseph, and Moses, never again invested in the slave trade, but not John, who remained an unapologetic slave trader for years to come.

In 1773, Moses underwent a spiritual conversion, becoming both a Quaker and an abolitionist. It was only a matter of time before Moses and John had a very public falling-out. Under thinly veiled pseudonyms, the two began attacking each other in print. Moses condemned slavery as a sin, while John insisted that the slave trade "had been permitted by the Supreme Governor of all things from time immemorial, and whenever I am convinced as you are, that it's wrong in the sight of God, I will immediately desist." That had been back in 1786. By 1789, when Moses founded the Providence Society for Promoting the Abolition of Slavery, John was an even more adamant defender of the slave trade, going so far as to claim, "There is no more crime in bringing off a cargo of slaves than in bringing off a cargo of jackasses." John, a big man with a loud raspy voice, took great delight in exposing what he felt were the self-serving pieties of New England's Quakers. When Moses urged his fellow Rhode Islanders to invest in the textile industry as an alternative to the slave trade, his brother gleefully reminded him where the cotton for a textile mill came from: "the labor of the slaves."

As John would have no doubt enjoyed bringing to his brother's attention, even Rhode Island College was hopelessly enmeshed in slavery. Not only the Browns but slaveholding families throughout the country, including that of Henry Laurens from Charleston—a former president of the Continental Congress and one of the foremost slave traders in the United States—had donated money to the college. Enslaved workers had built the College Edifice with lumber donated by Lopez and Rivera, the largest slave-trading firm in Newport.

On that wet dark night in August 1790, when Washington crested the hill and saw the college ablaze with light, he witnessed a spectacle that has been repeated on special occasions many times since. Every commencement week, the lights go on in the windows of University Hall just as they did in Washington's honor. By the beginning of the twenty-first century, Brown's commencements were being overseen by the Ivy League's first African American president, Ruth Simmons. In 2003, Simmons commissioned a study to investigate the university's link to slavery. Its findings, published in a document titled *Slavery and Justice*, set a precedent that many colleges and universities have followed since.

Having come from a family with close ties to Brown (not only was my father virtually raised on the campus, but his grandfather had served as the college's librarian from 1893 to 1930), I was aware of the Brown family's connection to slavery. In the 1990s, I'd even co-written an unproduced screenplay set at a Brown-like college that includes a lachrymose confession by one of the characters about his family's slave-trading past. So when I first heard about Brown's highly controversial decision to explore the university's association with slavery, I must admit to thinking, what more is there to know? Well, let me tell you, I had no idea about how intimately involved not just Brown but all of Rhode Island was in southern slavery.

Yes, there were slave traders in Newport, Bristol, and Providence, but most of the state's slavery connections were more indirect. Rhode Island's farmers and merchants provided plantation owners in the Caribbean and the southern states with beef, butter, hay, horses, candles, salt cod, barrel hoops and staves, timber, and shoes. Other Rhode Islanders were in the rum distillery business, purchasing slave-produced sugar and molasses from the Caribbean and distilling it into the rum that was then used to trade for slaves in Africa. More than any other northern state, Rhode Island served as, in the words of the *Slavery and Justice* report, "the commissary of the Atlantic plantation complex."

It was a tragic irony that Moses Brown, the high-minded Quaker abolitionist and textile manufacturer, not John Brown, the unrepentant slave trader, created one of Rhode Island's most enduring and pervasive connections to the slaveholding South. During the same year that Washington visited Providence, Moses opened America's first water-driven cotton-spinning mill in the next town over, Pawtucket. Designed and built by Samuel Slater, the British émigré we met in a previous chapter who reverse engineered the mills he'd seen in England, what is today called the Old Slater Mill is touted as the birthplace of the American Industrial Revolution.

As Moses's brother John was quick to point out, the mill in Pawtucket depended on slave-grown cotton. What no one could have foreseen was that in just three years, with Eli Whitney's refinement of the cotton gin, the South's cotton-producing capability and slave population would grow exponentially, and with it, Rhode Island's textile industry. By the outbreak of the Civil War, three hundred textile firms had opened in the state.

Of course, a version of this phenomenon was happening all across New England. But once again, things were a little different in Rhode Island. As larger, more sophisticated mills appeared in Massachusetts, many Rhode Island textile manufacturers decided to specialize in the cheapest cloth possible: the coarse, cotton-wool blend used by southern planters to clothe their enslaved workers. Known as Negro cloth, this quickly became a Rhode Island specialty, as did the cloth used to make slave blankets and the sacks used for collecting cotton, known as bagging. One of the largest producers of this cloth was a company founded by Quaker abolitionists, the Peace Dale Manufacturing Company in southwestern Rhode Island. Today the thought of a company founded by abolitionists supplying plantation owners with cloth for their slaves might seem patently absurd. However, in antebellum America, as in all times and places, contradictions that might seem obvious more than a century later were by no means so troubling at the time, especially when people's livelihoods were involved.

The very premise of Rhode Island back in the seventeenth century had been tolerance, equality, and political autonomy—hence the outsized Independent Man atop the statehouse—but that did not prevent the state from becoming what was in essence a northern outpost of southern slavery. According to the Brown report, "It is hard to imagine any eighteenth-century Rhode Islander whose livelihood was not entangled, directly or indirectly, with slavery." And it wasn't just Rhode Island. As the Brown report also makes clear, slavery was a nationwide sin. Whether it was cotton, rum, or sugar, every state in the Union depended on goods produced by enslaved workers in the South and the Caribbean.

It was still raining when Washington awoke the next morning. According to Brown family lore, John, who had reluctantly embraced the Federalist cause when it became clear his business interests would suffer if Rhode Island did not join the Union, took the president for a ride in his chariot.

John was very proud of his chariot, which had a single, forward-facing seat. It had been built at immense expense in Philadelphia and represented the state of the art in carriage design. Washington might have taken note. As we have already seen, when it came time for his southern tour the following spring, he would be tricked out in a brand-new carriage built in Philadelphia.

In any event, it must have been a very crowded chariot. Washington was over six feet and so was John, who unlike the president was a man of considerable girth. Where Washington was dignified and aloof, John was brusque and energetic (a squirrel with a nut in his paw was his personal mascot). In the only portrait that exists, John has the big-nosed, pinched-face look of the English comic actor Rowan Atkinson's Mr. Bean but with a linebacker's body.

John Brown reveled in confrontation. In 1772, the captain of the British revenue cutter *Gaspee* began searching Rhode Island vessels for undeclared goods. When the *Gaspee* grounded on a shoal in Narragansett Bay, Brown organized and led a boarding party. After capturing the crew, he and his compatriots burned the ship to the waterline, an outrageous stunt that Rhode Islanders look to today as the true start of the American Revolution, a year and a half before the Boston Tea Party. That morning in August 1790, Brown took Washington to see a new ship he was building on India Point—the giant nine-hundred-ton *President Washington*.

Washington undoubtedly enjoyed the ride to India Point, but it would be John's brother Moses to whom he would actually listen in the years to come. In January 1794, in the first year of his second term as president, Washington took the extraordinary step of mentioning the Rhode Island Quakers' petition to ban the slave trade in his remarks before the Senate. Four years after declining to take up the Quaker Warner Mifflin's proposal about slavery, Washington had decided that the time was right to put the weight of the presidency behind the issue.

It's an event that is rarely mentioned by Washington's biographers; it's only because of Charles Rappleye's *Sons of Providence*, an excellent account of the relationship between John and Moses, that I became aware of Washington's decision to take up the Quaker cause. Soon after Washington's speech, a senator from Georgia challenged the mere mention of the petition by the president. "Is it regular," he asked, "that petitions . . . should be introduced by members of the executive branch?" But with help from Rhode Island senator Theodore Foster, the petition was taken up by Congress, and on March 22 "an act to prohibit the carrying on the slave trade from the United States to any foreign place or country" became law. Moses traveled to Philadelphia for the debates in Congress and reported that the president "appeared clear and decided for suppressing the trade." Washington, it turns out, did not wait until the very end of his life to make his views on slavery public. He did it during his second term as president, and we have John's brother Moses to thank for helping to make it happen.

We were looking for a parking space on the edges of the Brown campus when we drove by a famous building at the corner of Power and Benefit streets: the converted carriage house in which the Providence mayor Buddy Cianci reputedly put out the butt of a cigarette on the face of the man he believed to be his wife's lover, an act that helped land the disgraced mayor in jail.

My dad spoke up. "That's where my father kept his car."

"What?"

"Yes, he rented a space in that carriage house when it used to be a garage. John Brown's chariot was in a corner all by itself."

I couldn't believe it. Today the restored chariot is on display in the back of the John Brown House and is recognized as one of the finest examples of a carriage of its type in the United States. But as recently as the 1930s and 1940s, when my father had known it, the carriage was nothing special—a curious artifact gathering dust in the corner.

We parked near my father's old house on Benevolent Street, just a block away from the main campus. Then it was on to the college green and University Hall. When I was a freshman in 1974, in a kind of last gasp of the campus unrest of the 1960s, Brown undergraduates occupied University Hall. I don't remember the source of the outrage, because the war in Vietnam was pretty much over by then, but Brown students continue to have a penchant for activism that would have made Moses proud. His brother John, not so much.

It was so hot that we did our best to stay in the shadows of the buildings and trees. We walked past University Hall, which had served as a barracks and hospital for the allied French army during the Revolution, into what is known as the quiet part of the campus facing the two libraries, the Rockefeller, where Melissa and I did most of our studying, and the John Hay, which now houses rare books and special collections. The John Hay (named for a Brown graduate who was one of Abraham Lincoln's two private secretaries) was built with funds provided by Andrew Carnegie and opened in 1910 by Harry Lyman Koopman, my great-grandfather, the librarian. My dad said the librarians set up a bucket brigade of undergraduates to pass the books from the original library (now the economics department) diagonally across the street to the John Hay. When it came to books of greater value, my great-grandfather personally transported them—in a wheelbarrow.

One of the recommendations of the Slavery and Justice project had been to create "a living site of memory, inviting reflection and fresh discovery, without provoking paralysis or shame." It was here, in the quiet part of campus, that we found the university's slavery memorial. By that time I had let Dora off the leash, and as she flushed squirrel after squirrel into the trees (making it a much less quiet part of campus), we all studied the sculpture. It took a while to figure out what was being depicted. Beside a columnar plinth with a panel summarizing the findings of the slavery study was the top of a giant bronze dome with the links of a chain reaching to about eye level. We gradually realized this was a buried ball and chain and that the top link of the chain was broken in half. The ends of the broken link had been finished with silver mirrors that reflected the sky above, an apparent expression of hope attached to the buried legacy of slavery. It was an evocative and moving monument, but to my mind the most important part of the Slavery and Justice project wasn't the memorial but the history the report revealed.

I later took a walking tour of eighteenth-century Providence with a volunteer at the Rhode Island Historical Society, a former postman from Pawtucket named Scott Alexander. At the Market House near where Washington disembarked, Scott told me of how public perceptions of Rhode Island's role in the slave trade had undergone a dramatic change in recent years. "The Brown study changed everything," Scott said. "It broke the ice." That's just it, I think. History doesn't sit still, frozen on its pedestal like a statue. It's ongoing; it's dynamic; it keeps breaking ice.

Today the metaphorical ice seems to be breaking all around us. Old assumptions about the country's history—that slavery was simply an unfortunate footnote to an otherwise unblemished story of freedom and prosperity—have proven inadequate and downright harmful. A reckoning is going on in which many Americans have come to wonder whether *anything* from our country's history is worth saving. People from the past—even from just a few decades ago—will inevitably fail to meet the evolving standards of the present. That does not mean they failed to meet, in their own imperfect way, the challenges of their own time as best they could.

What I think we forget is that this is not the first time America has faced division and upheaval. In 1776, the old values that once guided this country (such as deference to a distant monarch) were upended and a new order created. America was born in a revolution and will continue to be defined by that revolution as each generation renews the struggle to measure up to the ideals with which this country began—that all of us are created equal.

Washington returned from his chariot ride in the rain with a bee in his bonnet. By 9:00 a.m. the sky had cleared, and with his entourage following behind, the president set out on a four-hour hike across Providence that, according to a congressman from South Carolina, "completely fatigued the company which formed his escort." They walked up the hill to the Edifice and "visited all the apartments of the college," including the roof, where they admired "the beautiful and extensive prospect" of the city and harbor below. Then they headed out of town for a two-mile walk to India Point to take another look at John Brown's *President Washington*. After paying their respects at the residences of several distinguished citizens, including John Brown's house, they returned to the Golden Ball, where Washington received addresses from the town, the college, and the local chapter of the Society of the Cincinnati.

The president was scheduled to head back to New York that evening. But first there was a final dinner at the statehouse. There were two hundred people gathered inside and "an immense crowd" outside, watching the festivities through the open windows. After dinner there were toasts. The second toast was to "the president of the United States." According to the newspaper, the place went wild: "The whole company within and without gave three huzzas and a long clapping of hands." At the conclusion of the toasts, Washington rose from his chair and, "with a considerable crowd of citizens, walked down to the wharf where he and his suite embarked for New York."

By all accounts, the presidential trip to Providence and Newport had been a big success. In a few short days, Washington had won over some of the staunchest Anti-Federalists in New England. "This visit was gratifying to the citizens as it was unexpected," an observer wrote in *The Pennsylvania Packet.* "There never was, perhaps, a greater exhibition of sincere public happiness than upon this occasion; every individual thought he beheld a friend and patron; a father or brother after a long absence; and on his part, the president seemed to feel the joy of a father on the return of the prodigal son. We have little room to doubt that his visit to the state of Rhode Island will be productive of happy effects, for whatever aversion the citizens of the state may have hitherto had to the new government, they must now feel a confidence in the administration of one who possesses their universal esteem."

We were on the highway, headed back to Cape Cod, when my father said, apropos of nothing, "You know what I'm most proud of?" I told him I didn't have a clue. "The time I saved our house in Pittsburgh." He explained that a few years after we moved in, he realized that a gap was developing where the third-story wall met the ceiling. The house was collapsing into the cellar. So he purchased a screw jack, positioned it under the center beam in the basement, and began to ratchet up the house, one turn at a time. I tried to visualize it: the incredible weight of an old brick house opposed by this solitary vector of force until the gap in the upper story closed to the point that the wall and the ceiling were united once again. "I was an English professor," he said. "We couldn't have afforded to hire a carpenter to fix it properly." My father had quietly, painstakingly, saved our family's house, and now, sixty years later, he was proud of what he'd done.

We left it at that, but I inevitably began to think of Washington and his tour of the thirteen states. With each ride into a different town, each address, each toast, and each night in another tavern, he was shoring up the country for the long haul ahead. Still to come, however, was the toughest journey of them all—to the South.

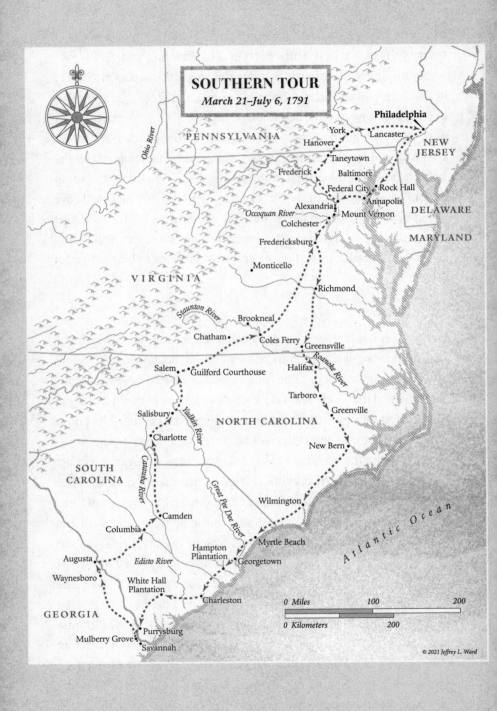

SOUTHERN TOUR
March 21–July 6, 1791

PENNSYLVANIA

Ohio River

York
Lancaster

Philadelphia

NEW JERSEY

Hanover

Taneytown

Frederick

Baltimore

Federal City
Rock Hall

Alexandria
Occoquan River
Colchester
Mount Vernon

DELAWARE

Annapolis

MARYLAND

Fredericksburg

VIRGINIA

Monticello

Richmond

Staunton River

Brookneal

Chatham
Coles Ferry
Greensville

Roanoke River

Salem
Guilford Courthouse
Halifax

Salisbury
Yadkin River

Tarboro

Greenville

NORTH CAROLINA

Charlotte

New Bern

Catawba River

SOUTH CAROLINA

Great Pee Dee River

Wilmington

Camden

Columbia

Hampton
Plantation

Myrtle Beach

Augusta

Edisto River

Georgetown

Waynesboro

White Hall
Plantation

Charleston

GEORGIA

Purrysburg

Mulberry Grove
Savannah

Atlantic Ocean

0 Miles   100   200

0 Kilometers   200

© 2021 Jeffrey L. Ward

Part IV

◇

SOUTH

The schooner *Lynx*.

CHAPTER 13

Terra Incognita

Until the spring of 1791, Washington's presidential travels had taken him to familiar territory. His visit to Providence, Rhode Island, for example, had marked the fourth time he'd been to that city. But it was going to be different when he headed south.

Being a Virginian, Washington was considered a southerner. Yes, he lived on the Potomac, but he hadn't spent any significant time in North Carolina and had never been to South Carolina or Georgia. The truth was, he knew New England and the Middle Atlantic much better than he did his own region. By venturing south, Washington was heading into terra incognita, and not just in a geographic sense.

As part of the legislative deal that put the nation's future capital on the Potomac River, the temporary capital had moved from New York to Philadelphia in the fall of 1790. Since then, Alexander Hamilton had successfully shepherded two new budget proposals through Congress: a controversial tax on whiskey and an even more contentious plan to create a national bank. Both measures had prompted sometimes vociferous opposition from the southern states. Virginia congressman James Madison had claimed the bank proposal was unconstitutional, a position supported by Washington's own attorney general, Edmund Randolph, and his secretary of state, Thomas Jefferson. Hamilton had responded with a vigorous thirteen-thousand-word defense of the bank legislation, and Washington had ultimately signed the bill into law. Given the controversy surrounding these two measures, Washington didn't know what to expect when, come the spring, he headed south.

He had yet another and perhaps even more important reason for making the southern tour. Under the terms of the legislative compromise that had created a new federal capital on the Potomac River (known as the Residency Act), it was up to Washington to oversee the construction of the actual city. It wasn't going to be easy, especially because Congress was unwilling to help finance the project. Both Maryland and Virginia had promised to kick in a total of $192,000, but that would not come close to purchasing the land and building the city in less than ten years. Before the project could proceed, Washington needed to meet with the landowners on the Potomac as well as a surveyor and an architect. After the initial meetings at the beginning of the southern tour, he would meet with them a second time on his way back to Philadelphia. With luck the tour would not only help bring the southern states into the fold but lay the groundwork for a new Federal City.

What made Washington's southern tour so extraordinary was that people in America almost never journeyed across such vast distances by land, opting instead to travel by what was the eighteenth-century equivalent of I-95: the sea. Normally a person in Philadelphia bound for Charleston or Savannah would have taken a packet similar to the one on which Washington had sailed from New York to Newport. But, of course, Washington's priority was not speed. He was making this trip to see as much of the country and its people as possible, and to do that he needed to travel by land.

Washington spent much of the winter of 1791 gathering information in preparation for his journey. From North Carolina came an ominous warning. Even though the people were "generally disposed to think favorably of the federal government . . . , considerable pains had been taken to misrepresent them. Some of the Antifederal gentlemen are as violent, or more so than ever." One of the most powerful political figures in the state, Willie (pronounced Wiley) Jones from Halifax, had been heard to say that "he reveres very much the character of General Washington, but he will not invite the president of the United States to dine with him."

No matter what Washington's reception proved to be, he knew the southern tour was going to be a grueling physical challenge—a more than eighteen-hundred-mile, three-month marathon as he made his way as far south as Savannah, Georgia, before heading inland to Augusta and then north across the high country of the Carolinas to Virginia and, eventually, Philadelphia. As he could attest after his tours of New England, Long Island, and the Middle Atlantic, the roads throughout America were terrible. During his return to Philadelphia from Mount Vernon just a few months before, his baggage wagon had flipped over twice. But he knew the worst was yet to come.

That winter he sought the advice of several southern congressmen and a Supreme Court justice from North Carolina, James Iredell, who had traveled widely in the region. They provided written descriptions of the roads and accommodations and even a sketch map of the alternate routes to Charleston. Iredell reported that the taverns along the coast were "in general, very bad." When it came to the roads, heavy sand was the problem—burying the carriage wheels and exhausting the horses. But it would be during Washington's return through the interior of the country that he would encounter the greatest challenges of the journey. Houses, let alone taverns, were few and far between in what was known as up-country Georgia. Then there was the red clay of the Carolinas. Add a little rain, which was all too common in the spring, and the roads became slippery wallows of muck. "The accommodations are very wretched," Iredell warned, "and the country a very miserable one."

That winter, Washington ordered the construction of a new and lighter carriage, which was to be painted a cream white. Although he called the carriage his chariot, to distinguish it from the larger, much more ornate vehicle he used in Philadelphia, the new carriage was larger than John Brown's chariot, with an extra rear-facing seat, making it technically "a light traveling coach." In an age before modern shock absorbers, the carriage's body was suspended on thick leather straps that prevented the vehicle from shattering to pieces on the uneven roads. To keep the carriage's center of gravity as low as possible, Washington's scientifically minded secretary of state advised some modifications. "By lowering the hang of your carriage, and exchanging the coachman for two postilions," Jefferson believed the presidential carriage would be "better prepared for [the bad roads] to come—a circumstance which I confess to you appeared to me essential for your safety, of which no one on earth more sincerely prays both from public and private regard."

Adding to the challenge was the season of the year. "Let me hope you will not forget the pestilential effects of the southern sun in the hot season," Henry Lee cautioned from Alexandria. Washington had initially determined that he must leave Philadelphia before the middle of March in order to avoid "the warm and sickly months." But it was late in the month before he was able to leave the city. Even if all went as well as it possibly could (and when had that ever happened?), it would be early July before he returned to Philadelphia.

He planned what he called his "line of march" with all the military precision of the general he'd once been. He provided the members of his cabinet with a detailed itinerary so that correspondence could reach him throughout the tour. He sent a memo to his secretary of war, Henry Knox, granting him the authority to act on sixteen pending cases, many of them relating to an upcoming military campaign against the Native peoples in the Ohio River valley, who were becoming increasingly and violently opposed to white settlement in the region. If some problem arose during his absence, "of which the probability is but too strong," his cabinet members should "hold consultation thereon, to determine whether they are of such a nature as to require my personal attendance at the seat of government." If need be, "I will return immediately from any place at which the information may reach me." But, of course, if he was in South Carolina or Georgia when he received the message to return, it could take a month for him to reach Philadelphia.

By then Washington's secretary Tobias Lear was married; in fact, Lear and his wife, Polly, had just had a son. While Lear remained in Philadelphia and provided Washington with weekly, sometimes daily reports, William Jackson, a native of Charleston, would accompany him on the southern tour. John Fagan would serve as coachman and James Hurley as postilion, while his valet William Osborne, servant John Mauld, and footman Fiedes Imhoff rode on horses beside the carriage, as did Jackson. The same enslaved servants who had accompanied him during his New England tour, Giles and Paris, both wearing showy red livery with new tasseled hats, were responsible for the baggage wagon and Washington's white charger Prescott.

There is a long-standing tradition that a dog also accompanied Washington on his southern tour—a greyhound named Cornwallis. As we shall see, the evidence supporting this assertion is sketchy, to say the least. However, because Melissa and I were traveling with a dog, this was one "tradition" I wasn't going to scrutinize too carefully. Yes, I decided, for now I'd assume Washington set out from Philadelphia on March 21 with his own version of Dora.

Much like Washington, Melissa and I spent the weeks before our own journey fussing with our itinerary. We were scheduled to leave in early March, then take a monthlong pause midway through the tour so that I could attend to some speaking commitments and we could check in with our dads on Cape Cod. Then it would be back on the road until we reached Philadelphia in the middle of May.

Melissa and I weren't southerners by any means, but we had both spent some time in the South. Melissa's first job out of college had been as an intern at the Valentine museum in Richmond, Virginia, while I attended graduate school in English at Duke University in Durham, North Carolina. By Thanksgiving, Melissa and I were engaged and had decided to move in together. But where were we going to live? I wasn't particularly happy at Duke, and Melissa wasn't particularly happy at the Valentine, and we were in a quandary. At a Burger King in Richmond we decided to spin for it, a technique we've used ever since to make important decisions. Laying an empty but still ice-filled cup of soda on its side, we spun it like a top. If the straw poking out of the cup's lid pointed at Melissa, I'd move to Richmond. If it pointed at me, Melissa would move to Durham. We spun the cup, and it pointed at me. I was really unhappy at Duke; I could see my father's life flashing before my eyes; I needed to get out of the ivory tower and experience life. So I insisted that we spin it again. Once again, the straw pointed at me. We spun the cup a third time with the same result, and Melissa moved to Durham.

I never took to academia, but Melissa and I both came to love Durham. The minor-league baseball franchise, the Durham Bulls, had just been revived (it was the spring of 1980), and we went to games as often as we could. We developed a lifelong love of hush puppies and college basketball. Melissa found a job as a legal secretary at a law firm run by a state representative named Paul Pulley. Paul had been a football star at UNC and now owned a summer home on Pamlico Sound and a cruising sailboat he liked to race every weekend. We joked that Melissa had been hired not because of her nearly nonexistent typing skills but because she could set a spinnaker, and it didn't hurt that her fiancé was also a sailor. That summer, driving with Paul and his wife in his giant Cadillac to the coast every Friday evening, was one of the best we'd ever had. When I was offered a job at a sailing magazine in Connecticut, I was happy to leave graduate school but sad to leave North Carolina. People didn't seem to have as much fun in Darien.

On a bright blue morning in May, Melissa, Dora, and I arrived in the town of Rock Hall on Maryland's Eastern Shore. We parked at the site of the old ferry landing and looked out across the Chesapeake. On our left was the Chesapeake Bay Bridge. Somewhere beyond the bridge on the opposite shore was Annapolis. Normally Washington would have bypassed the Eastern Shore altogether and traveled to Annapolis via Baltimore. But with all the rain, the roads had been terrible, and "receiving unfavorable accounts" of the conditions around Baltimore, he had decided to take the ferry at Rock Hall and sail to Annapolis, about thirty miles away.

Just the day before, Melissa, Dora, and I had also taken a thirty-mile ferry ride—on a steel ship named the *Eagle* capable of carrying 768 passengers and 52 vehicles that completed the voyage from Nantucket to the mainland in two and a half hours. Washington, of course, didn't have it so easy. Getting a carriage, a baggage wagon, 10 horses, 8 persons, and a dog across the Chesapeake in 1791 required 4 vessels. It soon became apparent that even this armada wasn't enough to accommodate everyone, and Paris and 2 horses were left to wait for the next boat to Annapolis. By the end of the tour, Paris had become, Washington claimed, "self-willed and impudent . . . , [doing] nothing he was ordered, and everything he was forbid." One can only wonder whether Paris's change of temperament began on the dock at Rock Hall as he watched the rest of his traveling companions leave without him.

One of the boats was bigger than the rest, so Washington ended up on that vessel, along with his carriage and two horses. As it turned out, he should have taken a different boat.

That evening in Philadelphia, about 150 miles to the northeast, Martha Washington had a premonition. "We had a very severe thundergust here on Thursday evening," Lear later reported, "and were not without our apprehensions that you might be crossing the bay at that time, which proved too true."

The voyage began well enough, with a light breeze that after a few hours faded to what Washington described as "a stark calm." Then, much as Melissa and I'd experienced on the way to Newport, but with night coming on, they were hit by a terrific storm. Soon it was "immensely dark, with heavy and variable squalls of wind, constant lightning and tremendous thunder." As if the conditions weren't bad enough, it quickly became apparent that the sailors on Washington's vessel had "no knowledge of the channel" leading to Annapolis between Greenbury Point to the north and Horn Point to the south. Soon they were hard aground. "With much exertion and difficulty," they were able to continue sailing through the squalls and flashes of lightning, only to run aground again about a mile from Annapolis. This time, they were stuck for good.

It made for a miserable night as Washington, "in my great coat and boots," tried to sleep in a berth that was "not long enough for me by the head, and much cramped." By the morning they were "still fast aground." Luckily, a small sailboat was sighted headed their way from Annapolis, and Washington and his baggage were soon on dry land. The other vessels, he learned, had arrived the previous night without incident; Paris and the two horses sailed in the following day, by which time Washington's carriage had finally made it ashore.

Melissa and I arrived in Annapolis in the afternoon. Our hotel was up on the hill, just across from the statehouse. Leaving Dora in the room, we climbed the stairs of the capitol and were soon in the hall where on December 23, 1783, Washington had surrendered his military commission to the Continental Congress. In the middle of the almost empty room was a bronze statue of the general, holding the commission in his hand. There he stood, all alone at an extraordinary moment in our nation's history. The war had been won, but the country was bankrupt, and no one knew what the future held. Until then, revolutions had invariably ended with a military coup. By voluntarily handing in his commission, Washington had done his best to prevent some dictator from seizing power in America.

But as he eventually came to realize, surrendering ultimate power had not been enough to ensure the preservation of the United States. A new and stronger national government needed to be created to prevent the thirteen states from lapsing into thirteen different countries.

And Washington was the only person the American people trusted at the head of the new government. Now here he was in Annapolis, exhausted by a harrowing night at sea, back in the building where his path to the presidency had begun eight years before. Of course, Washington's southern diary contains no reference to that historic moment, although he does observe that the statehouse "seems to be much out of repair."

We sat down for dinner that evening at a restaurant on the waterfront with outdoor seating. Dora had just lain down at our feet when we noticed a familiar sight: two wooden masts looming above the dockside trees with colorful pennants streaming from their tops. One said *"Egan"*; the other said *"Lynx."* This was a familiar sight, yes, but in completely the wrong place; it was the *Lynx*, a replica of an American schooner captured by the British during the War of 1812. Every summer, the *Lynx* comes to Nantucket to help fulfill the educational mission of the Egan Maritime Institute, an island organization I had helped found about twenty-five years earlier. Here it was in Annapolis after a winter in Florida and Georgia, headed north just as Melissa and I began our journey in the opposite direction. After dinner we walked down to the dock and wished Captain Peacock and his crew a safe passage to Nantucket. The next morning they were gone.

Washington spent most of his time in Annapolis prepping for the real estate deal that would either make or break his plans for a capital city on the Potomac River. Washington saw the construction of the Federal City as the physical culmination of his quest to create a durable union. It simply wouldn't do to turn either New York or Philadelphia into the nation's capital; the country needed its own designated national district, and as it so happened, the Potomac was at the almost precise midpoint between Maine to the north and Georgia to the south. Washington was also convinced that the river was destined to become the artery down which the commerce of the West would flow to the East. From his perspective, all convergences led to the Potomac, and he was willing to risk his reputation as a national hero to make sure the capital ended up on this river.

And risk it he did, especially when he sought additional legislation that allowed the federal district to include Alexandria, a town in which he owned considerable property. In addition to the 1,200 acres Washington owned in the federal district, his nine-year-old step-grandson, Washy, was due to inherit a 950-acre plot of land just across the river in Arlington, Virginia. Making appearances even worse, when Congress passed the Residency Act, which immediately increased the value of land along this portion of the Potomac, Washington raised the rents he charged his tenants in the region.

For Washington, who'd been away from home for six straight years during the Revolution and then for an additional two years before the war's conclusion, it must have seemed like his just deserts to be able to build a city—and the country's capital—from scratch on the river that flowed past Mount Vernon, only seventeen miles away. But in this instance, Washington's long-held obsession with the Potomac blinded him to the impropriety of a president's overseeing the construction of a city in the virtual backyard of his home—a city built with slave labor on land bought and sold by his friends and relatives. Washington didn't want to be king, but there was a truly monarchical sense of privilege about the making of Washington, D.C. As John Adams later wrote, the creation of a city on the Potomac "raised the value of [Washington's] property and that of his family a thousand percent at an expense to the public of more than his whole fortune." The Potomac's commercial potential had been a nearly lifelong fixation of Washington's, but the river had also opened a chink in the once impenetrable armor of his reputation.

But to dismiss the establishment of Washington, D.C., as a tawdry get-rich scheme is to ignore the inherent idealism of Washington's vision of the United States. Washington wasn't an eighteenth-century Robert Moses, a public official recklessly in thrall to power and ambition; if Washington was in thrall to anything, it was his youthful conviction that the Potomac was the embodiment of America's destiny as a continental empire—a conviction that dated back to when at twenty-two years old he canoed down a 170-mile length of the Potomac to the Great Falls, about 15 miles upriver of modern-day Washington, D.C. How could he not, when presented with the opportunity thirty-seven years later, build the nation's capital on this wondrous river that meant so much to him?

Until the end of his life, Washington, a man who prided himself on his impartiality, remained convinced that the construction of the capital on the Potomac was in the nation's best interests. And who knows, maybe he was right. And yet, as a congressman at the time wisely commented concerning the president's preoccupation with what became Washington, D.C., "almost all men form their opinions by their interest without always knowing the governing principle of their motives or actions."

We had lunch in Georgetown at a restaurant with a patio overlooking the canal that was eventually built beside the Potomac—a tree-lined memorial to just how misguided Washington's hopes for the river proved to be. He'd been overly optimistic about the cost of making the Potomac navigable. The company he'd helped found in 1785 never turned a profit. In 1821 (by which time the Erie Canal was being dug beside the Mohawk River in New York), a commission determined that the only way the Potomac valley could be used successfully for water transportation was to construct a similar canal. Unfortunately, that was beyond the capabilities of the Potomac Company, and Washington's brainchild was disbanded. (In 1828, with coal emerging as the cash crop of western Virginia and Pennsylvania, a Maryland-based company began building the Chesapeake and Ohio Canal from Cumberland, Maryland, to Washington, D.C., which operated until 1924 and is now the basis of a 184.5-mile national historic park.) In the end, Washington was a victim of what one historian has called Potomac Fever: "a delusion-inducing obsession with the grandeur and commercial future of the Potomac River." But no matter, the city he built beside the Potomac remains.

We were in the neighborhood to see the Old Stone House, built in 1765 and the oldest structure in Washington, D.C. Local residents back in the early twentieth century had claimed this was once Suter's Tavern, which had served as Washington's headquarters when he was planning the nation's capital, but such is not the case. The actual tavern had long since been demolished, but thanks to the confusion, preservationists insisted that the Old Stone House, now owned by the National Park Service, be saved. So traditional lore, even when mistaken, can serve a greater good.

Until Washington's arrival in Georgetown on March 28, the general assumption had been that the new Federal City was going to be a relatively modest affair. That winter, Washington asked Thomas Jefferson, who had already designed the Virginia capitol in Richmond, to draw a preliminary sketch of the capital city on the Potomac. Jefferson drew the plan of a hundred-acre village in what is now the Foggy Bottom section of D.C. After his seven years in Europe, Jefferson believed the capital of a primarily agrarian republic such as the United States should reflect the humble circumstances of its citizens; the architectural grandeur of Paris and London was to be avoided.

Not Washington, who anticipated a day when America's economy and cultural sophistication would rival anything in Europe. Having never been overseas, he could envision a monumental American capital without associating it with the monarchical excesses that so troubled his secretary of state. Tellingly, Washington turned to the Parisian-born architect Pierre Charles L'Enfant, who had overseen the refurbishing of Federal Hall in New York, to design him a capital worthy of his ambitions for the United States.

But first Washington had to persuade the landowners to sell the government their property at a reasonable price. There were two rival groups: those who owned the land in the Georgetown area and those who owned the land to the east, in the direction of what was then called the Eastern Branch of the Potomac and is now known as the Anacostia River. Assuming the city was going to be on the scale of Jefferson's drawing, the two groups were jockeying with each other to persuade Washington to place the two most important buildings—the capitol and the presidential mansion—on their respective pieces of land.

Washington had appointed three commissioners (one of whom was married to the widow of Martha's son) to oversee the creation of the city, but from the start the president was the one really calling the shots. The city was going to be bigger than any of the landowners had previously imagined. Congress had determined that a square, ten miles on each side, be set off as the federal district. With one tip of that square at the southernmost portion of Alexandria, Washington anticipated using most of that hundred-square-mile diamond. There was no need for the landowners, who were referred to as the proprietors, to be in competition with one another. There would be plenty of room for everyone. As Washington put it, "Philadelphia stood upon an area of three by two miles. . . . If the metropolis of *one state* occupied so much ground, what ought that of the United States to occupy?"

This was Washington's deal: The proprietors would deed to the government all the land the president wished to include within the Federal City. L'Enfant would draw a plan, and the proprietors would receive half the lots from their former holdings and get paid $66.67 an acre for the land where Washington decided to place the governmental buildings. Once the plans for the Federal City were made public, land values would skyrocket, providing the proprietors with the opportunity to sell their landholdings at a significant profit. In the meantime, the sale of government-owned lots would finance the construction of the governmental buildings. If the proprietors balked at these terms, Washington threatened to move the Federal City to a site higher up the Potomac, where the landowners were willing to make him an even better deal. The president told the proprietors to think about it that night, and they would reconvene the next morning.

Much to Washington's relief, the landowners "saw the propriety of my observations; and that whilst they were contending for the shadow they might lose the substance; and therefore mutually agreed and entered into the articles to surrender [the land] for public purposes." Washington was elated. "This business being thus happily finished and some directions given to the commissioners, the surveyor, and engineer with respect to the mode of laying out the district, surveying the grounds for the city and forming them into lots, I left Georgetown, dined in Alexandria, and reached Mount Vernon in the evening."

A week later, he was on his way south.

April – 1791.   92

Received an Address from the May
or, Aldermen & Common Council
of the City of Richmond at three
Oclock, & dined with the Governor
at four Oclock. –

    In the course of my enqui
ries – chiefly from Colo. Carringto
– I can not discover that any dis
contents prevail among the peo
ple at large, at the proceedings
of Congress. – The conduct of the
assembly respecting the assump
tion he thinks is condemned by
them as intemperate & unwise
– and he seems to have no doubt
but that the Excise law – as it is

A page from George Washington's diary of the southern tour.

CHAPTER 14

The Fellowship of the Past

We were headed to Washington's first significant stop after leaving Mount Vernon—Fredericksburg, the home of his sister Betty and his late mother, Mary, just across the Rappahannock River from the farmhouse where George and Betty had grown up. If Washington did, in fact, cut down the cherry tree, it had happened at what was known as Ferry Farm.

We were less than an hour from Fredericksburg when I suggested to Melissa that we stop for lunch. We had an appointment at Washington's mother's house, and it would be great if we had eaten and given Dora a quick walk before we arrived. Melissa whipped out her phone and found a restaurant at a quaint little town called Occoquan on the steep edge of the river for which it is named. Occoquan is an artsy community with a Main Street full of galleries and restaurants, and we sat down at the Tastefully Yours café. We had just opened up our menus when Melissa noticed a paragraph at the bottom of the page with the headline "Did Washington Drip Here?"

"Do you know anything about this?" she asked.

"Sounds like I should."

The menu told of an accident Washington had while crossing the Occoquan by ferry. It was all a little hard to follow, but somehow Washington ended up in the water. Because the restaurant had once been the home of the ferryman, the possibility existed that Washington had come here to dry off; hence the headline.

I suddenly realized I had completely forgotten about the incident that almost ended Washington's southern tour before he had even left Virginia. In my preoccupation with Fredericksburg, I had come close to overlooking the river crossing that made Washington's debacle on the stormy Chesapeake look like a walk in the park. Thanks to sheer luck—and Melissa's navigating—we were now in the vicinity of where that potential disaster had unfolded. As Steinbeck had so prophetically written, "We do not take a trip; a trip takes us."

Washington had left Mount Vernon feeling good about life. His plans for the Federal City were on track. After a week's rest, his horses were cutting capers again, just as they'd done when they departed from Philadelphia a few weeks before. Then, just ten miles later, while crossing the Occoquan River at Colchester (a once-thriving port that no longer exists), Washington's carriage almost ended up in the drink.

Ferry accidents happened all the time. In 1777, the highest-ranking French officer in the Continental army (before Lafayette became a major general) drowned when the horse he was sitting on leaped off the Schuylkill ferry. When a carriage was loaded onto a ferry, it was standard procedure to unhitch the horses, just in case they panicked during the crossing. Due to "the neglect of the person who stood before them," one of Washington's horses leaped off the ferry's bow while still attached to the other three. They were about fifty yards from shore and the water was deep. The sounds of the thrashing animal can only be imagined as the members of Washington's entourage frantically attempted to unhitch the horse from the others. But that was just the beginning of the nightmare. "This struggling frightened the [other three horses] in such a manner that one after another and in quick succession they all got overboard, harnessed and fastened" and dragging the carriage along with them. "Providentially, indeed, miraculously," Washington wrote, "by the exertions of the people who went off in boats and jumped into the river as soon as [the ferry] was forced into wading water—no damage was sustained by the horses, carriage, or harness." It had been a lucky escape. It was not, however, an auspicious way to begin his southern tour.

George Washington didn't spring full blown from Liberty's forehead. He had a strong-willed mother named Mary. A widow since the age of thirty-five, Mary Ball Washington had raised her son George and his four siblings in a modest riverside home, its clapboards painted red to look like brick. In 1772, at the age of sixty-two, she moved into a smaller house in Fredericksburg next door to her daughter Betty and son-in-law, Fielding Lewis.

In March 1789, just before Washington departed for his inauguration in New York, he visited his mother for the last time. She had been suffering from breast cancer for years. By the time Mary said goodbye to her eldest son, the tumor had broken through the skin, and she was taking mercury and arsenic to dull the pain.

Michelle Hamilton, manager of the Mary Washington House—a very simple, story-and-a-half building with a beautiful garden in back—explained that Washington's mother made a point of getting out of bed before greeting her son. Michelle took us to the room where the last farewell probably occurred. Washington had come to ask for his mother's blessing before he left for New York. "Go wherever God sends you," Mary is claimed to have said, "but you have my blessing."

A few months later, it wasn't her own health she was worried about but that of her son in New York, who had been felled by his own tumor in June. "She wishes to hear from you," Betty wrote to her brother in July. "She will not believe you are well till she has it from under your hand." Unfortunately, Mary Washington died before her son had a chance to assure her he had recovered.

Mary cut quite a figure in Fredericksburg. Well into her seventies (she died at the relatively ancient age of eighty), she charged around town in a phaeton, a sporty open carriage with four oversized wheels pulled by a single horse. The enslaved workers at her daughter's house just a few blocks away claimed you could "set your watch" by her appearance with a basket of gingerbread for her grandchildren. On a hill about a quarter mile behind Mary's house was an outcropping of granite she called Meditation Rock, where she often took her grandchildren for Bible instruction. It was there, on the rocky hilltop, that she asked to be buried in an unmarked grave.

We stood with Michelle and her mother beside the rocks on a beautiful spring afternoon. There is now a monument to "Mary, the Mother of Washington," but her grave remains unmarked, its exact location long since forgotten. When in the early nineteenth century some civic leaders proposed to give her a proper tombstone, the plan was opposed and ultimately defeated by her grandchildren, who insisted that Mary wanted it just the way it was.

Washington and Mary had a complex, sometimes contentious relationship; the historian Samuel Eliot Morison went so far as to claim Washington's mother "opposed almost everything her son did for the public good." That, I think, is overly harsh. As one of Washington's cousins later wrote, "Of the mother I was ten times more afraid than I ever was of my own parents. She awed me in the midst of her kindness, for she was, indeed, truly kind." The unique duality of Washington's character—his indomitable, often intimidating determination mixed with an almost tender generosity—probably came from Mary. In the end, Washington and his mother were too much alike for their interactions to be anything but problematic. I could relate.

If my father has become the dissertation adviser I never had (he has read and commented on just about everything I have ever written), my mother—who wrote poetry and journaled all her life—was the writer I wanted to be. When I was in my twenties, I sent my parents an admittedly terrible poem about the hikes we used to take as a family in the rugged country to the north of Pittsburgh. Mom responded with a devastatingly beautiful poem of her own about the coal mine we had come across during one of those hikes. No other commentary was necessary. She was a much better poet than I would ever be.

Almost twenty years later, when Melissa and I and the kids arrived at my parents' house around the time of my fortieth birthday, Mom greeted me with a question: "When are you going to grow up?" I stared at her in disbelief. By then I had spent the last ten years at home helping to raise my children; I'd written my first work of history and was about to become the director of a new maritime organization. Wasn't that enough? And yet, deep down, I knew exactly what she meant. I had not yet found my voice as a writer.

The next year I read *Into Thin Air* and *The Perfect Storm* and realized that the tale of the *Essex*, the Nantucket whaleship that had been sunk by a whale in 1820, was something more than an incident from the island's past; it was a survival tale with universal relevance. Three years later I published *In the Heart of the Sea*. If not for my mother's seemingly impossible expectations, I might still be the contented director of a modest maritime institute on Nantucket.

My mom was diagnosed with congestive heart failure seventeen years before she died. In the final year of her life, my dad had a cancer scare and went in for surgery. I spent the day with Mom in the waiting room, and at one point she turned to me and said, "We never thought he might die first." My mother passed away six months later, and my father is still with us. A part of me is convinced that, like my career as a writer, she willed it to happen.

That evening we arrived at the swankiest digs of our travels—the surprisingly dog-friendly Jefferson Hotel in Richmond. The lobby is really something. There you stand beneath an ornate rotunda of stained glass, looking up at a statue of Thomas Jefferson on a marble pedestal. As Melissa checked us in, I kept trying to get Dora to notice the figure of Jefferson looming above us, but she was more interested in the bronze alligator in the corner of what is called Jefferson's Palm Court. In the old days, there was a small pool beside Jefferson's statue that was the habitat of a live alligator named Old Pompey. (Oh, how I would have loved to have seen Dora's reaction to a live alligator!) Pompey died in 1948, and the bronze alligator Dora was sniffing was just one of several scattered throughout the hotel in Pompey's memory. Watching Dora examine the bronze reptile, I realized that an alligator was not a bad spirit animal for Thomas Jefferson.

Just a few weeks before, Melissa and I had visited Jefferson's Monticello during a work-related trip to Washington, D.C. After taking a shuttle bus up the hill, we were waiting beneath a grove of trees for the tour to begin when ink-black clouds suddenly appeared to the southwest and the wind began to build. Our guide warned us about the inclement weather protocol. If a thunderstorm should erupt, we'd be moved to the shelter of the building's entryway as they cleared everyone else off the mountain. Thanks to the storm, we were about to have our own, virtually private tour of Monticello.

By the time we'd made it to the front door, it was pouring rain. Then came a deafening crack of thunder. I looked up at the compass on the ceiling of the portico, which was wired to the wind vane overhead. It jittered frantically in the terrible gusts. Just as we were ushered through the entryway, an upper-story door slammed shut, causing several people in our tour to cry out in surprise. Once inside I looked to my left, and there was a bust of Alexander Hamilton. Then I noticed the much larger bust of Jefferson himself on the other side of the entrance hall. The two men appeared to be eyeing each other warily over the heads of the visitors as outside the thunderstorm raged.

While Washington was away on his southern tour, Jefferson and

Hamilton were back in Philadelphia serving together in his cabinet with apparent congeniality. Washington was not yet aware of the growing rift between them. Some of it was jealousy on Jefferson's part. Hamilton, fourteen years Jefferson's junior, had seized the spotlight—scoring success after success as his financial proposals sailed through Congress and he built a branch of government that was larger than all the other branches combined. There were five hundred employees in the Treasury Department; Jefferson's State Department had six.

But there was also a philosophical divide between the two men. Hamilton had based many of his financial proposals, especially the national bank, on the British model. Jefferson, on the other hand, looked to the growing revolutionary fervor in France as more in keeping with what had been started in America in 1776. Their opposing views on Britain and France were, of course, only one of their many differences. Making matters worse, from Jefferson's perspective, was that Hamilton was quickly emerging as Washington's most trusted cabinet member.

Within a year, the antagonism between Jefferson and Hamilton had become impossible for Washington to ignore. But all efforts to reconcile the two also proved impossible, particularly as Jefferson, with the help of James Madison, began covertly to undermine Hamilton's (and Washington's) policies. Hamilton called Jefferson "a man of sublimated and paradoxical imagination—cherishing notions incompatible with regular and firm government." For his part, Jefferson claimed that "Hamilton was not only a monarchist, but for a monarchy bottomed on corruption." It was an animosity that ended only in 1804, with Hamilton's death at the hands of Jefferson's vice president, Aaron Burr.

During our tour of Monticello, I couldn't help but wonder what kind of person would place a bust of his greatest adversary—an adversary shot in a duel by his own vice president!—in the entrance hall of his home? Jefferson apparently relished the juxtaposition of his own bust and that of Hamilton, telling visitors with a bemused smile that he and Hamilton were "opposed in death as in life."

When Jefferson placed the bust in his entry hall, he clearly felt he had bested his nemesis. It was Jefferson, after all, who followed Washington as the next two-term president of the United States (after John Adams's single term), followed, in turn, by the two-term presidencies of Jefferson's two acolytes, Madison and James Monroe, thus creating what was in effect a Jeffersonian political dynasty spanning twenty-five years.

But today, as we enter the third decade of the twenty-first century, you have to wonder. The United States has become what Hamilton—not Jefferson—envisioned: a commercial superpower where the credit-based economic system Jefferson so distrusted is an accepted part of daily life. If not a full-fledged abolitionist, Hamilton, the vice president of the New York Manumission Society, publicly opposed slavery. Jefferson, on the other hand, suggested in *Notes on the State of Virginia* that Blacks were intellectually inferior to whites; it's also been proven that he fathered several children by his enslaved servant Sally Hemings. But perhaps the biggest nail in the coffin of Jefferson's reputation has been the immensely popular musical by Lin-Manuel Miranda, in which Jefferson (first played by the Black American actor Daveed Diggs) is portrayed as a scheming poseur. I know I was projecting, but on that stormy afternoon at Monticello, I could swear there was the slightest hint of a smirk on the marble lips of Alexander Hamilton.

And then, more than a year after our visit to Monticello, came word that a researcher had discovered evidence that Alexander Hamilton, despite his public stance against slavery, owned at least one enslaved servant at the time of his death. When I heard the news I immediately thought back to the entrance hall at Monticello and wondered who, if anyone, was smiling now?

The Civil War is just about everywhere you look in Richmond, which is not surprising given that the city served as the capital of the Confederacy. Take Monument Avenue, for example, which at the time of our visit was still dominated by five colossal Confederate memorials.

In 1996, a statue of the African American tennis star Arthur Ashe had been added to the collection, but it was the twelve-ton, twenty-one-foot-high Robert E. Lee atop a forty-foot pedestal that ruled the avenue. In 2017, Richmond's mayor, Levar Stoney, announced the formation of a commission to study the issue of what to do with the Confederate statues on Monument Avenue. Rather than steal them away in the dead of night, as had happened in Baltimore, the commission's report, which was published in the summer of 2018, advised that most of the statues remain where they were, but with the addition of signage to put them in their historical context. The one exception was the recommendation to remove the statue of the Confederate president, Jefferson Davis, which was surrounded by chiseled text glorifying the so-called Lost Cause.

That was how things stood in May 2019. Then, just a year later—as I'm writing this—demonstrations erupted all over the country in reaction to the death of George Floyd, a Black American who was killed in an altercation with police in Minneapolis. On the night of June 10, protesters in Richmond toppled Jefferson Davis to the ground. Just the week before, Mayor Stoney and Virginia's governor, Ralph Northam, had vowed to remove all the Confederate statues, but in the case of the Confederate president the protesters weren't willing to wait. "If anyone's going to lead by example," a Richmond protester was quoted as saying, "it needs to be us." Years of discussion and planning had been superseded by the events of a single night. No matter what happens to the other, now-graffiti-covered Confederate statues, the citizens of Richmond had made their feelings known.

Americans have a history of making their feelings known. On July 9, 1776, after a public reading of the newly adopted Declaration of Independence, a crowd of New Yorkers flooded onto the Bowling Green in Lower Manhattan and pulled down the two-ton equestrian statue of King George III. According to legend, the statue was eventually melted down into more than forty thousand lead musket balls that were then used to oppose the forces under the command of the British king. In the meantime, a group of loyalists secreted away the statue's decapitated head and sent it back to London. The horse's tail was also preserved and is now at the New-York Historical Society. King George's empty pedestal remained in place until 1818, when it was finally removed in the aftermath of the War of 1812. Today, the only vestige of the monument that once dominated the Bowling Green is the wrought-iron fence that surrounded it. If you look carefully, you can still see where the royal crowns that topped each fence post were sawed off by the protesters in 1776. As the example of New York City's King George monument demonstrates, history isn't being lost when a statue is toppled to the ground; history is being made.

In the spring of 1791, almost exactly 229 years before protesters descended on Richmond's Monument Avenue, the people of Virginia also gathered in the streets—not in anger, but in celebration. President George Washington was coming to town. Melissa and I heard the details from Jamie Bosket, president of the Virginia Museum of History and Culture in Richmond. He and his staff showed us several documents related to Washington's southern tour, starting with a diary kept by a lawyer staying in a small Virginia town on the day before the president's expected arrival. "Great anxiety in the people to see General Washington," he wrote. "Strange is that impulse which is felt by almost every breast to see the face of a great gentleman." The next day the lawyer records, "All crowding the way where they expect him to pass, anxious to see the savior of their country and the object of their love."

Washington was a celebrity, and he used that star power to win as much support as possible for a federal government that many Virginians were predisposed to distrust. It wasn't going to be easy in the years ahead—just look at the growing tension in his own cabinet—but only Washington could have formed an enduring national government in a country created by a revolution. As a southerner with the political agenda of a northerner, he was uniquely qualified to be the leader both Federalists and Anti-Federalists could abide. It's a metaphor as tangled as the history of this country, but Washington's administration was able to hold in suspension (if only for a few years) the combustible mixture that would ultimately erupt into the two-party system. Without Washington there would have been no pause between the upheaval of the Revolution and the more measured chaos of a republic struggling to reach some kind of consensus. If either John Adams or Thomas Jefferson had been our first president—associated as they were with the extremes of the eighteenth-century political spectrum—they would have had little chance of reaching across the Federalist/Anti-Federalist divide to form a sustainable government.

As Jefferson was quick to point out, a certain amount of turmoil is essential in a free society. Protests had sparked the American Revolution, and protests would continue to define the United States as each generation has struggled to live up to the ideals set forth in the Declaration of Independence. But as Washington had come to appreciate during his first term as president, aspirations alone don't create workable change.

Washington wasn't the greatest thinker of his day—we'll let Jefferson and Hamilton tussle over that crown—but he got things done. When Jefferson became president in 1801, he issued a memo to his department heads explaining that he was going to base the daily work flow of the executive branch along the lines established by Washington, who required his cabinet members to share their official correspondence with him. "By this means," Jefferson wrote, "he was always in accurate possession of all facts and proceedings in every part of the Union, and to whatsoever department they related; he formed a central point for the different branches, preserved a unity of object and action among them, exercised that participation in the gestation of affairs which his office made incumbent on him, and met himself the due responsibility for whatever was done." Whether he was in his presidential mansion or on the road, Washington was in constant search "of all facts and proceedings in every part of the Union." This is a leader working incredibly hard to build something to withstand the test of time.

The next object Jamie showed us at the Virginia Museum of History and Culture was what Melissa and I considered the Holy Grail: George Washington's southern journal. Actually, it was just a portion of the journal that had been donated to the museum in the nineteenth century by Supreme Court chief justice John Marshall, who had used it as source material while writing the first extensive biography of Washington. The journal was about the same size and dimensions as a reporter's notebook. The pages were unlined, but that had not prevented Washington from filling the notebook with absolutely straight lines of text. The handwriting was familiar—rounded and readable—but what impressed me were how few corrections there were; the words just flowed from page to page. Melissa and I had wondered whether Washington used all the time on the road to catch up on his journal, but the handwriting was so precise and perfect that there was no way he had written a word of it while sitting in a jostling carriage. No, Washington had put pen to paper either before he went to bed or before he set out in the morning—often as early as 4:00 a.m.

We had hoped to visit the Valentine museum, where Melissa had interned in the fall of 1979, but it was closed. While Melissa and Dora went for a walk in downtown Richmond, I visited the White House of the Confederacy—the home of Jefferson Davis and now a museum. I had expected the place to be filled with hagiographic references to the Old South. I quickly realized, however, that if the museum had started out that way when it was founded in 1896, this was no longer a historical house with a point to prove. I joined the tour well after it had started. The young African American docent led us into what looked like Davis's dining room. And there, enshrined in the middle of the far wall, was a portrait of George Washington. A man wearing a yarmulke asked about the painting. The docent explained that Confederate leaders liked to believe Washington would have approved of their cause. In fact, on the seal of the Confederacy was an engraving of the statue of Washington that stands beside the Virginia capitol along with the date the Confederacy was founded, which was, by no accident, on Washington's birthday—February 22, 1861.

The docent pointed out that such a claim ignores what Washington said in his Farewell Address—that the "National Union" was the basis of the country's "collective and individual happiness." Personally, I have no doubt that if Washington had magically come back to life on what would have been his 129th birthday, he would have been horrified that the southern states had seceded from the Union. At one point during Washington's presidency he was overheard insisting that if slavery should ever come to divide the United States, "he had made up his mind to remove and be of the Northern [portion]." The docent put it perfectly: "We'll never know, of course, but it may have been wishful thinking on Davis's part to think that George Washington would have supported the Confederacy."

When it comes to Washington and slavery, nothing is clear cut. While in Richmond he received the disturbing news from Philadelphia that would, in five years, contribute to Ona Judge's decision to slip out of the presidential residence, board a northbound vessel, and flee to New Hampshire. Washington's attorney general, Edmund Randolph, had informed Tobias Lear that according to Pennsylvania law any slave kept in the state for more than six months would be granted his or her freedom. This meant that the enslaved members of Washington's staff—including his chef Hercules, his valet Christopher Shields, and Ona Judge (all of whom had been in Philadelphia through the winter)—were within weeks of gaining their freedom. The law, however, had a loophole. If a slave should be taken across the state border, even for just a day, the clock would be reset when the slave returned to Pennsylvania, and another six months would have to pass before he or she attained freedom. Washington wrote to Lear that under the circumstances he saw no other option than to get the enslaved members of his staff across the state line "under pretext that may deceive both them and the public." Otherwise, he might be required to compensate the estate of Martha's deceased husband for the loss of the dower slaves in this group. "I shall not only lose the use of them," he wrote to Lear, "but may have to pay for them."

As Washington later learned, Lear and Martha had already come up with a plan. Hercules and Ona Judge's brother Austin would be sent to Mount Vernon, supposedly to cook for Washington on his return from the southern tour. In the meantime, Martha would take the rest of the enslaved members of the household on an excursion across the New Jersey border to Trenton. Lear was confident that "the matter may be managed very well." But he had a caveat. Before Lear started arranging for the slaves' transportation out of Pennsylvania, he wanted to remind Washington of a promise he had made regarding his slaves. "No consideration should induce me to take these steps to prolong the slavery of a human being," Lear wrote, "had I not the fullest confidence that they will at some future period be liberated." Nearly nine years later, when the former president lay dying in the arms of Tobias Lear, barely able to speak, Washington instructed Martha to destroy the will he had written at the beginning of the war and keep the will he had drafted just five months before in which he freed his slaves. By that time, however, two enslaved members of Washington's presidential household—Judge and, as we shall soon see, Hercules, the chef—had gained their freedom on their own.

William Loughton Smith was a congressman from South Carolina who had accompanied Washington on his trip to Rhode Island the previous summer. Now he was headed south on the same roads as Washington, just a couple of weeks behind the president. On April 22, he stopped at the site of the new Federal City, where he received a tour from the architect Pierre Charles L'Enfant. Smith, a Federalist from Charleston, was enraptured by what he saw. "I was delighted with my ride," he recorded in his own travel journal, "and returned to my tavern in the dusk of the evening well satisfied that the place selected unites more advantages for the place intended than any spot I have seen in America."

Like Washington, Smith was doing his best to learn what the American people thought of the new government. Unlike Washington, Smith was able to travel incognito through the southern portions of Virginia to the North Carolina border. One night he stayed at a tavern where there was "a great deal of conversation on public topics, in the course of which they spoke their minds freely." Once the conversation had reached a stopping point, Smith retired to his room to dress for dinner. When he returned, a Colonel Morton said, "We suppose, sir, from your acquaintance with the proceedings of Congress that you probably are a member of that body." Smith admitted that such was indeed the case. "Had we known who you were," the colonel replied, "we should have spoken with more reserve about Congress." Smith insisted that "it was on that account I had not discovered who I was, in order to hear their opinions about government with freedom—that I wished to have the sentiments of the people . . . , as our object was only to promote their welfare and obtain their approbation."

Washington also attempted to discover what he could about "the sentiments of the people." However, the fact that he was the president of the United States made it much more difficult to find out what people actually thought. No one—particularly amid the festivities surrounding this southern tour—wanted to tell him what he didn't want to hear. When Washington had visited Connecticut, Massachusetts, and New Hampshire, he'd still been in the process of putting together a government. Since then, his government's political agenda had come into clearer and increasingly controversial focus. More than ever before, Washington needed to know what the people thought about what he was doing.

One of his political appointees in Richmond, the Revolutionary War veteran Colonel Edward Carrington, reported that the new tax on whiskey "may be executed without difficulty—nay . . . , it will become popular in a little time." Repeating a refrain Washington would hear throughout the tour, Carrington insisted that the people were "favorable toward the general government and that they only require to have matters explained to them in order to obtain their full assent to measures adopted by it." Even if Washington was getting an overly rosy view of the true temper of the American populace, this did not diminish what I would call the Washington effect: the positive impact his immense popularity had on even the most skeptical of citizens. He had seen it most recently in Rhode Island, and he would see it again in the Carolinas and Georgia. Blinkered to whatever discontents might be brewing, Washington worked tirelessly to promote his administration's political agenda everywhere he went.

Washington left Virginia in a hurry. After a night at a tavern that elicited one of his few words of (faint) praise about his accommodations during the entire tour (he commended it for its "tolerable clean beds"), he made it as far as a tavern in Greensville County when it started to rain. Prudence dictated that he remain there for the night. Then he noticed "the crowds" beginning to assemble that "would have . . . soon made the house [where he intended to stay] too noisy to be agreeable." Washington was making this tour so that he could be seen by as many people as possible, but he also needed to maintain at least a modicum of privacy when it came to his nighttime accommodations. The prospect of getting mobbed in Greensville induced him to climb back into his carriage and keep going.

A few miles later, it began "to rain violently." In desperation, he stopped at the next available tavern, but it had no stables for the horses and "no rooms or beds which appeared tolerable." He had no choice but to push on through the downpour to Halifax, North Carolina, almost fifty miles from where he had started in the morning. Well after six in the evening, after crossing the rain-swollen Roanoke River in a ferry that could barely accommodate his carriage, he rolled into Halifax, the home of the Anti-Federalist Willie Jones. As a state politician later reported, "The reception of the president at Halifax was not such as we could wish."

But in one sense, it was exactly the reception Washington wanted—as quiet and low key as possible—as he eased himself into the state that rivaled Rhode Island in its lack of enthusiasm for the Constitution. Washington had succeeded in getting far enough ahead of schedule that no one knew he was coming. The respite continued in Tarboro, where he was received "by as good a salute as could be given by one piece of artillery." The next morning he left Tarboro unbothered by the dust that would have otherwise been kicked up by the company of cavalry that had planned to escort him over the next eighty miles to New Bern. It was not until he reached what he termed "a trifling place called Greenville," twenty-five miles down the road, that the light horse troop caught up with him.

By that point Washington had entered a landscape that was new and utterly strange to him: the domain of the longleaf pine—a species of tree most of us in the twenty-first century have never seen but that in the eighteenth century covered an estimated ninety million acres, all the way south from North Carolina to Florida and as far west as Texas. An individual longleaf pine tree could live for up to five hundred years and grow to a width of 3 feet and a height of 110 feet. The longleaf was incredibly adaptable; it could grow in dry, sandy soil and in muddy swamps. With thick bark, huge pine cones, and a long taproot anchoring it in the ground, the longleaf was amazingly resistant to fire. In fact the species depended on fire (caused by frequent lightning strikes) to scour the land of smaller plants and add nutrients to the soil. With branches that grew relatively high up on its arrow-straight trunk, the longleaf created open forests of shadow-flecked grassland, thick with pine needles. If it was windy, the canopy of branches overhead created an unearthly roar, as if waves were crashing in the air up above.

There was an unnerving sameness about the terrain, and many were the times, particularly early in the history of North Carolina, when inhabitants became so disoriented among the shadowy trees that muskets and cannons had to be fired to help them find their way home. Washington, like many travelers, regarded these majestic forests as some of "the most barren country I ever beheld." But even he had to admit there was a peculiar beauty about a longleaf forest. "The appearances of it are agreeable," he wrote, "resembling a lawn well covered with evergreens and a good verdure below from a broom of coarse grass which having sprung since the burning of the woods, had a neat and handsome look, especially as there were parts entirely open and others with ponds of water which contributed not a little to the beauty of the scene."

Melissa, Dora, and I had our own encounter with a young longleaf pine forest at the Green Swamp Preserve in the southern edge of the state, just past Wilmington. The temperature was getting into the eighties by the time we parked at the preserve, but once we'd ventured into the forest, it was surprisingly cool. The branches overhead provided shade, and the afternoon breeze had plenty of room to circulate among the well-distanced trees. Dora showed a fondness for the pineapple-sized pine cones. They made for great chew toys. A sign alerted us to the presence of Venus flytraps. Having seen *Little Shop of Horrors*, I imagined a plant the size of a Buick, but no, these were tiny little things—miniature green bear traps among the grass, a few inches high. Melissa took up a pine needle (which had to be eight inches long) and placed the tip of it between the jaws of one of the plants. Sure enough, they closed around the pine needle with a greedy suddenness.

The longleaf pine forests that once dominated the South were doomed as soon as Europeans arrived on America's shores. If you wanted to build and maintain an oceangoing ship, you needed two products derived from the pine tree—tar and pitch. Tar preserved the rope rigging against degradation from salt water and sunlight, while pitch kept the ship's hull from leaking. It had been that way for literally thousands of years. God Himself instructed Noah to smear the seams of his ark with pitch. First you slowly burned the resin-filled wood of a pine tree in a kiln to produce tar. Then you boiled the tar in a cauldron to create pitch. There were, of course, pine trees in

Europe, but none of them could compare with the American longleaf pine, which had high levels of oleoresin, the key ingredient in making naval stores. By the nineteenth century, North Carolina was providing 90 percent of America's tar and pitch, which have been described as the petrochemicals of their day. There are varying accounts of where the term "Tar Heel" came from, but it might have been coined during the Civil War, when it was said tenacious Carolina soldiers put tar on their heels "to make them stick better in the next fight."

But it was not just the country's lust for tar and pitch that caused the end of the longleaf pine forests; there was also the emergence of fire prevention. The longleaf pine depends on frequent fires to keep the ground clear. But as naturally caused fires became less frequent, the subsequent growth of shrubs and rival tree species began to choke out the longleafs. Today it is the faster-growing and far less noble loblolly pines that dominate the Carolina landscape.

Except when it comes to my dog, I'm not one to anthropomorphize the nonhuman world, but I must admit to having been surprisingly moved by a 1908 poem by Anne McQueen I found on the walls of the history museum in New Bern titled "The Cry of the Pine":

All through the land are the forests dying,
One piece of silver a tree-life buying.
Listen! The great trees moan to each other!
"The axe has scarred us too, my brother—
We die, we die!"

———

Washington's determination to rely on only public accommodations was sorely tested in the Carolinas. There simply weren't enough taverns. After a night at an establishment run by Shadrack "Shade" Allen, south of Greenville, he stopped at a place about fifteen miles down the road owned by Shade's brother John. Assuming that tavern keeping was an Allen family tradition, Washington ordered breakfast. John Allen's wife, Ann, might have appeared unusually flustered by the request, but that didn't prevent her from putting together an immense spread of country ham, fried and broiled chicken, turkey, sausages, eggs cooked several ways, waffles, battercakes, and hot soda biscuits. Washington's entourage launched into the meal with a will, but Washington himself was not all that hungry, eating only a single boiled egg. When Washington offered to pay for all the food his party had consumed, he was distressed to learn that this was no tavern; it was John Allen's home. "We were very kindly and well entertained," Washington recorded in his diary, "without knowing it was at [Allen's] expense until it was too late to rectify the mistake." In later years Ann Allen was often teased that Washington barely touched the food she'd offered him. "Well," she'd respond with a laugh, "there was glory enough anyway in having General Washington as my guest."

In New Bern and Wilmington, Washington received the warm, festive welcomes that had become de rigueur to the north. There were addresses, dinners, and at the old governor's mansion in New Bern, known as the Palace, a ball. In Wilmington, which, like New Bern, was situated on a tidal river, Washington asked the proprietor of the local tavern about the quality of the city's drinking water. Washington had "noticed the very flat and swampy nature of the surrounding country" and assumed it must be difficult to secure a reliable source of potable water. The proprietor, a man named Lal Dorsey, looked at him somewhat sheepishly. "I'm afraid I can't help you," he said. "You see, I haven't drunk water in forty years!"

The only reason why I knew about Lal Dorsey was that a research librarian at Wilmington's New Hanover County Public Library named Travis Souther had sent me an account of the tradition, along with half a dozen other stories about Washington's visit while I was preparing for our travels. It was thanks to Travis that I have a newspaper story with the best headline ever written about George Washington's southern tour: "Boy Scrapes Face on Tree, Finds Washington Memorial." Under the dateline of July 2, 1949, the story tells of how a boy playing in Wilmington's Pembroke Jones Park ran into a tree and gashed his face on something sharp. "When city employees in the park examined the tree to see what had caused the cut," the reporter recounted, "they found a tiny metal prong, and on scraping away the bark uncovered a plaque of either brass or copper." The inscription revealed that the tree had been planted in 1925 by the Daughters of the American Revolution to commemorate Washington's visit to Wilmington.

I wanted to thank Travis Souther personally for all his help. While Melissa and Dora waited double-parked outside the library, I sprinted up to the History Room on the second floor. By that point in our travels, Melissa and I had realized that we had the same rumpled sartorial aesthetic as librarians, museum archivists, and historical society volunteers: L.L.Bean meets JCPenney. And sure enough, Travis looked like a younger version of me: blue collared button-down shirt, chinos, and glasses. Looking at Travis and his similarly dressed boss, I thought, these are my people. Call it whatever you want—the Fellowship of the Past, perhaps?—but these are the folks who keep history—especially local history—alive.

Peter Manigault and friends at his plantation outside Charleston, South Carolina.

CHAPTER 15

"Follow the Yellow Brick Road"

With the possible exception of chasing a squirrel up a tree, there is nothing Dora likes more than a beach. On a sixty-degree afternoon in March, Dora discovered the famous Grand Strand of South Carolina's Myrtle Beach. The tide was out and the beach—unfettered by the breakwaters that chop up the Florida coastline to the south—stood before us much as it did for Washington in 1790: a sixteen-mile stretch of hard, absolutely level sand, perfect for a horse-drawn carriage.

Back then, only the Withers family lived on what Washington called Long Bay. When in 1822 a hurricane washed the Witherses' house and eighteen persons out to sea, the surviving family members decided to abandon this section of unprotected coast, leaving the beach empty of human habitation until the late nineteenth century. Not until 1901 was the first hotel built on what the developers had renamed Myrtle Beach for the native shrubs growing along the edges of the sand. I don't know about you, but when I think of Myrtle Beach, I don't think of waxy bushes; I think of high-rises, beach bars, and carnival rides—all of which were clearly visible to our right. Keeping my focus on the sand and water to the left, while ignoring the occasional beachgoer in flip-flops glaring disapprovingly at Dora as she romped through the chest-high surf, I tried to imagine George on the beach.

Washington liked to exercise each morning on Prescott, so it's likely the two of them were galloping ahead of the cream-colored carriage and baggage wagon as the greyhound Cornwallis loped beside his master on his big white horse. If Cornwallis was anything like Dora, his tongue lolled out of his grinning mouth as he scanned the water's edge for unsuspecting shorebirds to harass. Given the firmness of the beach—it was said that a horse's hoof didn't even make an impression on the sand—it was definitely the fastest any of them would go during the three months of the southern tour. You've got to think it was an exhilarating experience for everyone involved—horses and people alike—with whoops of joy and possibly a neigh or two breaking up the stillness of the otherwise empty beach. Unfortunately, all Washington records of the frolic by the bay is that they "passed along with ease and celerity."

Once they'd reached the end of the beach and passed through yet another shadow-flecked section of longleaf pine forest, they found themselves in the low country of South Carolina—an absolutely flat terrain (one traveler compared it with a bowling alley) that blossomed into a seemingly unending series of rice fields. "These fields in early spring," a local wrote, are "covered with the young rice, springing green from the dark earth and intersected by innumerable ditches, the water gleaming bright in the sunshine." Washington was enraptured by what he saw: an agricultural paradise that he later described to the governor of South Carolina, Charles Pinckney, as "a fairyland."

For a farmer from tidewater Virginia, where tobacco had exhausted much of the land by the end of the eighteenth century, it was almost unimaginable: a cash crop of immense value that had no negative impact on the fertility of the soil. This was the way it worked: a planter bought several hundred acres of swampland along the edge of a tidal river, brought in a gang of enslaved workers (many of whom had been taken from a rice-growing section of West Africa and there-fore already knew what they were doing), and set them to work clear-ing and draining the swamp, digging ditches, and building sluice gates called trunks to control the flow of river water into and out of the rice field. In this section of the Carolina delta country, the incom-ing tide pushed fresh river water up into fields so that the young rice plants could grow to maturity. When the time came to harvest the rice, the trunks were opened and the fields drained with the outgoing tide. A single acre of land was, according to Washington's reckoning, capable of producing close to two thousand pounds of rice.

Left unsaid about this fairyland was the incredible amount of physical labor involved in clearing the land and tending the rice. It wasn't until Melissa and I reached Georgetown, about forty miles south of Myrtle Beach at the confluence of a virtual constellation of rivers, that we began to get a proper appreciation for the human cost of growing rice in the eighteenth century.

The Rice Museum—located in Georgetown's Old Market Building—is a museum of a museum: a throwback to the era of the diorama, a kind of waterless aquarium of history in which visitors gaze through pane after pane of cloudy glass at still-life depictions of how the eighteenth century was imagined in the mid-1970s. It's a tough sell in an era of Xboxes and IMAX, but not if you have a docent like Wally Zeddun, who had us riveted from the start. "Slave labor was not cheap labor," Wally said. "It was *forced* labor, which meant that you could make people do inhuman tasks and effectively work them to death. Rice was unbelievably labor intensive."

First Wally showed us a diorama of what a rice plantation looked like before the land was drained. There was a man poling a dugout canoe through a gloomy swamp full of alligators and venomous snakes. Then Wally showed us a group of field hands clearing the drained land—chopping down the huge trees and assembling the brush into piles to be burned. Then it became time to dig the ditches through the fertile soil and build the trunks—another Herculean task, especially in ninety-degree temperatures beside a mosquito-infested river. But planting and harvesting the rice were just as backbreaking—a grueling regime that reduced an enslaved person's life expectancy by decades. Even worse was the alternative low-country crop, indigo, a plant that produces a blue dye. Wally said the chemicals used to manufacture the dye were so toxic that an indigo worker might be dead after just five years in the trade.

The slave-labor camps of the low country, otherwise known as rice and indigo plantations, were in constant need of replenishment. Prior to the Revolution, South Carolina imported twice as many enslaved Africans as Virginia did. By the 1780s, Virginia's enslaved population had become self-sustaining, allowing the state to stop the importation of slaves from Africa; not South Carolina, which imported ten thousand additional enslaved laborers in that same decade. Over a four-year span in the early nineteenth century, forty thousand Africans were landed in Charleston. In parts of the Carolina low country as much as 85 percent of the population was Black. In 1774, a white planter not far from Georgetown reported to a white friend, "I slept last night . . . at least four miles distant from any white person—like the tyrant of some Asiatic Isle, the only free man on an island of slaves."

There is a drawing from that same period (see page 214) of eight planters sitting around a table, smoking, drinking, and laughing it up late into the night as an enslaved house servant leans wearily against a window seat beside a parrot in its cage. There is something terrifying about the hilarity inside that dimly lit room in the face of the suffering all around. An hour later we were standing if not in that room, then in one just like it.

We were now at Hampton Plantation, where Washington was entertained after a festive day in Georgetown. It is an amazing house, built in 1730 by the French Huguenot refugee Noe Serre of black cypress and yellow pine on a high brick foundation, with two flanking wings added a few decades later. Originally, the house had faced the Santee

River, but as the road to Charleston became more of a highway than the river, the decision was made to reverse the orientation of the house with the construction of a grand, south-facing porch. According to a tradition passed along by Archibald Rutledge, a descendant of the original owners who sold the house to the state in 1971, the porch's wide cypress steps were not finished until just a few days before Washington's arrival. The home's owner at the time, the widow Harriott Pinckney Horry, insisted that not until the president mounted the new set of stairs would anyone else be allowed to set foot on them.

As Archibald Rutledge explains in an article about Washington's visit to Hampton, the French Huguenots who settled the Santee delta (known as the French Santee) in the eighteenth century tended to be short in stature. Francis Marion, the Swamp Fox of legend (who used the house as a refuge during the war), was not even five feet tall. At well over six feet, Washington appears to have made quite an impression as he climbed the porch's gleaming white staircase. "The General was a noble giant," one of Rutledge's diminutive ancestors wrote in wonder. "He had the largest hands and feet of any man I ever saw."

Standing smack dab in front of the new porch, which jutted from the side of the house like the portico of a Greek temple, was the other great tree of the South—a live oak. Where the longleaf pine is all about verticality, a live oak has branches that seem to defy gravity as they reach out horizontally from a wide, thick trunk. The wood of a live oak is extraordinarily dense and heavy. The wood's grain structure is also incredibly strong, which made it ideal for the interior planking and structural timbers of an eighteenth-century warship. As a result of the shipping industries' voracious appetite for this sturdy wood, Congress would enact legislation in 1817 prohibiting the unauthorized felling of live oaks on federal land—the first instance of government-mandated environmental protection in U.S. history.

On that spring day at Hampton Plantation, Washington's hostess, Harriott Horry, pointed to the live oak in front of her house and explained that now that the porch was completed, she was thinking about cutting the tree down. Harriott's mother, Eliza Lucas Pinckney, who was also standing on the porch that day, had already advised her daughter against it, insisting that a live oak tree, with its outspread branches festooned with Spanish moss, should be regarded "with the reverential esteem of a Druid." In this instance, Washington, the supposed destroyer of his father's cherry tree, sided with Harriott's mother. Don't cut down the tree, he advised, "as an oak is a thing no man can make." To this day, the live oak, now a veritable monster of a tree, still stands in front of the house at Hampton Plantation.

One of the tragic ironies of the French Santee in the eighteenth century is that a group of persecuted exiles from Catholic France, the Huguenots, had come to this section of South Carolina in search of religious freedom only to enmesh themselves in a system of absolute oppression. In the back hallway of Hampton Plantation is a plaque titled "Names of the Enslaved." There are hundreds of names on the list, each accompanied by the slave's appraised worth. Soon after Harriott's husband, Daniel, died in 1785, the furnishings in his house were valued at 833 pounds. His slaves? Fifteen thousand two hundred nineteen pounds. Of course, the Civil War changed all that, but not as radically as many northerners imagined. A significant number of Hampton's former enslaved people became tenant farmers, working one day a week for the owner in exchange for a place to stay. As Sue Alston, the daughter of a slave at Hampton, put it, "The Yankee bust the old slavery chain, but he did not take the rope away, as my grandfather say, didn't take the rope away because maybe the people would go too far."

Dora had waited patiently in the shade during our tour of Hampton. By the time we returned to the car, she was in desperate need of a walk. We'd driven about a quarter mile down the Old King's Highway, when we decided to pull over and go for a stroll in the sultry air.

Another highway had long since become the route of choice, and this single-lane road of sand surrounded by an empty pine forest was much as it had been when Washington's entourage passed through on its way to Charleston.

For an old road, it was amazingly straight. It was also in amazingly good condition—hard and smooth and without the roller coaster of potholes that plague the sandy, unpaved roads on Nantucket. According to Archibald Rutledge, the local plantation owners used to race their horses down this road, galloping side by side through the pines.

Dora was ahead of us sniffing something at the side of the road. Neither one of us thought much of it until we got a little closer and simultaneously realized that Dora was nose to nose with the uplifted head of a large black snake.

A word about Melissa and snakes. When Melissa was a little girl, she and her two sisters and brother went on a camping trip with their parents to the upper Hudson River valley. The campsite was on the edge of the shallow, rock-studded river, and while their mother prepared lunch, the children followed their father out to a small island in the middle of the river. It was a warm sunny day, and they were all perched on a large flat stone when one of them realized that snakes were sunning themselves on the surrounding rocks. Not just a few snakes—*hundreds of snakes*. Until then the snakes had been motionless, but now they were moving, slipping into the river and wriggling through the ankle-deep water. *The snakes were everywhere!* All four children began to scream. With a child in each arm and the other two hanging off his back, Melissa's father carried his hysterical children to the riverbank. To this day, Melissa and her siblings cannot stand the sight of a snake. (Melissa's father, now ninety-four, isn't enamored of them either.) Needless to say, Melissa was not happy to see her beloved dog staring into the eyes of a snake the size of a boa constrictor.

Melissa grabbed my arm and let loose a visceral cry of horror. "Dora!" she shouted. "Come here!"

I sprinted ahead, and by the time I reached Dora, the snake had slithered away. As you might expect, it proved to be a very brief walk in the pine barrens.

About ten miles down the road, we came upon St. James Santee Episcopal Church. The parish was founded in 1706 by the original French Huguenot settlers. This little church was built out of brick in 1768 and has wonderfully tapered columns, also made of brick, holding up a portico that looks like a smaller version of the porch at Hampton Plantation. In his book *Home by the River*, Archibald Rutledge writes of how "in the old days this church was the gathering place for the whole wide rural community. . . . They came in coaches and carriages; in 'chariots,' as some said, but the young blades always rode their thoroughbreds." Now that the King's Highway no longer has any traffic to speak of, the church sits in virtual abandonment amid the woods. We had found, in the middle of seeming nowhere, a silent witness to Washington's passing entourage. We peered through the church's windows and could make out what Rutledge describes as "its high-backed cypress pews, its massive pulpit and communion rail of San Domingo mahogany, and its indefinable air of austere sanctity."

As we continued through the pines toward Charleston, I called my father to let him know about our progress so far. He reminded me that I had relatives who once lived in Charleston. In the 1940s and 1950s, my dad's uncle Karl Koopman, son of the Brown librarian, had been the librarian at The Citadel. My dad also reminded me that Karl's wife, Martha, a great favorite of my mother's, had driven the bookmobile for the Charleston public library.

When we were growing up in Pittsburgh, my parents used to tell us stories about Karl and Martha. Karl, the librarian at a military college, apparently had somewhat conservative political beliefs (his life's work, according to my father, was a history of Brown football through 1950), while Martha was more, shall we say, left wing. My mom used to correspond with Martha and would tell us about how she drove her bus full of books into the rural communities outside Charleston. I definitely needed to find out more about this couple—my dad wanted pictures!—and promised to look into it once we arrived in Charleston.

As I'm writing this, I've just had the pleasure of watching *The Wizard of Oz* for what may be, incredibly, only the fourth or fifth time. When my brother, Sam, and I were growing up in Pittsburgh, we had a tiny black-and-white TV set, so I'd never properly experienced Dorothy's arrival in Munchkinland until I watched the movie with my own kids. I remember shouting out, "Oh my God, Munchkinland is in color!" While I was watching the movie last night, I realized that Dorothy's welcome by the Munchkins—with all its glitz and razzle-dazzle—was essentially what Washington experienced in Charleston.

Instead of the mayor of Munchkinland, Washington was received by the intendant of Charleston, Arnoldus Vanderhorst, who greeted him on the carpeted steps of Prioleau's Wharf clutching a six-foot black staff crowned in gold. Accompanying Vanderhorst were the city's twelve wardens, each with his own silver-crowned staff. I can't help but wonder whether Vanderhorst had the same mustache and slick of curly hair as the Munchkin mayor, who along with his own group of councillors regales Dorothy with a song that comically echoes what Washington had just heard from the singers in the boats that escorted him across the Cooper River to Charleston. (You know the ditty, with its enthusiastic claims that Dorothy will be "Hiss-tooory!" and have her own bust in the Munchkin "Hall of Faaaame!") Soon Washington was standing on the balcony of the city's commercial and cultural center, the Exchange, watching various civic groups and military organizations parade past. Instead of the Lullaby League and (my favorite) the Lollipop Guild, there were the city's clergy and the Society of the Cincinnati. But, of course, Charleston in 1791 was no Munchkinland. Sustained by the ruthless exploitation of enslaved labor, Charleston was the grandest and wealthiest city Washington had ever seen.

The low-country planters with mansions in Charleston and Savannah were, to a certain extent, political anomalies in the largely Anti-Federalist South. To get their rice to market, they needed the infrastructure—such as wharves for oceangoing ships—that only a city could provide. Unlike the family farmers in North Carolina and the up-country to the west, these coastal planters had a much higher tolerance for the taxes that came with a strong federal government. The receptions Washington received in Savannah and particularly Charleston put even New York and Boston to shame. Just about every day and every night of Washington's weeklong stay in Charleston, there was yet another dinner, speech, or ball. Instead of listening and persuading, he was being wined and dined. Ten days later, once he'd made it to Savannah, Washington apologized to Tobias Lear for not writing to him while in Charleston, "but the continual hurry into which I was thrown by entertainments—visits—and ceremonies of one kind or another, scarcely allowed me a moment that I could call my own."

It was exhausting and repetitive to be sure, but there was no one better equipped for this relentless treadmill of entertainment than Washington. He was by now fifty-nine years old and rail thin, with his lips fastened like a Venus flytrap around those dentures inside his mouth, but when he put on his black velvet suit and strapped on his sword, he could still command a room. His charisma was his superpower, and he enjoyed showing it off. Take, for example, this account of the president working the room during a concert at the Exchange: "He gratified the company greatly by frequently standing up, and with charming ease and dignity walked about the room anticipating the wishes of every spectator. . . . The heartfelt satisfaction depicted on every countenance was reflected from one which beams with benignity on all." You can't help but feel bad for the musicians who were trying to entertain the crowd while the man of the hour chatted it up with the audience. But as was probably obvious to all, the real entertainment that night was not the music but the president of the United States.

What is it about seeing the world from a great height that makes you feel as if you were sharing the earth with its former inhabitants? Melissa and I were standing on the octagonal arcade at the top of St. Michael's Church. We were 186 feet over Charleston, with only the church's spire and weathervane above us. Standing beside us were C. J. Cantwell, the St. Michael's tower captain, and David Preston, a history professor at The Citadel and the author of a terrific book about Braddock's defeat on the outskirts of my old hometown of Pittsburgh. It was David who had helped arrange the tour of St. Michael's.

I clutched the beautifully carved balustrade with white knuckles. (Along with horses, heights scare me.) CJ instructed us to stay on the south side of the platform so that the tourists on Broad Street wouldn't see us. Otherwise they'd track her down and demand their own visit to the top. As Melissa and I could testify, climbing the steep spiral staircase inside the tower of St. Michael's was not easy. I didn't know how Washington, the giant of Hampton, had managed it. Clearly, he didn't suffer from claustrophobia or, once he reached the tower's viewing platform, acrophobia.

There we were—high up over the city with the clouds. Even if the height was unnerving (at least for me), there was a wondrous sense of standing beside Washington and enjoying the same spectacular view. Ahead of us was the historic core of the city—divided into a leafy grid, the magisterial houses competing with one another for the sea breezes blowing in from the harbor and the ocean beyond. Washington wrote of how the view from the tower revealed Charleston "in one view and to advantage. The gardens and green trees, which are interspersed, adding much to the beauty of the prospect."

David not only got us to the top of St. Michael's; during a tour of The Citadel, he introduced me to an archivist named Tessa Updike, who found all sorts of information about Uncle Karl. During the eighteen years of Uncle Karl's tenure, the library's collection grew from ten thousand to seventy-five thousand volumes. Tessa even found the photo my father was hoping for. There they are at the time of Karl's retirement: Karl in his officer's uniform (he retired from The Citadel as a lieutenant colonel) and Martha in a long formal dress, standing with the college's president, General Mark Clark, and a very old cocker spaniel. Only the cocker spaniel, which I assumed belonged to the general, looked as if he were enjoying himself.

It wasn't until I made a trip to Martha's former employer, the Charleston County Public Library, that I secured a picture of her in action. A research librarian named Dot had already sent me a bunch of great articles about Washington's time in Charleston. I decided to pay her a visit.

Dot and her co-worker Marianne were delighted to learn that I was related to a former Charleston librarian and quickly located several pictures of Martha and her bookmobile, a 1940s woody station wagon full of books. They found an interview with two women who used to work for Martha back in the 1950s. One of Martha's former co-workers remembered setting up shop at the edge of a field, where two curious horses came over to the fence and breathed down her neck as she sat at a card table checking out books. Another remembered the time at what she called Cocos Swamps. "Those little children's parents couldn't even read," she told the interviewer. "There was one little boy who promptly sat down on the grass and said, 'I love my book.'"

That evening over dinner I told Melissa what I'd discovered about Great-aunt Martha. Melissa was quick to remind me that I wasn't the only one to have a librarian in the family. Her mother, Elizabeth (to whom Melissa bears a striking physical resemblance), was an elementary school librarian. Melissa recounted how during the last week of every summer vacation she accompanied her mother to her school and helped her process new books—gluing the pocket for the library card on the back page, stamping the name of the library inside the front and back cover boards as well as on the top edges of the pages, placing the catalog number on the lower portion of the spine, and adding a clear plastic cover over the book jacket.

But Melissa's library connection went back even further than that. When she was just eight years old she used to ride her bike to the West Falmouth Library, a tiny two-room building less than a mile from her house. The librarian, Mrs. Hennessey, would give Melissa a cart of books to return to the stacks. "The books were arranged alphabetically by author," Melissa said, "and with every book, I'd recite my ABCs to make sure I was putting it in the right place." This was in the 1960s, and one awful day Mrs. Hennessey learned that her son Arthur had been killed in Vietnam. "I was too young to understand much about death," Melissa remembered, "but I could tell how sad it made Mrs. Hennessey." A year later a monument in Arthur Hennessey's memory was placed on the green on Falmouth's Main Street, and during a Memorial Day ceremony Melissa was given the honor of laying a posy on the bronze plaque bearing the name of Mrs. Hennessey's son.

While in Charleston, Washington got some more disturbing news from up north. His dreams for the Federal City on the Potomac were in jeopardy. Claiming that the deed Washington wanted them to sign "goes far beyond our idea of what was the spirit of the agreement," the landowners refused to go forward. "The pain which this occurrence occasions me," Washington wrote to the three commissioners, "is the more sensibly felt as I had taken pleasure during my journey through the several states to relate the agreement and to speak of it on every proper occasion." In other words, Washington had been bragging about the deal for more than a month now, only to hear it had fallen through. After fulminating about how the landowners were in the wrong, he told the commissioners that when he returned to Georgetown in June, he "should be exceedingly pleased to find all difficulties removed." With the chances of that happening close to zilch, Washington was already steeling himself for an epic confrontation on the Potomac.

Nearly everywhere you go in downtown Charleston, you'll overhear someone conducting a history tour. There's much to talk about, of course, but one story seems to be repeated over and over again: the tale of George Washington, the painter, and the horse's rear end. It goes something like this: While Washington was in Charleston, the city fathers requested that he have his portrait painted by the renowned American artist John Trumbull. Upon the president's return to Philadelphia, Trumbull labored over a large canvas depicting Washington on the eve of the second Battle of Trenton. Before sending the completed painting to Charleston, Trumbull showed it to South Carolina congressman William Loughton Smith. Smith had an objection. The Charlestonians, he explained, were expecting a portrait of the president as they had seen him during his southern tour. Whether or not Trumbull was miffed by Smith's criticism, he agreed to give it a second try, ultimately creating the painting that now hangs in the assembly room of Charleston City Hall. It's a terrific painting that shows Washington in his general's uniform just before he crossed the Cooper River. You can see the familiar skyline of Charleston in the background, and there, standing behind his master, is his white charger Prescott.

But there is just one thing: it's not the horse's head in the foreground but the opposite end. What's more, Prescott's tail is erect—as if he were about to relieve himself on . . . *the city of Charleston*! Was Trumbull expressing, not so subtly, his frustration with the painting's sponsors? According to legend, Trumbull made sure he got paid before he added the backward-facing horse.

The thing of it is, there is no evidence that the purchasers of the painting were affronted by Prescott's hindquarters. When we were at the Colony House in Newport, I saw another painting of Washington standing beside a horse's heinie, this one by Gilbert Stuart's daughter

George Washington and Prescott by John Trumbull.

Jane. I think those of us in the twenty-first century are way too sensitive about seeing a horse's behind on prominent display. Back in the eighteenth century it was like looking at the rear fender of a car—nothing to cause offense.

But, hey, if it gives the tour guides of Charleston something to talk about, that's just fine with me. Nantucket has the scarred forehead of Ahab's White Whale; Charleston has the gleaming flanks of Washington's White Horse. Perhaps the tour guide we overheard on Broad Street put it best: "Over time people have come to love that horse's butt. It's a part of the city."

About thirty-three miles south of Charleston, we stopped at the Edisto Nature Trail, which looked like just the place for a mid-morning ramble. Suddenly it was as if we were in the midst of the diorama of a low-country swamp we'd seen at the Rice Museum in Georgetown. Instead of standing in a dugout canoe, Melissa and I were on an elevated wooden walkway that led to the mucky edge of the Edisto River. Back when we were living in Durham, Melissa assumed that any creek or river south of the Mason-Dixon Line was brimming with water moccasins. Since Dora's encounter with the snake a few days before, Melissa was even more dogmatic in that conviction. It didn't help matters when Dora bolted down the wooden boardwalk and disappeared around the bend. Both of us imagined her jumping into the river and taking on an alligator.

I ran ahead and quickly put Dora on the leash. I couldn't believe how wild this country was less than a quarter mile from the edge of the highway: a lush semitropical swamp full of trees dripping Spanish moss. Archibald Rutledge wrote of the time he went hunting along the Santee River in what he assumed was a primeval patch of wilderness "with immense canebrakes . . . and towering trees," only to discover that "it had once been cultivated." He found ancient canals, old banks, and cypress trunks, no longer functioning but still structurally sound. It was "a haunted region," Rutledge wrote, "for there is no earthly loneliness like that created by man's abandonment of what he once . . . considered secure and permanent." When we came upon the remains of an old railroad bed, I knew exactly what Rutledge had meant. Nature grew at a hothouse pace down here in the low country.

About twenty miles later we came upon three men sitting beside the road in lawn chairs. Behind them were two metal barrels that looked to function as sources of heat in the colder months. There weren't any cars behind us, so I pulled in beside them and lowered the window. I explained that we were following George Washington and that he had once traveled down this road.

"Of course he did," the one on the right said. "This used to be *the* road through here."

The middle one spoke up. "It was worth your life to get across this street back then, there were so many cars. Then came 95 around 1968."

I introduced them to Melissa and Dora. "I can tell that dog belongs to your wife," the one on the left said as the other two laughed.

"Have you been here all your lives?" I asked.

"Yup," the one on the right said, "and I'm about to turn sixty-nine years old."

There was a faded sign that said "Vacancy" in what looked to be an old parking lot just ahead of them. I asked if there had once been a motel over there. "Oh, yes. People from all over used to stay there on their way up and down the country. Now it's just us."

A few more miles down the road we passed a giant billboard that read "Sherman and His Army: Terrorists, Arsonists, Thieves." Clearly, the War of Northern Aggression had not ended in this section of South Carolina.

When we were at Mount Vernon, we'd visited Washington's distillery, which had been the largest and most sophisticated in the country. It seemed kind of ironic that Washington decided to invest in a distillery in 1797 given that his administration had instituted the 1791 tax on spirits that sparked what became known as the Whiskey Rebellion in western Pennsylvania. During a recent trip to Pittsburgh,

I'd visited Braddock's Field, a place where seven thousand armed protesters gathered in opposition to the tax on whiskey. Washington
responded to the unrest by dispatching an army of almost thirteen
thousand soldiers under the command of Light Horse Harry Lee.
Washington even made a point of traveling to western Maryland and
Pennsylvania to review the troops, becoming the only sitting U.S.
president to lead an army in the field.

The rebellion quickly folded, and Washington won kudos for
dealing with the crisis in such a decisive manner. But as Steve Bashore,
who runs the distillery at Mount Vernon, discovered when he gave a
presentation in Pittsburgh, the citizens of western Pennsylvania have
not forgotten what happened in 1794. The questions Steve fielded
after his talk were pointed and in some cases angry. "There are plenty
of people in Pennsylvania," he told me, "who still resent how Washington handled the Whiskey Rebellion." As evidenced by the billboard we'd just passed in South Carolina, Americans have long
memories when the federal government responds to an insurrection
with an overwhelming show of force.

Washington spent the third night of his journey between Charleston
and Savannah at White Hall Plantation on Hazzard Creek, a tributary
of the Broad River. White Hall was owned by Judge Thomas Heyward, who had also owned the house in which Washington had stayed
in Charleston. Washington recorded that he was "kindly and hospitably entertained" by the judge while noting that he'd once again been
forced to stay at a private residence, "there being no public houses" on
this portion of the road to Savannah.

White Hall Plantation was in what is today the town of Ridge-
land, where we stopped at Cooler's Grocery. I talked with Oregon
Cooler, who has worked at the store for forty-seven years. Yates Cooler
was behind the register. "All my life," Oregon said, "people have talked
about how George Washington slept here." "What was he doing?"

Yates asked. "Campaigning for president? Vote for me, I'm George Washington!"

Oregon showed me a picture of the store's founder, Grandfather Cooler, in front of a simple wooden structure that later burned down when a car crashed into it. The store is now made out of cinder block. Oregon said that what's left of White Hall Plantation, which was burned by Sherman's army, is now owned by a corporation. She's been given the keys to the gate, and back in January 2018, when it snowed for the first time in recent memory, she and her husband and granddaughter drove out to the brick ruins of the plantation. She took out her iPad and showed me some pictures she had taken that day. Live oak trees still lined the road leading to where the main house had been—now a weedy wasteland of rubble.

After picking up a lunch of fried chicken, cream corn, collard greens, and fried okra at Dukes Barbeque, which has a drive-through window, we parked in the shade beside the Old Charleston Road—a sandy single-lane road just like the old road we'd followed from Hampton Plantation to Charleston. An hour later we came to the town of Purrysburg on the Savannah River. It was here that Washington boarded a boat and headed down the river to the city about twenty-five miles away. Melissa, Dora, and I went to the Piggly Wiggly to buy some groceries in preparation for our weekend stay in Savannah. It was Friday, March 15, and Savannah, we'd been warned, hosted one of the largest St. Patrick's Day parades in the United States (second only to Chicago). "The city will be pretty much shut down," a local historian had cautioned me. "It will be a sea of green."

And so, after a day following South Carolina's dusty version of the Yellow Brick Road, we drove into the Emerald City of Savannah.

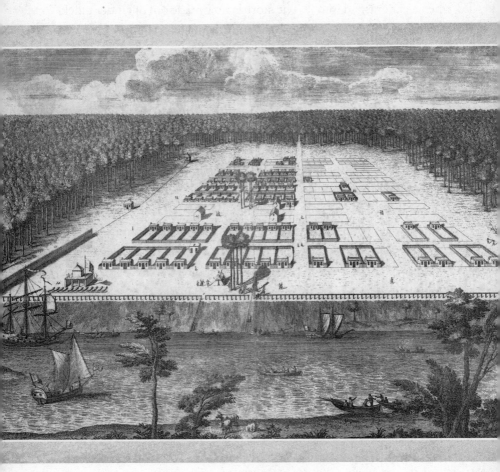

View of Savannah by Peter Gordon.

CHAPTER 16

"Eleven O'Clock Sunday Morning"

On Saturday morning of St. Patrick's Day weekend, we set out through the already party-crazed streets of Savannah. At the waterfront we discovered the Coast Guard's *Eagle*, a tall ship that makes the *Lynx*, the Nantucket-based schooner we'd seen in Annapolis, look like a dinghy by comparison. A female cadet came over to pet Dora, who immediately rolled over onto her back. As often happens, Dora quickly attracted a small crowd of women and young girls eager to pat her tummy. The cadet said that before they arrived the previous night, the *Eagle*'s crew had no idea St. Patrick's Day was such a big deal in Savannah. Although Melissa and I had been warned about two weeks before—enabling us to secure one of the last available rooms in the city—we still had trouble comprehending the magnitude of the celebration unfolding around us.

The historic center of Savannah is divided into twenty-four squares, as if New York's Central Park had been broken up into manageable rectangles and parceled at regular intervals throughout the old, residential heart of the city. Most of these squares have their own fountains. On that St. Patrick's Day weekend, the water in those fountains was a radioactive green. There were booths selling wristbands for drinks. Everyone, it seemed, was clutching a to-go cup of beer, and it was eleven in the morning.

Savannah sits on a plateau overlooking the river that shares its name. There's an engraving of the settlement made in 1734, soon after the city was founded. The artist had been sitting on a hill on the other side of the river, where he had a panoramic view of the naked plain of Savannah, recently hacked out of a wilderness of longleaf pine, the shadowy edges of which can still be seen encircling the clearing. The fifty-foot-high riverbank is so steep that ropes are being used to haul cargo up from the ships secured to the foot of the embankment.

It's been said that Savannah was the first planned community in America. Georgia's founder, James Oglethorpe, envisioned the city as a refuge for the urban poor of England where they could create a classless society without slavery and, if you can believe it, without alcohol. In that 1734 sketch you can already see the system of squares that still dominates the city today. Oglethorpe hoped to create a network of cooperative communities within the settlement, and inhabitants were limited in the amount of land they could own. Instead of the usual southern crops of rice and tobacco, which relied on enslaved Africans to perform the labor, Oglethorpe hoped to create a profitable silk industry, initially requiring that landowners plant a certain number of mulberry trees (silkworms depend on the mulberry leaves for food) per acre. One of the gatherings Washington attended while in Savannah was at the Filature, named for the process of securing silk from the green cocoons that once filled the barnlike structure's loft. The other alternative crop Oglethorpe hoped to nurture was cotton, which was first planted in Georgia in 1733. At that time, the process of separating the cotton fibers from the seeds was so laborious that the crop proved less profitable than initially hoped. But of course, all that would change by the end of the century.

Within a decade of the colony's founding, Oglethorpe's dream of an agrarian, slave-free paradise was no more. Initially the state was seen as a buffer between the Carolinas and Spanish-occupied Florida, which had become a haven for fugitive slaves. But when Georgia, the supposed buffer, became the slave refuge, Carolina planters grew irritated with the new colony's slavery ban. In addition, Georgia's settlers started to envy the economic success of the low-country planters to the north. Within a decade Georgia was a slave colony just like the rest of the South.

It's a consummate irony, of course, that a city founded as alcohol free is now anything but. Instead of dropping the glimmering ball on New Year's Eve, Savannahians used to raise a huge, strobe-lit to-go cup in what was known as the Up the Cup ceremony. That Saturday a local resident said to me, "We like to pride ourselves on our history, but come on—look around you! This is more like Vegas." And yet, thanks to those omnipresent squares, each one bristling with historical plaques, the past—even amid the tumult of a St. Patrick's Day weekend—is still right there with you.

And besides, as Washington could have testified, Savannahians have been enjoying themselves for centuries. Take, for example, the ball at the Filature. Washington retired at eleven, but the party continued until three in the morning. The next day, the festivities resumed in a specially constructed "bower" overlooking the river. Laurel and bay leaves had been wrapped around three rows of pillars, and the view was spectacular. Instead of today's enormous container ships sliding up and down the Savannah River, Washington's eye feasted on the "extensive . . . rice lands above and below the town." Two hundred people had been packed inside that arbor, but Washington remained his usual, imperturbable self. One partygoer later wrote of how you needed to meet the president face-to-face to fully appreciate "the intelligent serenity of his countenance, the unaffected ease and dignity of his deportment."

So many toasts were given during Washington's visit to Savannah— each accompanied by a blast of cannon fire—that he decided the city's artillery unit deserved a special gift. Soon after Washington's return to Philadelphia, he sent two of the fieldpieces captured from the

British at Yorktown to Savannah's Chatham Artillery Company. Today the "Washington Guns" can be seen beneath a protective canopy on Bay Street, yet another nodal point of history that even Dora found of interest as she sniffed the surrounding wrought-iron fence.

Dora, it turned out, does not like St. Patrick's Day parades. She was fine with the quieter floats—one of my favorites was titled "Savannah for Morons": a roofless bus full of twentysomethings shouting, "Happy Thanksgiving! Merry Christmas! Don't do drugs unless it's on purpose!" The pounding drums of the high school marching bands, on the other hand, were a little much for Dora. But it was the Sons of Confederate Veterans who pushed her over the edge.

It began well enough as we watched a man and a woman with gray shirts and floppy brown hats walk past with a banner reading "Southern Loyalty Not Hate." The trouble started when the men behind them, each with a bayonet attached to the barrel of his rifle, paused in front of us, raised their weapons, and fired into the sky. A thick cloud of suitably gray powder smoke rolled over us as Dora tugged desperately on the leash. Melissa and I agreed that it was time for a tactical retreat to our hotel room.

The next day, a Sunday, was clear but very cold—just forty degrees, in fact. Melissa and I felt like the only ambulatory people in Savannah as we walked with Dora to Wright Square for a 10:00 a.m. history tour with Vaughnette Goode-Walker. Vaughnette was dressed in an ankle-length red coat, red gloves, a white shawl, and a pink knit cap pulled over her braids. In one hand she held an enormous walking stick that she described as her "Rasta man made of wood."

We began at the monument to Tomo-Chi-Chi, chief of the Yamacraw Indians and "co-partner" with James Oglethorpe. Vaughnette said it was the only monument in Savannah memorializing the region's original inhabitants. From there we plunged into the wide back alleys of the city, the pathways of Savannah's African Americans in the nineteenth century, whom Vaughnette described as the "urban

Vaughnette Goode-Walker at Savannah's Wright Square.

people." She explained that on the first Tuesday of every month slave auctions were held on the steps of the Chatham County Courthouse. In March 1859, however, there was an auction like no other. Vaughnette showed us a transcription of the ad that appeared in the local newspapers. "Long Cotton and Rice Negroes," it read. "A Gang of 460 Negroes. Accustomed to the culture of rice and provisions, among who are a number of good mechanics and house servants, will be sold . . . by Joseph Bryan."

Bryan was the foremost slave dealer in Savannah. Even for Bryan, this was a big sale. Pierce Mease Butler of Philadelphia, an absentee owner of two plantations in the vicinity of Georgia's St. Simons Island, had run up tremendous gambling debts and needed cash. So he put up for auction half the enslaved people he'd inherited from his uncle. There was so much interest in the sale—prospective buyers came from as far away as Louisiana—that the auction had to be moved from Bryan's place of business on Johnson Square to a racetrack a couple of miles outside the city.

The auction lasted for two days and was conducted in a driving rain. A reporter from the *New-York Tribune* posing as a "Negro speculator" later wrote an account of the auction. He described a young man unsuccessfully pleading with the crowd to buy both himself and his fiancée. He told of how a group of buyers insisted that a pregnant mother remove the blanket she'd wrapped around her midriff so they could get a better look at her. "The expression on the faces of all who stepped on the block was always the same," the reporter wrote, "more anguish than it is in the power of words to express . . . , crushed hopes and broken hearts." The auction netted $303,850 (about $9.5 million in today's dollars) for Pierce Mease Butler. In appreciation, Butler gave each of his former slaves a dollar. In the African American community, the auction is still remembered today as the "Weeping Time."

Vaughnette also told us the story of the *Wanderer*, the last ship to deliver enslaved Africans to Georgia in 1858, the year before the Butler slave auction and more than half a century after Congress had officially banned the importation of slaves. The leading investor behind the voyage was Charles Augustus Lafayette Lamar, one of a growing number of extremists in the South, known as the fire-eaters, who not only defended slavery but claimed it was essential to the financial and moral health of the nation. Even Lamar's father insisted his son was "so impulsive and so crazy on the Negro question that I can make no impression on him."

Lamar went to extraordinary lengths to secure the fastest sailing vessel he could find—the 106-foot *Wanderer*, built at Washington's former spy capital of Setauket on the north shore of Long Island and modeled on the *America*, the schooner that had won the first America's Cup race in England in 1851. In 1858, the *Wanderer*, equipped with suspiciously oversized water tanks and flying the pennant of the New York Yacht Club (Lamar's partner in the venture, William Corrie, was a member), departed from New York Harbor bound for the mouth of the Congo River.

Somehow the ship's captain packed 487 enslaved African men, women, and children onto this little vessel. I've spent considerable time aboard the schooner *Lynx* of Nantucket, which is just a little smaller than the *Wanderer*. I cannot conceive how that many people could have been jammed into a hundred-foot schooner. By the time the *Wanderer* reached Jekyll Island on the Georgia coast, 78 of the captives had died. In hopes of avoiding detection, Lamar divided up the 409 survivors into smaller groups that were sent to auctions in Florida and South Carolina, as well as Savannah and Augusta. Inevitably, the Africans' filed teeth and distinctive tattoos alerted authorities to the fact that these slaves had not been born in the United States.

Within the year, Lamar and the *Wanderer*'s captain and crew were on trial in Savannah. (By then the members of the New York Yacht Club had passed two resolutions—the first erasing the name *Wanderer* from their list of vessels, the second expelling Lamar's partner, William Corrie, from the club.) To no one's surprise in Savannah, Lamar and everyone associated with the *Wanderer* were found not guilty. "It was the O.J. trial of 1858," Vaughnette said. "You must acquit." Seven years later, Charles Augustus Lafayette Lamar was shot and killed while leading a charge against Union soldiers during the last engage-ment of the Civil War, seven days after Lee's surrender at Appomattox.

Vaughnette, Melissa, and I sat on a park bench on Johnson Square with Dora at our feet. Behind us was Christ Church, where Washing-ton attended a Sunday service on the morning he left Savannah. Vaughnette gestured at the beautiful, tree-shaded square. "This was one of the largest slave yards in America," she said, "and it all hap-pened in front of a church." We could hear the service going on in-side. "Today most of Savannah is Black," she continued, "but not in the historic district." She looked at her watch. "Eleven o'clock Sunday morning. The most segregated hour in America."

About thirteen miles out of Savannah, we stopped at a historical plaque marking the location of Mulberry Grove Plantation, owned in 1791 by the widow of the Revolutionary War hero Nathanael Greene. At the conflict's nadir in the autumn of 1781, after the fall of Charles-ton to the British and General Horatio Gates's devastating defeat at the hands of Lord Cornwallis in Camden, Washington decided that Greene was the only one of his generals capable of turning the war around in the South. A former Quaker from Rhode Island, Greene did exactly that. He didn't have enough soldiers or money, but somehow he succeeded in driving the British from the Carolinas and Georgia.

In appreciation of Greene's efforts, the state of Georgia awarded him Mulberry Grove, a plantation on the Savannah River. In 1786, five years before Washington's visit, Nathanael Greene died of sun-stroke, leaving his wife, Caty, with five children and the debts he'd amassed to feed his army during the war—debts he had been forced to guarantee personally. When Washington stopped at Mulberry Grove on the way both to and from Savannah, Caty was waiting to hear about a petition she'd filed in Congress seeking relief from her deceased husband's debts.

Caty had known Washington since the beginning of the Revolu-tion. Her oldest son had been named for him. At one point during the war, when the army was in winter quarters in New Jersey, the Greenes hosted a dance in their living room. Nathanael reported approvingly that Caty and the commander in chief had danced together for three hours straight.

Ribald traditions have sprung up over what occurred between Washington and Caty at Mulberry Grove. As one local historian has noted, "The president made his companions wait outside." I think it's unlikely that anything untoward happened during those two stopovers. Caty was beautiful, that's for sure, but she was also a dazzling conversationalist. Her daughter Cornelia claimed her mother possessed "the most remarkable combination of intellectual power and physical beauty I have personally encountered in womanhood." Perhaps Caty's husband, Nathanael, gave her the finest tribute: "Her flowing tongue and cheerful countenance quite triumph over my grave face." The widow of the Revolutionary War officer whom Washington regarded (along with Lafayette) as a surrogate son, Caty was just the person with whom the president could talk freely before and after the hullabaloo in Savannah. In any event, within the year, Washington had signed the legislation relieving Caty of her husband's war debts.

Mulberry Plantation had a noteworthy history even before the state awarded the property to Nathanael Greene. The first boatload of enslaved workers ferried across the Savannah River into the then slave-free colony of Georgia had arrived at what became Mulberry Grove. In 1792, just a year after Washington's visit, Caty invited a recent graduate of Yale, who had come south to tutor the children of a neighbor, to live at Mulberry Grove. His name was Eli Whitney. The following year, Whitney, with (it's been claimed) Caty's input, created a new version of a cotton engine (or "gin" for short) with a wire-toothed cylinder that separated the fiber from the seed with unprecedented efficiency. Although modern academics have debunked the claim that Eli Whitney "invented" the cotton gin (a technology that had existed for centuries), there is little doubt that the version of the device he perfected at Mulberry Grove changed the nation.

Just look at the numbers. In 1790, Georgia and South Carolina produced 1.5 million pounds of cotton. Seventy years later, at the beginning of the Civil War, the South produced 2.3 billion pounds of cotton, accounting for 60 percent of the United States' exports by revenue. Over that same period the number of the enslaved in the country went from 700,000 to 3 million.

Mulberry Grove was burned by Sherman's army, and the land is now owned by the Georgia Ports Authority. Melissa and I weren't able to explore the plantation property that afternoon, but thanks to Vaughnette, who had an iPad with her during our tour, we'd seen the pictures she'd taken while visiting the long-abandoned site. Like White Hill Plantation back in South Carolina, all that was left was a corridor of live oaks leading to a heap of blasted brick.

As we stood there beside the historical plaque for Mulberry Plantation, it felt as if we had reached a kind of ground zero. Here, at a plantation once owned by a lapsed Quaker from Rhode Island who'd led the American Revolutionary forces in the battle for liberty and freedom in the South, a Connecticut Yankee with a mechanical bent had, with the help of the recently deceased general's brilliant wife, created the machine that assured the enslavement of millions of human beings.

Looking into the woods across from the plaque, I was tempted to believe that a monster had been born in Mulberry Grove. But it was worse than that. A monster is singular and slayable. What haunts America is more pervasive, more stubborn, and often invisible. It is the legacy of slavery, and it is everywhere.

Savannah marked the southernmost point of Washington's tour. His next major stop, Augusta, about 130 miles up the Savannah River, was north even of Charleston. From here on, he was in the homestretch. And yet by heading inland into the up-country, Washington was venturing into what might be perceived as enemy territory. Unlike the plantation owners of the low country, the farmers to the west were deeply suspicious of what Washington's new government was up to—particularly when it came to the tax on whiskey. In Piney Woods, South Carolina, where Washington would spend his first night after leaving Augusta, a grand jury had recently declared that the excise tax was "repugnant to the condition and liberties of a free people . . . [and] will bear very and unequally hard on the inhabitants of the southern states . . . [especially] those who live in the interior country." The days of glad-handing in Charleston and Savannah were over. Now it was time for Washington to start changing people's minds.

The city of Augusta first came into being back in 1736 when a fort was built just below the fall line of the Savannah River. An Indian trading post had existed at this spot for decades, and Governor Oglethorpe wanted to ensure that Georgia, not South Carolina, received most of the deer pelts being sent down the river. Augusta (named for the mother of King George III) was built at the convergence of two old Indian trading paths. What became known as Washington Road led to the homeland of the Cherokees, while Wrightsboro Road led to the Creeks.

During the Revolution, Augusta was far enough from British-occupied Savannah that it could serve as Georgia's patriot capital, a position it still held when Washington rolled into town on May 18. The president had actual governmental business to conduct in Augusta regarding the return of fugitive slaves from Spanish-held Florida. While Georgians were eager to get their slaves back, Washington didn't want the negotiations to imperil the United States' relations with Spain. What most concerned him were ongoing attempts by a shadowy group of land speculators (which included the former Virginia governor Patrick Henry) to persuade Georgia's governor, Edward Telfair, and the state legislature to sell them what were called the Yazoo lands—a huge tract stretching west all the way to the Mississippi River. That large groups of Native peoples lived on those lands did not concern the speculators.

Despite having participated himself in a similar landgrab after the Seven Years' War, Washington was dead set against this particular scheme and believed it "must involve the country in trouble, perhaps in blood." Three years after his visit to Augusta, the Georgia legislature perpetrated the Yazoo land scandal by authorizing the sale of forty million acres. When the sordid details of the transaction became known (legislators had been bribed), the law was repealed. This created a legal mess that ultimately forced Georgia to cede what became the states of Mississippi and Alabama to the federal government.

It was in Augusta that tragedy struck Washington's entourage. Cornwallis, the president's faithful greyhound, unexpectedly died, apparently worn out by the unrelenting pace of the southern tour. "Washington's heart was as tender as a woman's," one account read, "as those of us can testify who saw how the loss of a favorite pet could work upon his responsive feelings."

It was in Augusta that I began to have my doubts about the whole idea of Washington's canine companion (especially one named for his great British rival). Bill Kirby is a writer for *The Augusta Chronicle*. Awhile back, he wanted to retire, but his editors offered him his dream gig: write three columns a week about anything he wanted as long as Monday's column touched on history. I first became aware of Bill when he mentioned my latest book about the Revolution in one of his columns. We'd started to correspond, and he'd provided me with a pouch full of newspaper clippings about Washington's visit. Soon after our arrival in Augusta, Bill took Melissa, Dora, and me on a tour of the city's historical hot spots, and the conversation inevitably turned to Washington's dog.

Bill pointed out that everything we know about Cornwallis comes from an article in an 1892 issue of *The Augusta Chronicle*. According to the story, recent roadwork had led to the discovery of a buried gravestone that read "Here lies the dust of Cornwallis, the favorite of George Washington, whose recent visit to this colony shall ever be among its proudest memories." Beneath the marble gravestone they found a small brick vault with the remains of a large dog.

There are a few strange things about this story. For one, the gravestone refers to Georgia as a colony—a word that no God-fearing

American in 1791 would have dared use. The other is that no one can find the location of this grave site. Then Bill provided the clincher. "Nat," he said, "did you notice the date of the article?" I hadn't. "April 1, 1892." He let that sink in. "It was all an April Fools' Day joke!" So forget everything I've told you until now about George Washington's dog Cornwallis.

But that isn't the only bogus tradition about Washington that comes from Augusta. None other than Parson Weems, the minister who wrote the famous myth-brimming biography of George Washington, once lived and preached in the city. The fifth edition of Weems's ever-expanding biography of the first president—the first to include the story about the young Washington cutting down the cherry tree—was published when Weems was in Augusta. One of the articles Bill had sent me had the headline "'Pa, I Can't Tell a Lie' Originated Here in 1807." When you combine Weems's cherry tree with the invention of Cornwallis the dog, Augusta is a veritable font of misinformation about George Washington.

Our conversation with Bill strayed to other topics. "Before they invented Florida," he explained, "northerners came to Augusta." That's one of the reasons why Augusta National, one of the premier golf courses in the world, is in the vicinity. On the other side of the river is a legacy of a different sort—the Savannah River Site, a former hydrogen bomb plant, long since decommissioned, but a lasting source of radioactive contamination that has leached into the water table, spawning, according to some recent, undoubtedly spurious accounts, huge pink alligators and mutant spiders.

But for many Augustans, the darkest stain on the region's reputation comes from the novel *Tobacco Road*, published in 1932 by Erskine Caldwell. *Tobacco Road* is set in rural Georgia just outside Augusta during the Depression. The Lesters, a family of white sharecroppers, are depicted as stupid, lascivious, and cruel. The teenage daughter has a cleft lip that the father is too lazy to have fixed; the woman pursuing the older brother has a nose without any cartilage that makes her look like a pig. It's a world of grotesques—hideous and sometimes comical—and in the 1930s Augustans were furious with Erskine Caldwell. "There's an actual Tobacco Road here," Bill said, "and there was talk of changing the name to something else—just because of Caldwell's book."

During dinner at an Italian restaurant called Augustino's, Bill talked about his own southern heritage. He's the eight-times-great-nephew of Patrick Henry, but it's the relative who was a "waiter" in the Revolution whom he's most proud of. "If you needed to empty a chamber pot," Bill said, "you called on my ancestor. That's why there are more Kirbys than Custers. Obscurity has its benefits."

George Washington was unimpressed by the up-country of South Carolina, describing it as "a pine barren of the worst sort." Hills abounded, and the roads were heavy with sand. By the time he reached Columbia, one of his horses had come up lame, or foundered, requiring that he stay an extra day in the state capital—a newly established town with a "large and commodious, but unfinished" statehouse. For Washington, who was attempting to create a new capital of his own, Columbia was a cautionary tale. If this statehouse amid the long-leaf pines was any indication, creating a city from scratch would not happen overnight.

That said, Washington apparently liked the look of South Carolina's capitol. When he was ultimately forced to fire the architect Pierre Charles L'Enfant (who quickly proved unwilling to take criticism), he chose the young Irish architect who designed the statehouse in Columbia, James Hoban, to design the Federal City's executive mansion, otherwise known as the White House.

Our own journey to Columbia was everything Washington's wasn't. The peach trees were in bloom, and the purple-pink blossoms made the leisurely, two-hour journey a delight. There were also plenty of pecan trees just beginning to green up, and four miles east of Lexington we came upon a noted sycamore—a descendant of the tree that supposedly sheltered Washington as he attended to his lame horse. Back then someone with an ax had cut two blazes in the sycamore's trunk to help travelers find their way to Columbia. To this day, Route 1 is called Two Notch Road.

We arrived in Columbia in time for lunch, then went for a stroll on the grounds of the Greek Revival statehouse that replaced Hoban's original structure. It was only after the shootings at the Emanuel AME Church in Charleston in 2015, in which nine persons (including the state senator Clementa Pinckney) were killed, that the Confederate standard was taken down from a flagstaff on the statehouse grounds. Even then it didn't happen until after the Black activist Bree Newsome scaled the thirty-foot pole and pulled down the flag. Newsome was arrested, but the point had been made, and a Confederate battle flag no longer flies beside the South Carolina statehouse.

The capitol is surrounded by a veritable sculpture garden of figures from the Revolutionary and Civil Wars. That afternoon, about twenty third graders were running excitedly from monument to monument on a scavenger hunt. "Hey, here's the Swamp Fox!" one of the students shouted. "I know about him." A chaperone pointed at a statue of the Confederate general Wade Hampton. "Hey, we didn't have to come all this way to see that guy. We've got a Wade Hampton Avenue back home."

For the most part, the kids and their chaperones seemed oblivious to the controversy surrounding Confederate statues such as these. But then an African American student brought me up short. "Nice dog," he said, pointing to Dora. Before I could thank him, he said, "I think you should name him Frederick Douglass." Clearly someone in this school group was looking for an alternative historical figure to venerate.

Near the statehouse's massive front steps we found the surprisingly diminutive bronze figure of George Washington, holding a cane missing its lower half. A plaque claimed Union soldiers had damaged the statue, which remained in its present state of disrepair as a pointed reminder of the havoc the Yankees had inflicted not only on the South but, in this case, on the memory of the country's first president.

It was in Columbia that Washington put the proverbial pedal to the metal, leaving at the ungodly hour of four in the morning. For the rest of the southern tour, Washington remained in a hurry, bursting out of the blocks every morning before daylight. Years later, his step-grandson, Washy Custis, recounted how Washington's blistering pace during the tail end of the southern tour "astonished everyone," claiming that the many Revolutionary War veterans who flocked to his anticipated stops shouted out to the young people hurrying along with them, "Push on, my boys, if you wish to see him; for we, who ought to know, can assure you that he is never behind time, but always punctual to the moment."

George Washington's punctuality is, I think, one of his more endearing characteristics. People make fun of those who are impulsively punctual. I should know, I'm one of those sorry sorts who always arrives at meetings on time (but never a minute early) and hasn't met a deadline he didn't like. It's a particularly embarrassing trait given my line of work; writers are supposed to be too lost in the clouds to adhere to the timetables of others. (The novelist Charles Portis refers to punctuality as "the puniest of the virtues.") At the beginning of one of my favorite movies of all time, the mockumentary *This Is Spinal Tap*, the filmmaker Marty DiBergi (played by Rob Reiner) tells us about the first time he saw the English rock band Spinal Tap. "I remember being knocked out by their, their exuberance," he recounts, "their raw power—and their punctuality." As the joke implies, a true rock star is always late. But not George Washington.

The peso Washington cut in half to pay for breakfast at Nathan Barr's tavern.

CHAPTER 17

"A Cat May Look on a King"

One of the great benefits of the southern tour, from Washington's perspective, was that it finally gave him the chance to visit the sites of the many crucial battles fought in the Carolinas and Georgia. Already the former general had inspected the still torn-up terrain outside Charleston and Savannah. Now, with his arrival in Camden, the oldest inland town in South Carolina, he had hit Revolutionary War pay dirt.

In 1780, Lord Cornwallis—the British general, not the fictive greyhound of Augusta—turned Camden into one of the fortified bases from which he launched his own southern campaign. That summer, Cornwallis defeated Horatio Gates at a vicious battle fought five and a half miles north of Camden. The following year, Nathanael Greene fought Cornwallis's second-in-command, Lord Rawdon, at the Battle of Hobkirk's Hill, even closer to the town center. It was only appropriate that our tour guide in Camden was a retired army officer named Rick Wise.

Rick had commanded a multiple launch rocket system (MLRS) battery in Desert Storm. He then volunteered for the war in Iraq. He would have preferred to have been in combat ("I've always been a pointy-end-of-the-stick kind of guy," he said), but ended up serving as a staff officer in the multinational force headquartered at Saddam Hussein's palace in the Green Zone. "Every time I saw a dusty Humvee," he said, "I felt guilty."

Rick, who now drives my dream car, a red Camaro, said he got his love of history from his grandmother. "She used to tell stories about 'Uncle Francis,' the Swamp Fox," he recounted. "Francis Marion was a short dude with dark hair—I'm thinking Jamie Farr from *M*A*S*H*." Rick is no Maxwell Q. Klinger. Tall, with an athlete's build, he was wearing aviator sunglasses and a dark blue baseball cap with a crescent moon on the front (the personal logo of the South Carolina Revolutionary War hero William Moultrie) and the word "Liberty." He said he was at work on a master's degree in military history and had hopes of waiving the language requirement. "I speak English as a second language," he explained. "My first is Southern."

Rick joined us in our Honda Pilot for a quick tour of downtown Camden, then led us in his Camaro to the scene of Horatio Gates's defeat. The battlefield is on the edge of the Old Catawba Road to Charlotte—a single-lane dirt road similar to the one we had followed to and from Charleston. The battle was fought in the midst of an ancient longleaf pine forest, and efforts are under way to reestablish the pines, which now have the gangly, adolescent look of the shaggy-topped trees imagined by Dr. Seuss in *The Lorax*. Rick said that at the time of the fighting in 1780 the trees were so big that two men could hide behind each trunk. When Washington visited the site eleven years later, he could see how the musket balls had chewed up the tree bark and horse skeletons still littered the ground.

Rick explained that the two armies met around dawn after marching hard all night. A light fog hung in the air, and when the British regulars charged out of the mist shouting "Huzzah!" with their bayonets fixed, the American militiamen turned and ran "like scalded dogs." It wasn't long before Gates was leading them in full retreat. Unfortunately, the American commander neglected to inform Major General Johann DeKalb that he had abandoned the field. DeKalb had been a mentor to the young Lafayette and was one of the most respected officers in the Continental army. Even after his horse had been killed, DeKalb continued fighting until he lay in a bloody heap at the base of a pine tree.

Rick took us to the spot where DeKalb, who'd been shot three times and repeatedly stabbed, was found by Cornwallis. "I am sorry to see you so badly wounded," the British general reportedly said. It took three days for DeKalb to die. When Washington visited the site of DeKalb's grave in Camden, he knelt down on his cloak and prayed. As he understood better than any president ever has, the country's independence had come at a cost.

The next day, after an early morning sprint of about twenty miles, Washington pulled into the tavern owned by Nathan Barr for breakfast. Once Washington had finished his bowl of corn mush and milk—just the meal for someone without a tooth in his head—he decided to give Barr's young daughter a nice tip.

At this early stage in the country's history, the United States had not yet begun to mint its own coins. In order to cover expenses during the southern tour, Washington had requisitioned four hundred dollars' worth of Spanish pesos from the U.S. Treasury that were kept in a strongbox beneath the coach driver's seat. The cost of breakfast at a tavern in South Carolina had been set by the state at the equivalent of a British shilling. Washington asked Major Jackson for one of the Spanish coins in the strongbox, cut the peso in half with his sword, and left the half-moon of silver in the bottom of his bowl. This was four bits (or half a Spanish piece of eight) and worth about two shillings—basically double the price of the breakfast. Many years later, Barr's daughter, then in her seventies, gave the four bits left by Washington to a relative who eventually donated the chopped coin to Wofford College in nearby Spartanburg, making it one of the few Washington traditions that has actually been documented.

As Washington made his way north toward the South Carolina border, he noticed that the surrounding countryside had taken a turn for the better. The sandy pine barrens had given way to a more lush landscape of rolling hills and rocky-bottomed rivers. The soil was now "a greasy red" with forests of large oak, hickory, and chestnut trees intermixed with the first meadows he'd seen since leaving Virginia. Washington had entered the Carolina Piedmont—the region between the coastal flatlands to the east and the Appalachian Mountains to the west, and the home of the Catawba.

Once Melissa, Dora, and I had driven across the bridge over the Catawba River—a vast sheet of languid brown water—we took the exit for the Catawba Reservation and Cultural Center. On our way to the reservation we passed a historical plaque marking the location of a tavern owned by Major Robert Crawford. This was where, the sign read, "President George Washington spent his last night in South Carolina on his southern tour, May 27, 1791. Here Washington was met by a delegation of the chiefs of the Catawba Nation, who set forth their apprehensions that attempts would be made to deprive them of their land."

Washington had a history with the Catawba. As a British officer during the Seven Years' War, he had sent large amounts of trade goods to the tribe. More than two hundred Catawba warriors—heralded as "the bravest fellows on the continent"—had fought for the British against the French and their Native allies. A decade later during the Revolution, the Catawba chose to back the United States, an alliance that cost them dearly when the British burned their village in 1781. Now that the Catawba were allied with a republic instead of a monarchy, they changed how they addressed their tribal leader. While it had been King Hagler whom Washington had dealt with during the Seven Years' War, it was Hagler's successor, General New River, with whom the president met at Crawford's tavern.

The Catawba were cultural shape-shifters. As disease ravaged the tribes throughout the Piedmont in the seventeenth and early eighteenth centuries, the Catawba welcomed refugees from a wide variety of Native groups. At one point more than twenty different languages were spoken among the Catawba. In 1763, this polyglot people were granted a fifteen-mile square of land by the Crown. By the time of

Washington's visit, the tribe had begun leasing large tracts of their land to white farmers. Although this provided the Catawba with a source of income, tribal leaders feared their tenants might begin to manipulate the legal system to take control of what was rightly Catawba land. Washington assured General New River that under the new constitution the federal government had the sole right to negotiate Indian treaties and that the Catawba had nothing to worry about. But as time would prove, the Catawba were more than justified in their concerns.

Washington, in typical fashion, gives the barest of details about his meeting with General New River. Fortunately, a Methodist minister visited the tribe just a month and a half before Washington's encounter, and his account provides a vivid picture of the Catawba leader as "a tall, grave old man . . . with a mighty staff in his hand. Round his neck he wore a narrow piece of leather . . . adorned with a great variety of bits of silver." New River and his people "wore silver nose-rings from the middle gristle of the nose and some of them had little silver hearts hanging from the rings." The Catawba dressed much like their white neighbors, with some of the men "even wearing ruffles and very showy suits of clothes made of cotton."

At the Catawba museum I talked with Kassidy Plyler, whose Catawba name is Dances Like a Butterfly. She told of how one of her relatives met her future husband, the son of a wealthy farmer, on the ferry across the Catawba River. Back then, before 1965, it was illegal for a Catawba to marry a white person. Kassidy said her aunt used to talk about how "her daddy lied about his race to get married."

For centuries the Catawba have been renowned for their pottery, and in the gift shop I bought a small clay duck for Melissa (who was back in the car with Dora on a telephone call)—the perfect gift, I reasoned, for the owner of a duck-tolling retriever. While I was paying for my purchase, I asked Kassidy if she knew anything about George Washington's visit in 1791. She directed me to her boss, Wenonah Haire, who suggested I talk with the Charlotte-based sculptor Chas Fagan. Fagan had recently completed a pair of statues—one of the

Catawba leader King Hagler, the other of Hagler's white neighbor and friend Thomas Spratt—that are now a part of the city of Charlotte's Trail of History, a sequence of memorials highlighting important characters from the region's past. Melissa and I were scheduled to spend the night at an Airbnb in a suburb of Charlotte and resolved to visit the statues of Hagler and Spratt the next morning.

At the edge of a park near the highway we found them: two seven-and-a-half-foot figures standing on a rock. There they stood—two self-possessed human beings gazing at the world with a companionable dignity. Chas Fagan later told me about how he had worked with the Catawba while researching his subjects. In keeping with the tribe's wishes, he'd modeled Hagler's face on the members of the Harris family, whose ancestor Peter Harris had been adopted at a young age by Thomas Spratt shortly after Harris's parents died in a smallpox epidemic. At the end of an eventful life, which included fighting in the Revolution and even traveling to England as part of an early version of a Wild West show, Harris asked to be buried in the Spratt family cemetery, where his grave can still be found. In the archives, Fagan discovered references to the trade goods the young George Washington sent to the Catawba during the Seven Years' War and then made sure to include some of those goods as part of Hagler's clothing.

In *Moby-Dick*, Ishmael decides that the Polynesian harpooner Queequeg is "George Washington cannibalistically developed." While looking into the bronze eyes of Chas Fagan's rendering of the Catawba leader, I began to think of George Washington as King Hagler presidentially developed.

Washington had been profoundly influenced by his interactions with Native peoples. During the Seven Years' War a Seneca leader had given him the sobriquet Conotocarious, meaning Town Taker or Destroyer. According to Washy Custis, Washington's "peculiar" way of walking—"placing and taking up his feet . . . in a light elastic tread [with] precision and care"—was something he'd picked up from his Native allies during "his long service on the frontier." One of the

Thomas Spratt and the Catawba leader King Hagler by Chas Fagan.

soldiers in Washington's Life Guards was a Wampanoag named Simeon Simons who was a direct descendant of Massasoit, the Native leader whose alliance with the Pilgrims saved Plymouth Colony from annihilation. According to tradition, Simons served with Washington throughout the entire war and even returned with him to Mount Vernon before ending up back home in Griswold, Connecticut. After Simons's death, his friends recounted how "when Washington was the topic, Simeon was affected as if he was a dear, dear friend."

That said, Washington's record with Native peoples was definitely mixed. During the Revolution his Native name of Town Taker proved disturbingly prophetic when he launched a brutal campaign against the Iroquois in upstate New York that led to the destruction of more than forty villages. As Washington finished his southern tour, his administration was about to embark on a campaign against the Native peoples in what is today Ohio. (As a result of that campaign and the Indian removals of the following century, there are no federally recognized tribes currently in Ohio.) And yet, unlike many subsequent presidents, Washington insisted that existing Indian treaties be scrupulously adhered to. He was certainly not perfect in his dealings with Indian tribes, but that did not prevent many Native people of the time from considering him a friend. Five years after meeting with Washington at Crawford's tavern, General New River traveled more than four hundred miles to Mount Vernon, where he once again met with Washington. The Catawba experienced plenty of setbacks in the nineteenth and twentieth centuries, including the eventual loss of much of their land. But as I write this, the tribe is about to begin building a 1.8-million-square-foot casino and hotel on sixteen acres just across the North Carolina border at Kings Mountain.

And then there is the example of the Iroquois. Despite the Continental army's destructive campaign against them in northern New York, the Iroquois came to appreciate Washington's efforts on their behalf once he became president. Around the time of Washington's death, the Seneca spiritual leader Handsome Lake had a vision in which he saw a house suspended between the earth and the clouds.

On the house's porch with a dog at his side was George Washington—"the only white man so near the new world of our Creator."

In 1851, Ely S. Parker became sachem of the Iroquois Confederacy. During the induction ceremony a peace medal first given by George Washington to Parker's ancestor Red Jacket was draped around Parker's neck as evidence of the "bond of perpetual peace and friendship established and entered into between the people of the United States and the Six Nations of Indians." Before becoming America's first Native commissioner of Indian affairs, Parker served as secretary to General Ulysses S. Grant and was present at Appomattox for the surrender of Robert E. Lee. I can see it now: the Washington peace medal dangling from Parker's neck as he attends to the paperwork associated with the fall of the Confederacy, knowing that up there, in a house amid the clouds with his faithful dog at his side, President Washington is smiling.

Washington was escorted to his next stop, Salisbury, North Carolina, by yet another unwanted troop of cavalry. But he had to give the North Carolina militia their due; they were tenacious, even sending an advance guard into South Carolina to accompany him across the border.

Thanks to Charles Caldwell, who at nineteen was part of that advance guard, we have one of our few glimpses of Washington between stops of his southern tour. Caldwell and his compatriots had first come upon Washington's carriage speeding toward them from the south. Inside the carriage they found not the president but his secretary Major Jackson, who explained that Washington was somewhere behind, enjoying his morning exercise on Prescott. So the Carolina cavalrymen went looking for the president.

The road, Caldwell remembered, was "lined on each side by ancient forest trees," and up ahead, at the top of a steep hill, they saw him "on a magnificent milk-white charger." Washington and Prescott were advancing down the hill, and the charger's steps were "measured and proud, as if the noble animal was conscious of the character and standing of his rider." This was Washington in a rare moment of actually having fun—alone on his horse on a bright sunny morning, exploring an unknown land. No wonder the tour was so good for him. "I have been in the enjoyment of very good health during my journey," he reported to his former secretary David Humphreys, "and have rather gained flesh upon it." Melissa and I had a similar experience in the South, particularly when it came to gaining flesh.

On Main Street in Salisbury, North Carolina, there is a statue of a very different sort from what we'd seen in Charlotte—a sheet metal cutout of Washington and Betsy Brandon, a young local girl who is the subject of yet another questionable tradition about the president. The story goes like this: On his approach to Salisbury, Washington decided he needed some refreshment before he was greeted by the crowd up ahead, so he stopped at the house of the Brandon family. Washington knocked on the door, and a girl named Betsy appeared. She explained that the rest of the family had gone into town to see the president, leaving only Betsy to tend the house. "Oh, I do so wish I could see him!" she said. "Well, I think we can arrange that," Washington said. "If you'll make me a cup of coffee, I'll promise you a sight of George Washington."

Betsy dutifully provided the stranger with the coffee. "Now you must keep your promise," she said. "George Washington is now before you," he said.

Unfortunately, the documentary record makes this anecdote highly unlikely. There was a Betsy Brandon living in Salisbury in 1791, but she was a married woman with ten children. Much like the city of Augusta, Salisbury seems to have been a kind of hot zone for generating dubious stories about Washington. The town even has its own "only a man" tradition. As Washington walked through the streets around sunset, the citizens "clamored for a speech." The president reluctantly complied. "Shading his face from [the sun's] rays with his handkerchief," a local historian wrote, "[Washington] said with eloquent and touching simplicity, 'You see before you only an old gray-haired man.'" The people, of course, loved it, especially when Washington claimed he was "more pleased with the plain, frank earnest welcome of Salisbury than the gaudy and fantastic reception at Charleston." Hey, who knows—he might have actually said something like that.

The stone steps from which Washington supposedly delivered those remarks are now on the grounds of the Rowan Public Library. I, of course, used this as an opportunity to visit the library, where I was directed to two extraordinary letters—framed and on display near the circulation desk. The first was the address from the citizens of Salisbury to George Washington; the other was his reply, apparently the only document signed by Washington during the southern tour that is not at the Library of Congress. The letter from Washington (undoubtedly written by Major Jackson) was standard-issue boilerplate, but the letter from the Salisburians (if that's a word) was truly special:

> We have the honor to signify to you, the joy, which your presence after a tedious journey undertaken at an advanced period of life, affords to the inhabitants of this place. . . . Situated at a remote distance from the seat of government, deriving no advantage from the establishment of post roads and destitute of regular information, we are sometimes at a loss to form proper opinions of national measures. But we, nevertheless, boast that we have been and still are zealously attached to order and effective government.

This, of course, was exactly what Washington was hoping to hear—particularly in a part of the state that he had been warned "vehemently" objected to the recent tax on whiskey. Washington later claimed that when he heard complaints about the tax during his southern tour, he was always able to put the person's mind at ease when he explained the reasoning behind the legislation. The cynical among us might assume Washington was simply whistling in the dark. In truth, however, he seems to have done exactly as he claimed. Yes, the farmers in western Pennsylvania would ultimately rise up in revolt, but such would not be the case in the states Washington visited during the southern tour, where there would be scattered outbreaks of violence in the up-country but no widespread and long-lasting unrest. Was this due to the Washington effect? One can only wonder what might have happened if Washington had conducted a western tour to Pittsburgh. Might a personal appearance by the president in the fall of 1791 have prevented the Whiskey Rebellion of 1794?

The next morning we parked in the vast lot of Old Salem Museums and Gardens in Winston-Salem. Imagine if Sturbridge Village and Plimoth Plantation had a love child who moved to North Carolina. That's kind of what Old Salem is all about: a historic Moravian village where costumed interpreters tell you what life was like in a mostly closed religious community in the late eighteenth and early nineteenth centuries.

While Melissa and Dora went for a walk through the leafy heart of Old Salem, I pretended I was a member of a school group and stepped into the ticketing area. I paid for my ticket and proceeded to the Museum Center, where a class was being briefed by a docent. Three years before, the trustees of Old Salem hired a new executive director, Frank Vagnone from New York, who had a reputation for shaking things up in the museum world. Vagnone preaches the heretical doctrine that a house museum should treat the visitor, not the house and its objects, as the chief priority, a dogma elucidated in his co-written book *Anarchist's Guide to Historic House Museums*. As he later told me, "I'm not interested in historic sites as nostalgia. I'm interested in today. What can the site teach me that's relevant to me now?"

When it came to Old Salem, Vagnone felt the institution needed to confront the Moravians' reliance on slavery. "The Moravians were refugee immigrants," Vagnone said, "running from persecution and death in Europe and seeking the most remote place they could find in America. They wanted to be left alone, with the exception of trade." In this respect, Vagnone explained, enslaved people performed an essential function for the Moravians, who all spoke German. In addition to being carpenters and coopers, the enslaved workers operated as interpreters. Vagnone began to realize that a visitor to Old Salem needed to get to know the enslaved people who helped build the town. This insight birthed a program called Hidden Town, which explores the role slavery played at Old Salem. Clearly Vagnone was leading the institution in a new and exciting, if sobering, direction.

As the docent at the Museum Center addressed the kids, I noticed an information panel that described Washington's visit to Salem. "George Washington may have been our most famous visitor to Salem in the past, but today you are our most important guest." The panel also pointed out that in addition to the six members of Washington's "Paid Staff" there were two "Enslaved Staff," Giles and Paris. The kids were dismissed and let loose into the village as another group came to take their places. "Good luck," I said to the docent. "This is a good day," she said brightly, "about two hundred kids. We have eight-hundred-kid days."

I walked up the hill on a wide brick sidewalk. I watched as a female interpreter, in a blue dress and white apron and bonnet with a wicker basket in her hand, got out of her gray Chevy Malibu and started up the sidewalk to work. I made my way to the tavern, where Washington spent two nights and enjoyed being serenaded by the Moravian brass band. Salem was in a region known as Wachovia, named by the original Moravian purchasers for where they'd come from back in Austria. (When Melissa and I were living in Durham, our first credit card was with Wachovia bank, which a friend called "Watch over Ya" bank.) The Moravians were pacifists and simply wanted to be left alone during the Revolution. That, of course, resulted in their harassment by loyalists and patriots alike.

There were about two hundred residents of Salem, divided into smaller units called choirs, consisting of those of the same gender and stage of life. This meant that the married wives lived together, as did the married men. Because the sexes did not live together, the conjugal act was a bit of a challenge. Moravians were instructed to procreate in a designated room called a cabinet while focusing not on their partners but on their union with Christ.

Until that point, Washington's tour had had definite militaristic overtones. When he wasn't being escorted by a company of cavalry, he was meeting with members of the Society of the Cincinnati and other veterans or inspecting battlefields. All that changed in Salem. Out of respect for the Moravians' love of peace, he did not ride into town in his general's uniform atop his warhorse, entering instead in his cream-colored carriage and dressed in his muted brown suit. Instead of toasts and cannon fire, he listened to the tubas and trombones while savoring an otherwise quiet dinner at the tavern.

Washington seems to have enjoyed the visit and even decided to stay an extra day when he heard that the governor of North Carolina, Alexander Martin, was headed his way. He visited the Single Brothers' House, the Single Sisters' House, the Boys' School, and the shops of various tradesmen. What impressed him the most were the town's waterworks, which provided each building with the unheard-of luxury of running water. At the corner of the town green there is still an old hand pump. Once Melissa and Dora joined me, I started to work the pump's handle, and the sudden burst of water into the soapstone basin put Dora into immediate retreat.

My first priority, however, was the tavern, and I joined the fifth graders from Clayton, North Carolina, as we all crowded into the rear entrance. It was only appropriate that I was experiencing Old Salem with a group of schoolkids. During his visit, Washington sat in on a class taught by Samuel Kramsch, who was instructing his students in English. The children were taking turns reading Noah Webster's *American Spelling Book*, a collection of English proverbs and epigrams that, in addition to teaching the kids how to read and spell, provided instructive lessons. As Washington sat to the side, one of the children read, "As you make your bed so you must lie." The next child read a proverb dating back to the fourteenth century: "A cat may look on a king," meaning that anyone— no matter what his or her social standing—can behave as he or she wants before a superior. Once the boy had finished reading about the cat looking on a king, he turned to his teacher and said with the syntax of someone for whom English was a new language, "They think it now also." In other words, he and the other boys were now in the presence of the closest thing America had to royalty. Because Washington had had such an intriguing interaction with schoolkids while in Salem, I was eager to see what the experience was like for children today, particularly in a museum run by Frank Vagnone.

Next to the side entrance of the tavern was a barn and an informational panel with the headline "Hidden Town." It began with a quotation from a June 14, 1780, entry in the Salem community's collective diary: "Yesterday a family came in flight from Georgia bringing about 20 Negroes; like those who preceded them, they camped in the woods opposite the tavern, and the place looked like a Negro village." The panel then went on to talk about how "people of many cultures (English, Irish, French, German, Italian, and even Cherokee) came here to spend the night. . . . Some were slaveholders and brought enslaved individuals with them. These slaves would not have been allowed to stay in the tavern." Clearly Giles and Paris slept somewhere else.

Soon we were in one of the main rooms talking with a docent in period dress. He looked over the group of ten-year-olds, all of them clutching sheets of paper provided by their teachers. "How you-all doing?" the docent asked. "You-all seem a little groggy. What time did you get up, six in the morning?" "No," a girl piped up, "that was when we had to get to the bus. I had to get up at five." "Me too!" shouted several others. "Wow, no wonder you're tired." I thought of Washington hitting the road by 4:00 a.m.

The docent explained that we were in the public room and that in the eighteenth century only four persons would have been allowed there at a time—all of them white adult males. He spoke of the card games that were popular at the time and a puzzle called a tangram (a shape puzzle from China first brought to America by a sea captain). This was all very informative, but what the kids wanted to know was where had Washington slept.

The docent explained that his room would have been upstairs. The kids immediately rushed to the staircase, only to find a chain across it. A minor riot ensued. "Washington's room is up there," one kid complained to a chaperone, "and we can't get up the stairs!" The docent explained that no one knew for sure which of the rooms Washington had slept in, and those rooms were off-limits to school groups. "But we were told to find the bed he slept in," an indignant child insisted. When I later told Frank Vagnone about how the fifth graders and I had been denied access to the second floor, he admitted that dealing with large groups in the tavern can be a challenge and then assured me that there no longer is a chain across the stairwell.

We had also missed, it turned out, what might be the most thought-provoking part of the tavern—a room above the kitchen that has been identified as where the enslaved people who worked at the tavern slept. In the last few years the room, which had previously been used as a large storage closet, has been turned into the "Tavern Room of Reflection and Meditation," available, according to the museum's website, "for contemplation regarding the enslaved." The space is now furnished with original pews from an African church as well as two headstones. One item you won't see in the Tavern Room of Reflection and Meditation is a bronze plaque commemorating Washington's visit that had been found among the other objects originally stored in the room. Vagnone's leadership team determined that given the new focus of the space it was inappropriate to display a plaque commemorating a slaveholder, even if he was the country's first president.

Washington had only one more stop in North Carolina before the southern tour was officially over: Guilford Courthouse, about thirty miles to the east, where in March 1781 the armies under the command of Nathanael Greene and Lord Cornwallis battled each other to the bloody draw that set Cornwallis on the path to Yorktown. Washington was unusually grouchy that day. Maybe he was thinking back to the battle and wondering whether Greene had blown the opportunity to defeat the British army at Guilford Courthouse. If Greene had put his best Continental troops on the front line, rather than the North Carolina militia, who turned and ran soon after the fighting had started, Washington believed Cornwallis's army "must have been sorely galled in their advance, if not defeated."

I think the source of Washington's irritation that day had nothing to do with Nathanael Greene. I think it had everything to do with having traveled for almost three months and more than fifteen hundred miles. It was time for this particular journey to end. More than anything else, he wanted to go home. No more addresses. No more dinners. No more toasts. And please, no more escorts.

When yet another company of cavalry met his carriage at Guilford Courthouse, Washington turned to Governor Martin, who'd joined his entourage in Salem, and asked him to dismiss the light horse and "to countermand his orders for others to attend me through the state." But that wasn't all. Even though the governor planned "to have attended me to the [state] line," Washington "requested that he would not." It wasn't the most tactful move on Washington's part, but after eighty-three days on the road, he was done.

A few nights later, just after crossing the North Carolina border into Virginia, he reflected on what he'd seen during the southern tour. He wrote in depth about the quality and variety of the land, the crops grown and the goods produced for market, and the rivers. "Excepting the towns (and some gentlemen's seats along the road from Charleston to Savannah)," he observed, "there is not, within view of the whole road I traveled . . . , a single house which has anything of an elegant appearance. They are altogether of wood and chiefly of logs." The public accommodations were, in a word, "bad," but the people "appeared to be happy, contented and satisfied with the general government under which they were placed. . . . The discontents which it was supposed the last Revenue Act . . . would create subside as fast as the law is explained and little was said of the Banking Act." He could now report with confidence that in all thirteen of the original states a majority of the American people approved of what he had done so far. But before he could return to the presidential mansion in Philadelphia, he needed to persuade the landowners on the Potomac to live up to their agreement. His dreams of a Federal City depended on it.

George Washington interpreter Dean Malissa at Mount Vernon.

CHAPTER 18

Muddy Freshets

On his second day back in Virginia, Washington crossed the Staunton River on the ferry owned by Isaac Coles, a wealthy planter and Anti-Federalist who had just finished a term in Congress. There was a tavern at the ferry landing, but Coles insisted that Washington stay at his house about a mile away. Because he was now off the clock as far as the southern tour, Washington readily agreed to Coles's offer of hospitality, leaving the rest of his entourage to fend for themselves at the tavern.

They came from different sides of the political fence, but Isaac and George appear to have enjoyed each other's company—so much so that Washington decided to spend an extra night. Isaac Coles ultimately moved thirty miles west to Chatham, Virginia, where he is buried in a family plot that now includes five subsequent generations of Coleses. Walter Coles V, eighty, is the present occupant of the property known as Coles Hill, and on the second floor of his Federal-style brick manor is the bed that Washington slept in for two nights in June 1791. I'd originally gotten in touch with Walter about the possibility of seeing the bed and talking with him about any family traditions related to the president's visit. It soon became clear, however, there was another, contemporary story connected with Walter Coles V that was pertinent to many of the issues Washington and the other founding fathers wrestled with when it came to the division of power between the federal government and the states.

About forty years ago, it was determined that Coles Hill sits atop one of the largest untapped deposits of uranium in the world, valued in 2011 at seven billion dollars. In the 1980s, when the Coles family began to explore the possibility of mining the uranium on their property, the Virginia legislature imposed a moratorium. As the value of uranium increased at the beginning of the twenty-first century, the Coles family formed a company called Virginia Uranium that took the state of Virginia all the way to the Supreme Court. When Melissa, Dora, and I arrived at Coles Hill in May 2019, Walter and his wife, Alice, were still awaiting the court's decision, which was due any day. But first things first. We needed to see the bed.

Walter was a proud Citadel graduate who'd been awarded the Bronze Star in Vietnam before beginning a long career in the Foreign Service. Walter and Alice had lived all over the world, but this ancient house, with twenty-eight-inch-thick walls and twelve-foot-high ceilings and built around 1817, was home. As Dora and their English setter, Letty, chased each other across the surrounding fields, Walter and Alice took us on a tour of their wonderful house.

The walls were covered with all sorts of paintings and historic documents, but what quickly caught my eye was a rusted and very bent harpoon. Walter explained that one of the more colorful characters in his family had been his great-uncle Russell Coles, a noted sports and nature writer in the early twentieth century who was a pal of Teddy Roosevelt's. The two regularly fished together, and Walter told of the time Russell took the president, whom he always called "Colonel," hunting for devil rays. First Russell spent a week at Roosevelt's home on Long Island teaching him how to hurl a harpoon. They then proceeded to Punta Gorda, Florida, where they set out in a small open boat. When a huge ray appeared off their bow, Russell shouted, "Iron him!" Teddy hurled the harpoon, and the mortally wounded ray lunged so severely that it twisted the harpoon's iron shaft like a piece of taffy. The bent harpoon at Walter's was the very one that had killed the devil ray; in fact, you could see it in the framed picture of Russell and TR with the dead ray—two tubby men with ropes around their waists to keep their pants up and big smiles on their faces.

On the second floor we found it: George Washington's bed. Until then, we'd seen only one other bed in which the president had slept— a surprisingly delicate piece of furniture at the Uxbridge Historical Society near the Massachusetts-Connecticut border. Washington had collapsed into the Uxbridge bed late on the night of November 6, 1789, after having been rebuffed at two different taverns in the vicinity. Whereas the Uxbridge bed was so lightly constructed that it looked as if it would have had a hard time accommodating someone over two hundred pounds, there were no such concerns about the Coleses' bed. Made of a dark sturdy wood, the bed had been built to last. Walter told of how an oxcart had delivered the bed from Norfolk to Isaac Coles's original house in Halifax, Virginia. He said the presidential visit wasn't something his family talked about much. There was, however, one tradition regarding the visit: "When one of the ladies in the Coles family was asked, many years later, what had been said at her table by the august George Washington, she replied that the only thing she could recall was that he *praised the pudding*!" Now, that's a tradition I can believe.

Instead of the past, Walter and Alice were living very much in the present, particularly when it came to their attempts to overturn the state's moratorium on mining uranium. It was kind of surreal to contemplate: a portion of this magnificent one-thousand-acre property, which had once been a tobacco plantation with between fifty and seventy enslaved workers and was now home to a small cattle and hay business, might one day become a uranium mine. Since the collapse of the tobacco, textile, and furniture industries, jobs in this part of Virginia were exceedingly hard to find, and Walter had been quoted as saying the mine would become "the engine of economic growth here." But, of course, you can't dig a uranium mine without serious environmental consequences, especially when it comes to the storage of the radioactive waste. Not only is the immediate area potentially impacted, but as was true with the former hydrogen bomb plant on the Savannah River, radioactive waste can contaminate the ground-water and affect communities many miles away. Walter said the Chatham community was split about fifty-fifty on the issue. "Some of my neighbors are investors," he said. "Others are dead set against it and were adamant at our meetings." What it came down to, he insisted, was his right to do what he wanted with his land.

There's little doubt that Walter's ancestor Isaac would have agreed with him, at least in principle. That was why they had fought a revolution—so individuals would have the freedom to do whatever they wanted with their property. The irony in the case of Virginia Uranium was that the federal government was supporting the Coleses' claim against the state's moratorium—just the opposite of the usual states' rights bias of an eighteenth-century Anti-Federalist from Virginia. And as it turned out, just a few weeks later the Supreme Court ruled in favor of the state's moratorium, meaning that for the time being all remains the same atop Coles Hill.

Walter had arranged for us to get a tour of the site of the house in which his six-times-great-grandfather had entertained the president. The house had burned down long ago, but we would be able to see the field in which Washington's horses had spent the day restoring themselves after almost three months of grueling travel. First, however, we were going to see the site of the ferry landing, where Isaac had greeted the president.

Both parcels of land are now owned by the retired Halifax County circuit court clerk Bobby Conner and his wife, Lucy. County clerk is an elected position, and Bobby had run unopposed in every election during his twenty-five-year career. Like Walter, Bobby's family has

lived in the region for a long time, and as we drove toward the river—
Bobby, Walter, and I in Bobby's Chevy Tahoe; Melissa, Lucy, and
Dora following in our Honda—Bobby pointed out how the ruts of the
old stagecoach road were still visible and paralleled the paved road we
were following.

We parked at the edge of a dense forest, where one of Bobby's
hired workers was waiting for us with a golf cart along with a member
of the Kell family, whose ancestors had once run the ferry. Bobby's
man had cut a path through the junglelike terrain to the river. As
some of us walked and others rode the cart through the dense green
woods, I felt like a Victorian explorer in South America or Africa; all
we needed were some pith helmets.

We soon came to what was left of the ferryman's house, with only
the old chimney emerging from the cellar hole. I picked up a brick
that lay on the ground, and Dora came over to me, her tail wagging
eagerly. I had no choice but to hurl the chunk of masonry, and soon
Dora was following us with a moss-covered brick in her mouth.

Near the edge of the Staunton River we found the hackberry tree
from which the ferry cable had once extended across the river. You
could see how the thick loop of stranded wire had long since been
enveloped by the tree's bark. Bobby said the key to a successful ferry
was keeping the landing open in the "muddy freshets." "You needed
a rocky creek bed for the crossing," he explained. "The buffalo found
them first, then the Indians, and after them, the pioneers." In the old
days, he said, all roads led to Coles Ferry. But with the proliferation
of bridges in the late nineteenth and early twentieth centuries, the
community that once existed at this rocky section of creek bed had
been abandoned.

Soon we were back in the cars and headed to the site of Isaac
Coles's house. After a brief time on a paved road, we turned onto an
unmowed field, the long grass brushing across the car's undercar-
riage as we bounced over the uneven terrain, eventually parking beside a large mud puddle. From there, it was a short hike through the
tall grass. Bobby warned us to check for ticks and chiggers once this

was over. Ticks I was familiar with, but chiggers? "Oh, they're nasty, awful things," Bobby said. I later learned that chiggers are microscopic insects whose saliva melts flesh. In men, they can create a condition known as summer penile syndrome. Luckily, the chigger season had not yet arrived in this portion of Virginia.

We came to a ridge overlooking a recently plowed field. "The Coleses always built on top of a knoll," Bobby said. The house was gone, but the many decorative trees and plantings that once surrounded the structure were still here—boxwoods, cedars, and azaleas grown to a wild profusion. In the furrows of the field we found shards of pottery and glass. "I wonder what Isaac and George talked about during those two days," Walter said. "Politics? Farming?"

If it was politics, they would have had plenty to discuss. Isaac Coles had voted against ratification at the Virginia Constitutional Convention and was a good friend of Thomas Jefferson, who had signed the deed to the Coleses' land in Chatham. As it so happened, Jefferson had recently stirred up some controversy back in Philadelphia. In April, he sent a copy of Thomas Paine's *The Rights of Man* to a printer in Philadelphia. Paine's book, a vehement defense of the French Revolution, had recently ignited a political firestorm in England, and Jefferson was eager for Paine's polemic to be printed in America. In a note to the printer, Jefferson said he hoped the book's publication would help oppose "the political heresies which have sprung up among us." To Jefferson's surprise (so he claimed), the note was published as a foreword to *The Rights of Man*.

In a letter to Washington, Jefferson claimed he was "sincerely mortified to be thus brought forward on the public stage." But you have to wonder. Jefferson admitted that his reference to "political heresies" was intended for Vice President John Adams, who he felt had become dangerously monarchical in his views. In his own defense, Jefferson insisted in his letter to Washington, "I certainly never made a secret of being anti-monarchical and anti-aristocratical." By 1791, these were the words of an Anti-Federalist spoiling for an ideological fight, hardly the measured words of a loyal cabinet member holding down the fort in Philadelphia.

The publication of the secretary of state's note unleashed a scorching, increasingly partisan newspaper debate that historians have since looked to as the point at which Jefferson first emerged as the country's most visible Anti-Federalist—an exceedingly strange position to be in, given that he was a member of Washington's cabinet. As John Adams wryly commented to Washington's secretary of war, Henry Knox, "It is thought rather early for electioneering." Washington never responded to Jefferson's letter, which just might be the least heartfelt apology ever written, choosing instead a strategy of "icy silence." Not lost on Washington was the fact that while he'd been away on his southern tour attempting to unite the country, his secretary of state in Philadelphia had been doing his apparent best to divide it.

It was, of course, absurd to accuse John Adams, or anyone else associated with Washington's administration, of plotting to establish a monarchy. But that did not prevent Jefferson and his fellow Republicans from returning to the claim over and over again. Even Washington's southern tour was viewed by the Republican press as an essentially monarchical exercise—despite the president's efforts to combat that very accusation. The Anti-Federalist newspaper editor Benjamin Franklin Bache claimed that the many addresses Washington received during his southern tour "savor too much of monarchy to be used by republicans, or to be received with pleasure by a president of a commonwealth." Another commentator insisted that the president's popularity was, in itself, antirepublican, referring to the "vileness of the adulation," while claiming that it cast "the utmost ridicule on the discernment of America." As Jefferson himself lamented, "Such is the popularity of the president that the people will support him in whatever he will do or will not do, without appealing to their own reason or to anything but their feelings toward him."

A part of Washington probably agreed with such criticism. As Caesar, Cromwell, and in a few years Napoleon would demonstrate, a leader could use his popularity to transform a republic into a dicta-torship. But as anyone who knew Washington understood, his only interest was in establishing a federal government that was strong enough to survive without him. If he could use his popularity to forge a durable union, so be it. But as was becoming increasingly apparent, the halcyon period Washington had enjoyed during the first two years of his presidency was about to end.

And, in fact, as Washington was finishing his southern tour, Jef-ferson and James Madison had already embarked on a tour of their own—to the new state of Vermont via New York City and Albany. In a letter to Washington, Jefferson claimed the purpose of the trip was "to get rid of a headache which is very troublesome, by giving more exercise to the body and less to the mind." But as Alexander Hamilton subsequently learned, Jefferson and Madison's journey also had a political agenda. According to Hamilton's friend Robert Troup, while in New York City, Jefferson and Madison were engaged in a "passion-ate courtship" of Robert Livingston, the chancellor of New York who had sworn in Washington at his inauguration, and Aaron Burr, Jef-ferson's future vice president. "If they succeed," Troup wrote wor-riedly, "they will tumble the fabric of the government in ruins to the ground."

What is remarkable is how long Washington continued to toler-ate Jefferson's insubordinate behavior. Part of it was Washington's seemingly naive hope that differences of political opinion could be discussed without forcing otherwise reasonable people to choose op-posing sides. For Washington, at least, it was not yet clear that Amer-ica's political scene was about to evolve into the combative two-party system we have today. As late as August of the following year, by which time the relationship between Jefferson and Hamilton had de-teriorated into open warfare, Washington wrote to his secretary of the Treasury, "It is to be regretted, exceedingly, that ... men of abilities—zealous patriots—having the same *general* objects in view, and the same upright intentions to prosecute them, will not exercise more charity in deciding on the opinions and actions of one another."

In the meantime, Jefferson, with the help of James Madison, continued to ramp up the attacks, particularly when it came to the economic programs put forward by the Treasury secretary. By the fall of 1791, Jefferson had hired the writer Philip Freneau, supposedly as a translator for the State Department but in reality to launch a new Anti-Federalist newspaper called the *National Gazette*, copies of which Freneau had the audacity to send to Washington's presidential residence. At one point during a cabinet meeting, when Henry Knox showed him a political cartoon in which Washington's head was about to be inserted into a guillotine, the normally reserved president erupted in fury. Thanks to Jefferson, who apparently had no qualms about the toll his underhanded actions were taking on both the president and his administration, we have an account of Washington's anguished soliloquy: *"By God*, he had rather be in his grave than in his present situation; that he had rather be on his farm than to be made *emperor of the world*; and yet they were charging him with wanting to be a king. That that *rascal Freneau* sent him three of his papers every day."

As Washington approached his fourth year as president, he had no interest in running for a second term. However, both sides—Federalists and Republicans—feared what would happen if Washington wasn't there to prevent the partisan struggle from ripping the embryonic country apart. Reluctantly Washington agreed to run a second time, only to immediately regret the decision when an Anti-Federalist majority was elected to Congress. Included in the opposition was Washington's obliging host for two days at the end of his southern tour, Virginia congressman Isaac Coles.

After lunch with Walter, Bobby, and Lucy at the Drug Store Grill in Brookneal (where I enjoyed the best pulled pork sandwich of my life), Melissa, Dora, and I were back on the road. Three hours later we were about 150 miles to the northeast and looking for yet another house in which the president had once slept.

By that point in our journey I had become increasingly irritated by the inevitable wisecracks involving the phrase "Washington slept here." After spending the last year and a half following Washington's tour across the country, both Melissa and I had come to realize how wrong it was to reduce Washington's travels to a historical joke. Every tavern and house in which he'd slept—both as a general and as a president—represented another day (and night) devoted to a nation that didn't even exist when he set out for the first meeting of the Continental Congress in 1774. Now, seventeen years later, he was approaching the end of his presidential travels without any sense of gratifying finality. He still had so much to do.

When Washington visited the town of Bumpass, Virginia, about 26 miles southwest of Fredericksburg, the house occupied by Sarah Macon Jerdone, known today as Jerdone Castle, sat on a hill over-looking the North Anna River. In the late 1960s, Virginia Electric and Power purchased 18,000 acres of adjoining property, cleared it of timber, and built a dam across the river. With the help of the rainfall associated with Hurricane Agnes, it took only 18 months for Lake Anna to be born. Over the years, 120 communities have sprung up along the lake's 200 miles of shoreline. Jerdone Castle still sits on its hill but is now virtually surrounded by the newly risen waters of Lake Anna.

When I was a teenager with a budding interest in sailing, our family used to summer at a little house in the woods of Underhill, Vermont. It was a beautiful part of the world, but the area's pleasures were lost on me. What I wanted more than anything else was to spend every waking moment sailing my Sunfish—the obsession I'd devel-oped during our all-too-brief visits to my grandparents' house on Cape Cod. Stranded in the mountains of Vermont, I fantasized that the waters of Lake Champlain, about twenty miles to the west, would magically begin to rise until our hilltop camp became an island. I would then sail out over the drowned land and explore the wave-washed edges of Mount Mansfield in my Sunfish.

As we drove toward Jerdone Castle, I realized that here, seventy-two miles south of Washington, D.C., my fantasy had been made real: the damming of the North Anna River had created a lake just like the one I had envisioned—a plethora of miraculous coves, each dotted with houses and backyard docks. How I would have loved to have grown up here on Lake Anna! When I came home from school, my Sunfish would have been waiting for me at the edge of our family's dock.

Later that night, at a motel in Thornburg, Virginia, I read about Lake Anna. The reason the river had been dammed, I discovered, was to create a reservoir to cool a nuclear power plant. There are two sections of the lake: the "cold" portion, whose waters are used to cool the reactor, and the "hot" portion, filled with the discharge from the plant. The houses and those wonderful docks are on the hot side where the water is fourteen degrees warmer than on the other side of the lake. So the lake of my adolescent fantasies was actually a cooling tank for a nuclear reactor—a fitting end to a day that had begun at an idyllic farm sitting atop 119 million pounds of uranium.

Washington arrived at Mount Vernon on the afternoon of Sunday, June 12. Against all odds, he had completed a journey of more than seventeen hundred miles without encountering any significant delays or disasters. Thanks to extensive planning and preparation, he had returned home eight days ahead of schedule, giving him two full weeks before his scheduled meeting in Georgetown to discuss the future of the Federal City.

In a letter to Alexander Hamilton, Washington was clearly proud of the efficiency with which he'd conducted the southern tour. It was also just as clear the record-setting journey had come at a cost to the enslaved members of his entourage. We don't know exactly what happened, but at some point during the tour the postilion Giles suffered an injury that made it impossible for him to mount a horse. For his part, Paris became so ill in Wilmington, North Carolina, that he'd been put under the care of a physician before eventually rejoining the entourage in Charleston. By the end of the tour, Paris had grown so uncooperative that Washington decided to leave both Paris and Giles at Mount Vernon. The last stretch of the journey, when they were on the road each morning by 4:00, must have been particularly arduous. Washington demanded an incredible amount of work from everyone around him, but as Giles and Paris could attest, the enslaved members of his staff, who were hardly in a position to complain (or quit), had no choice but to work to the point of physical exhaustion and, in the case of Giles, physical injury.

Waiting for Washington at Mount Vernon was his chef Hercules, who had been sent south because of the Pennsylvania laws regarding slavery. Before leaving the presidential mansion for Mount Vernon, Hercules had confronted Washington's secretary Tobias Lear. Hercules had learned of the real reason he was being sent home and, according to Lear, was "mortified to the last degree to think a suspicion could be entertained of his fidelity or attachment to you." Lear reported that "so much did the poor fellow's feelings appear to be touched that it left no doubt of his sincerity." Hercules's apparent sincerity might have really been an act. A few years later, on February 22, 1797—Washington's sixty-fifth birthday—Hercules fled Mount Vernon. When, a few months later, one of Washington's guests asked Hercules's daughter whether her father's disappearance had saddened her, she shook her head. "Oh, sir," she said, "I am very glad, because he is free now!"

When I awoke the morning we were to return to Mount Vernon, I was nervous. I was scheduled to have lunch with George Washington. After a year and a half following him across the country, I was about to speak with the man himself—well, sort of. Dean Malissa is the official George Washington interpreter at Mount Vernon. It had turned out that Dean was going to be working the museum's Wine

Festival that weekend, so we'd arranged to have lunch at the restaurant near the interpretive center.

Even when he's not dressed like George Washington, Dean commands a room. He's six feet four inches tall and has a deep, sonorous voice. At sixty-seven years old, with long gray hair tied in a ponytail, he looks as much like an aging rock star as the first president of the United States. But Dean's charisma is not intimidating. He's smart and affable. As we sat down at a table on the porch, I found myself thinking it would be hard to find a better twenty-first-century George Washington.

"This is the twilight zone for me," he said. "Even when I'm not in character, I'm always on at Mount Vernon." Dean is based in the Philadelphia area but obviously has an intimate connection with this place. "Those of us who are here routinely go about our duties, but every once in a while we have to stop and realize we are *here* at *Mount Vernon*."

He spoke of what a pleasure it was to inhabit someone from the eighteenth century. "People back then lived four lives in the time we live one," he said. "So much of our modern-day lives are lost to screen time, bubble gum of the mind. Back then people actually talked to each other face-to-face; they socialized. It heartens me, walking in their footsteps. The great frustration of my profession is that while I can study contemporary reports, consult everything that's been written about the man, I can never truly inhabit his world, walk in his shoes, share his beliefs. It's a humbling flaw. Before every performance I thank George Washington and ask for his approval. It's a gesture of respect."

Dean had spent his previous professional life as an executive for a firm selling the *V* (ventilation) in HVAC. "No razzle-dazzle," he said. The company had been founded by his grandfather, and after decades of constantly traveling in the Middle East and Asia, he realized he "wasn't having fun anymore." So he and his cousin decided to sell the company, and Dean retired at forty-six and took up acting. Much to his surprise, he almost immediately began to get hired.

Dean was performing as a colonial bass singer in the Liberty Tones in Philadelphia when he met the man who became his mentor, William Sommerfield, then the official Washington interpreter at Mount Vernon. "Bill was my Yoda. I was his Luke Skywalker, and eventually I became his handpicked successor."

Although performing George Washington is very different from his previous career in business, there are some important similarities. "I used to tell my sales and marketing guys that when it came to sales calls, you've got one hundred percent product knowledge, but you can use only three percent of that knowledge if it's going to be an effective pitch. You've got to have some social intelligence, read the room, your audience. It's the same thing a good teacher does.

"My job," he continued, "is to humanize this guy; that's my mission. I'm a storyteller. If I'm inaccessible, my interpretation fails. Academics dismiss historical interpreters, describe us with venom as 'simulacrums.' I use the word 'simulacrum' with defiance. Rather than calculate the weight of a pewter button, I'm trying to get at the essence of who Washington was." What Dean was describing was very much in line with Frank Vagnone's intention at Old Salem—"to elevate emotive experience to a standing equal with historical exactitude."

Dean asked about our trip so far. I talked about how the issue of Confederate statues had become a pervasive part of our own southern tour. Dean said that when he gives a presentation, there is rarely a question-and-answer period when he isn't asked about how he, as George Washington, reconciles slavery. "The first thing I do," he explained, "is acknowledge the strangeness of meeting someone from a different time. Then I ask the questioner a question: 'Does slavery exist in your own day and time?' The inevitable reply is an emphatic 'No.' Then you begin to hear murmurs in the audience. 'Actually,' I say, 'there are far more slaves in your world than in mine.' I then talk about how Washington's thinking about slavery evolved. Jefferson said a man of fifty can't wear the clothing of fifteen. The same applies to the way Washington's views changed as he progressed in life."

By that point, Dean and I had finished lunch, and we both had places we needed to be. But I had one final question. I knew that Dean was sixty-seven years old. George Washington died two months before his sixty-eighth birthday. What did that mean for Dean's future at Mount Vernon? While researching my book about the Battle of the Little Bighorn, I'd met plenty of Custer reenactors who were far older than the age (thirty-six) at which Custer was killed.

"You're right," Dean said, "I'll be historically dead next year." But like the man he was interpreting, Dean didn't seem particularly worried about his professional mortality. "When that threshold comes," he said, "I'll just walk through the door. In previous lives I've been a firefighter, a scuba diver, a stone sculptor, a corporate guy. I've left each one without looking back. There is something either very right or very wrong about me. I'll be able to pull the pin on this without jealousy or regret."

There's little doubt Washington enjoyed his two weeks at Mount Vernon, but already he was planning something extraordinary. Despite having devoted most of his life to creating this vast plantation, he was about to begin the process of breaking it apart. The way for a planter to project his holdings into the future was to will the entire plantation to a single heir. But Washington would spend what remained of his life gifting Mount Vernon's individual farms to his relatives. On top of that, he'd made the decision to free his slaves. When it came to the future of Mount Vernon, it was a recipe for disaster. By dividing his plantation into bits and pieces, Washington was ensuring its ultimate destruction. And sure enough, in just fifty years, his famous mansion house was on the verge of ruin.

Washington appears to have agreed with the character of Gloria in F. Scott Fitzgerald's *The Beautiful and Damned*. When Gloria and her fiancé, Anthony, visit "General Lee's old home" in Arlington, she objects to "making these houses show-places":

Beautiful things grow to a certain height and then they fail and fade off, breathing out memories as they decay. And just as any period decays in our minds, the things of that period should decay too, and in that way they're preserved for a while in the few hearts like mine that react to them. . . . Trying to preserve a century by keeping its relics up to date is like keeping a dying man alive by stimulants. . . . There's no beauty without poignancy and there's no poignancy without the feeling that it's going, men, names, books, houses—bound for dust—mortal.

I think if Washington had had his druthers, Mount Vernon would have been allowed to crumble to dust, leaving only his beloved trees to flourish on his hill overlooking the Potomac. No, Mount Vernon was never intended to last forever; his real legacy was to be the Federal City—what we call today Washington, D.C.

Mount Vernon circa 1858.

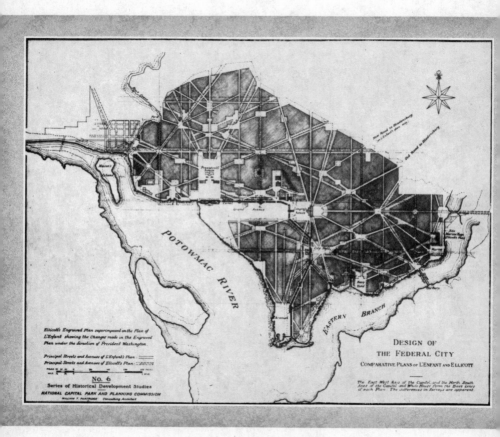

1792 plan of the Federal City.

CHAPTER 19

"The Devil's Own Roads"

On Monday, June 27, around 9:00 a.m., Washington arrived at Suter's Tavern in Georgetown to have it out with the land-owners. The last he'd heard, they'd rejected his offer to buy the ten-mile square of land that was to be the site of the Federal City. By the end of the day—once the president had had the chance to explain "the consequences of delay in this business"—the deal was back on. It was a good thing, too. While Washington had been away on his southern tour, the surveyor Andrew Ellicott had already begun laying out the boundary stones marking the capital's perimeter.

Ultimately, there would be forty of these stones placed at one-mile intervals. They have been called the country's first federal monuments, and today thirty-six of the original forty stones can still be found at or very near where they were first planted in the ground. In a city saturated with oversized monuments, these inconspicuous markers are a wonderful tonic for the soul—little timeworn nubs of sandstone, each encased in a protective iron cage. The boundary stones might be in the middle of a sidewalk or at the edge of a highway, but if you're willing to look for them, there they are. Melissa and I wanted to look.

On April 15, 1791, Washington's Masonic brethren in Alexandria laid a stone at the spot where the survey began—the southern tip of Alexandria at Jones Point. Today, Alexandria is no longer part of the District of Columbia. By the 1840s, there was talk of abolishing slavery in the nation's capital, and Alexandria, home to Franklin and Armfield, one of the largest slave-trading firms in the country, wanted no part of it. So, in 1847, through a process known as retrocession, Alexandria once again became a part of Virginia. (One can only imagine how this would have broken Washington's heart.) In the beginning, however, the laying out of the Federal City started here.

We parked under the Woodrow Wilson Bridge and walked over to a small dock on the Potomac River. On the opposite bank, about a mile away, was a strange sight: sitting on a swath of tarmac beside what looked like a mall at the edge of the river was Air Force One—as in the gigantic presidential jet in which Harrison Ford says to a very mean terrorist, "Get off my plane," before hurling the miscreant out an open rear door. We later learned that the mothballed jet is now a museum known as the Air Force One Experience. I couldn't help but wonder whether the jet has an informational panel explaining that the first mode of presidential travel was Washington's cream-colored carriage.

We followed a paved path into a grove of trees, and there it was— what looked like a miniature version of the Brant Point lighthouse on Nantucket. Directly ahead of the lighthouse, beneath a glass-paned hatch set in a cement retaining wall, was the boundary stone—not the original, but the one that had replaced the original in 1797. To get a better look, I jumped over the edge of the wall onto a raft of driftwood pinned against the barrier by the incoming tide and peered through the cloudy glass at the 222-year-old stone. It looked like a rotted tooth—appropriate, I guess, given the dental problems of our first president. So this was what Washington's journey had been leading him to: a stone fixed in the ground at the edge of the Potomac from which would blossom a capital city for all Americans, assuming (and it's a big assumption) our society lives up to the promises made in the Declaration of Independence.

The surveyor Andrew Ellicott had a free African American assistant named Benjamin Banneker. Banneker had been born on a farm outside Baltimore and quickly proved to have extraordinary mathematical and mechanical abilities. In his early twenties he built a functioning clock made entirely of wood, and by the time he accompanied Ellicott to Alexandria, he was publishing his own almanac. According to legend, it was Banneker who fixed the point of the first boundary stone by lying on the ground at night and plotting the movements of six different stars.

Banneker's presence among the surveying party did not go unnoticed. The *Georgetown Weekly Ledger* made note of "an Ethiopian, whose abilities, as a surveyor and an astronomer, clearly prove that Mr. Jefferson's concluding that race of men were void of mental endowments was without foundation." Later that summer, Banneker took the liberty of writing to Jefferson directly. Banneker praised Jefferson for the "true and invaluable doctrine" he set forth in the Declaration of Independence: "that all men are created equal, and that they are endowed by their creator with certain inalienable rights, that among these are life, liberty, and the pursuit of happiness." Then came the kicker: "But, Sir, how pitiable is it to reflect that although you were so fully convinced of the benevolence of the Father of mankind, and of his equal and impartial distribution of those rights and privileges which he had conferred upon them, that you should at the same time counteract his mercies, in detaining by fraud and violence so numerous a part of my brethren under groaning captivity and cruel oppression."

The day after Washington's meeting with the landowners, while his three commissioners prepared the necessary documents for signing,

Washington mounted his horse—I like to think it was his white charger Prescott—and went for the ride of his life. With the architect Pierre Charles L'Enfant and Andrew Ellicott accompanying him, Washington set out to "take a more perfect view of the ground in order to decide finally on the spots on which to place the public buildings." After two years of travel, after venturing as far north as Kittery Point, Maine, and as far south as Savannah, Georgia, Washington was about to inspect what would become the physical embodiment of the nation he now knew like no other person in America.

They rode to an abrupt rise of land known as Jenkins Hill, which L'Enfant had already described as "a pedestal waiting for a monument." The area was heavily wooded, but once it was cleared of trees, L'Enfant believed "no situation could stand in competition with this." This was where they would put the Capitol. In a republic it was only appropriate that the legislative body be at the city's center. Ahead of them, stretching toward the Potomac, would be a broad open area— what we now call the Mall—with, about a mile and a half away, the gardens of what L'Enfant envisioned as "the Presidential Palace" on the right.

They rode through forested, extremely wet terrain. Both Washington and L'Enfant saw the land as a tabula rasa on which to create a city of magnificent distances, with broad diagonal avenues breaking up the confining grid that Jefferson had proposed in his sketch of a modest town near the Potomac. L'Enfant, on the other hand, saw the Federal City as an undertaking worthy "of a grand empire . . . over whose progress the eyes of every other nation envying the opportunity denied them will stand judge." Washington could not have agreed more.

They didn't agree, however, on where to put the president's residence. Washington decided the building should be on a higher piece of land than L'Enfant originally suggested, giving the executive branch more of a parity with Congress on its highest of hills. Connecting the two buildings would be an avenue that for political reasons was named for the state where the nation's temporary capital was then located, Pennsylvania. Where Washington and L'Enfant saw a glorious future,

Ellicott, who was from Philadelphia, saw an unexceptional swamp. "This country bears no more proportion to the country about Philadelphia," he wrote to his wife, "than a crane does to a stall-fed Ox!"

That afternoon, Washington, with the help of a plan provided by L'Enfant, made a presentation to the landowners. There were two geographic factions among them, and the members of each faction wanted at least one of the two showpiece buildings on their parcel of land. To please both groups, Washington and L'Enfant had had to put a mile and a half between the Capitol and the White House. So that's one of the reasons why Washington, D.C., is such an expansive city— to please the original landowners. And pleased they were. "It was with much pleasure," Washington recorded in his diary, "that a general approbation of the measure seemed to pervade the whole."

Unfortunately, the good vibes were not to last. L'Enfant proved impossible to work with, and Washington's funding scheme—based on the rising value of the land—never really panned out. A lot of his friends—most famously Light Horse Harry Lee—lost a lot of money on Potomac real estate. For decades, partly because Jefferson and his Republican cohorts wanted it that way, Washington, D.C., remained a swampy group of villages clustered around two outsized, almost forlorn-looking palaces. It took a while, but in the end the nation's capital grew into something commensurate with Washington's (and L'Enfant's) original vision. As the Washington interpreter Dean Malissa had told me the day before at Mount Vernon, "Rule number one of American history: Don't mess with George Washington. You oppose him, you lose."

Leaving Dora in our air-conditioned hotel room in Alexandria (the temperature had climbed into the eighties), Melissa and I headed out on our own tour of Washington, D.C.

We started where Washington would have started, in Georgetown. A cooling breeze was now blowing down the Potomac as we walked past the lofty elegance of the Kennedy Center. Ahead of us, up a stone staircase, were a pair of gilt Pegasuses and the Lincoln Memorial, with the Washington Monument to our left. To our right, on the other side of the river, on a grassy hill overlooking Arlington National Cemetery, was the house Washington's step-grandson, George Washington Parke Custis, built when it became clear he wasn't going to inherit Mount Vernon. Washington appears to have taken an increasingly dim view of his step-grandson, who, according to Tobias Lear, had been spoiled rotten by Martha's constant reminders that he was destined to inherit the Custis fortune. Despite Washington's mounting frustrations with him, Washy maintained a reverent admiration for his step-grandfather, ultimately turning his new Greek Revival mansion into a kind of Washington memorial, with artifacts and a mural lionizing his famous ancestor by marriage.

Washington's worst fears for Washy seem to have been realized. Unlike Washington's favorite nephew, Bushrod, who ultimately became a Supreme Court justice and the new owner of Mount Vernon, Washy, high on his hill at Arlington, embodied the worst legacy of the Virginia planter. According to an account published in 1865, Custis fathered at least forty children by the women he'd enslaved, making him, by standard reckoning, a serial rapist. In the meantime, his legitimate daughter Mary became the bride of the young army officer Robert E. Lee. It would be at the Custis-Lee mansion in Arlington that Lee made the decision to reject President Lincoln's offer of command and lead instead the army of the Confederacy. Oh, how Washington's heart would have been broken once again!

Soon we were walking up the steps of the Lincoln Memorial. Lincoln greatly admired George Washington. During Lincoln's own pre-inaugural tour (by train instead of carriage), the president-in-waiting gave a speech in Trenton, New Jersey, in which he spoke of how as a young boy the reading of Parson Weems's biography of Washington changed his life. Lincoln movingly compared the challenge Washington had faced in 1776 with what awaited the country in 1861.

Melissa and I sat on the steps of the Lincoln Memorial and looked east. All around us people of different ages talked and laughed in many languages, some, like us, just hanging out, others, particularly the younger ones, loping up and down the steps. Up ahead of us, the Washington Monument was in a direct line with the Capitol on the opposite end of the Mall. In *The Beautiful and Damned*, F. Scott Fitzgerald complains of the city's "atmosphere of harsh repellent light, of distance without freedom, of pomp without splendor—it seemed a pasty-pale and self-conscious city." From an intellectual perspective, I knew what Fitzgerald meant. But that's not what Melissa and I felt on that spring afternoon on the steps of the Lincoln Memorial after a year and a half of following George Washington across the country.

We'd traveled to Boston, where Washington had made it clear that a president now outranked a governor, something that seems almost ludicrously obvious today—but only because Washington refused to accept John Hancock's dinner invitation in the fall of 1789. We'd sailed to Newport to see the synagogue that inspired one of the most eloquent defenses of religious freedom ever written. We'd seen the bed in which Washington had slept for two nights after successfully promoting a new economic program that many predicted would be roundly rejected in the South. And seemingly everywhere—from Portsmouth, New Hampshire, to Salisbury, North Carolina—were the stories of a president who insisted he was "only a man."

Washington was probably the most famous person in the world at the beginning of his presidency. He could have luxuriated in that fame and left it to his underlings to do the actual work. Instead, he had rolled up his sleeves and helped build a government designed to transcend the ego of any single individual. Melissa and I now knew how hard Washington had labored to create a lasting union of states and how important this city—despite all its coldness and formality—was to that effort.

Washington's great worry was that once he died, efforts would be made to abandon his plans for a capital city on the Potomac. Pennsylvanians had even gone to the extreme of building a new residence for the president in Philadelphia (which Washington indignantly refused to move into) in the hopes their city would become the country's permanent capital. Washington countered with an extreme measure of his own. The paper trail is sketchy, but there appears to be little doubt that it was his intention to be buried in a mausoleum beneath the rotunda of the Capitol—a calculated move to force subsequent administrations to complete the still-unfinished Capitol and keep the Federal City on the Potomac. On Washington's death in 1799, President John Adams requested that Martha make her husband's body available for removal from its resting place on Mount Vernon. In what must have been a prearranged deal, Martha agreed, with the stipulation that she be buried beside her husband in Washington, D.C.

But it never happened. It's probably unfair to say it was the fault of Thomas Jefferson, who was elected president the year after Washington's death, but I'll say it anyway. I know I have been tough on Jefferson until now, but in this instance I applaud his antimonarchical tendencies. All of us, at some point in our lives, need to be saved from ourselves—even George Washington. That's why actors need directors and writers need editors, and why presidents need political opponents. Let's face it, the United States would have been diminished by Washington's reinterment in a tomb beneath the Capitol's rotunda. Let autocracies like the former U.S.S.R., with its embalmed Lenin, celebrate their leaders' remains. America is a system of laws, not a cult of personality. Thank you, Thomas Jefferson, not only for the Declaration of Independence, but for helping to keep Washington's corpse where it belonged—at Mount Vernon.

Melissa and I walked on to the Washington Monument, surrounded by a circle of flags snapping in the wind. This magnificent obelisk—not a crypt in the bowels of the Capitol—is the memorial Washington deserved. Our next stop was the three-year-old National Museum of African American History and Culture, burnished and glinting in the afternoon sun. There was a huge line, and we gradually realized that the museum's popularity meant that it was necessary to reserve time-stamped tickets online. As we stood there, perplexed, a woman, perhaps a chaperone with a school group, walked up and handed us two tickets with 2:30 p.m. printed on them. "If someone asks," she said, "this never happened." Offering our heartfelt thanks, we followed the stream of people and entered the museum at almost precisely 2:30.

We were soon in a tightly packed crowd in the museum's purposely cramped depths, studying panels about the slave trade. Gradually, as we moved up through the building, the size of the rooms expanded and the crowding diminished. It was the same principle of compression and release the architect Frank Lloyd Wright regularly employed but resonant with a people's journey from bondage to freedom. The highlight from my perspective was when we came upon a statue of my new hero, Benjamin Banneker, the surveyor who had called Thomas Jefferson to task.

On our way out, Melissa stopped to talk to two women behind the information desk. They said the museum was by far the most popular in Washington, D.C., attracting between three thousand and five thousand people a day. "For a while there," one of them said, "we even outdid the Louvre in Paris." Did the museum's popularity forecast better things for our still racially divided nation? Only time would tell. It was on to the White House.

Washington laid the building's cornerstone on October 13, 1792. James Hoban, the designer of the South Carolina statehouse in Columbia, was the architect. Washington worked closely with Hoban, desperately trying to complete the structure for his Federalist successor, John Adams. During the War of 1812, when James Madison was president, the White House was occupied and burned by the British.

By the end of the war in 1815, which concluded on a surprisingly positive note with Andrew Jackson's victory at the Battle of New Orleans, the Federalist Party had, for all intents and purposes, ceased to exist. A series of meetings among New England Federalists during the war, known as the Hartford Convention, in which the possibility of secession had been discussed, put an end to the once proud party that looked to Washington as its standard-bearer. (As Washington might have warned them, bad things happen to those who oppose the Union.) Succeeding Madison was James Monroe, formerly one of Washington's harshest critics. Monroe had served a tumultuous tenure as Washington's ambassador to France, then published a scathing condemnation of his presidency called *A View of the Conduct of the Executive.* Washington's copy of Monroe's book still exists, and it's full of outraged marginalia. "Insanity in the extreme!" is one comment, followed by "A party man, lost to all sense of propriety." The day before his death, Washington complained bitterly to Tobias Lear about Monroe's recent election to the governorship of Virginia. He fell short of damning him with his dying breath, but there is no doubt that Washington despised James Monroe.

It is more than ironic, then, that on Monroe's election to the presidency after the War of 1812, he decided that the best course ahead was to emulate George Washington. Once the most partisan of Republicans, Monroe now insisted that "the chief magistrate of the country ought not to be head of a party, but of the nation itself." The White House was still under repair. Congress was in recess. Monroe resolved the time was right to set out on his own tour of the United States—something that hadn't been done since Washington's journey across the country at the beginning of *his* presidency.

Dean Malissa at present-day Mount Vernon could not have done a better job than Monroe of channeling George Washington. Having once served under Washington during the Revolutionary War (Monroe was badly wounded at Trenton), the new president decided it was only right that he bring along a buff and blue military uniform complete with a large *chapeau bras*—the kind of large flat hat made famous by Napoleon. It wasn't what Monroe had worn as a young army officer during the Revolution, but it was close enough. And as had proven true with Washington, the people loved it.

Once again, huge crowds greeted the president's arrival in every

city and town. But there was one possible exception: Boston, the historic stronghold of the Federalist Party. So Monroe resolved to pull
out all the stops. What he needed more than anything for his entry
into Boston was a proper horse, which was found for him—you can't
make this stuff up—at a circus! With his fake uniform and tricked-
out steed, Monroe rode into Boston, consciously evoking as best he
could the ghost of the first president.

Monroe had been with Washington at his darkest hour, during
the retreat through New Jersey that preceded the victory at Trenton.
"His countenance and manner made an impression on me which
time can never efface," Monroe wrote. "[He possessed] a deportment
so firm, so dignified, but yet so modest and composed I have never
seen in any other person."

Unless, of course, it was James Monroe in Boston in 1817. Abigail
Adams, whose son John Quincy was about to begin serving in Monroe's cabinet, was besotted: "The agreeable affability and unassuming manners of the president, with his polite attention to all orders
and ranks, has made a deep and lasting impression here." The newspaper editor Benjamin Russell, who as a young reporter had witnessed
Washington's political jousting with John Hancock back in 1789,
claimed that Monroe's presidential performance in Boston heralded
an era "of good feelings"—a phrase that has since come to define
Monroe's presidency. If imitation is the sincerest form of flattery,
Washington had—almost thirty years after his own tour of America—
thoroughly won over one of his harshest political critics. After decades of rancorous division, after yet another war with Britain, the
Union had endured.

I won't go into our journey from D.C. to Philadelphia other than to
say there were two highlights: visiting the Snack Food Capital of the
United States in Hanover, Pennsylvania, where we stopped at the factory store of our favorite potato chip manufacturer, Utz, and enjoying
ice cream served to us from a giant blue seventeen-foot-high shoe

originally built by Mahlon Haines, the "Shoe Wizard" of York. After a night in Lancaster, we headed into Philadelphia.

Washington had arrived to tolling bells and the usual happy crowds. He'd barely had a chance to park in front of the presidential residence before David Clark, the coach maker, was upon him, wanting to know how his handiwork had fared during the two-thousand-mile journey. As Clark crawled under the cream-colored carriage, John Fagan, the driver, shouted down to him from the box, "All right, Mr. Clark, all right, sir, not a bolt or screw started in a long journey and over the devil's own roads."

I had made an afternoon reservation for a carriage ride through Philadelphia's historic district. I had hoped to end our southern tour with all three of us in the very mode of conveyance that had transported Washington across the country. But I had two concerns. Would the driver let us bring a dog, and, just as important, would Dora be willing to climb into a horse-drawn carriage?

We found Todd, his appropriately white carriage, and his horse named Spot waiting for us on the corner of Fifth and Chestnut streets. Todd said he loved dogs. Dora, however, wasn't so sure she had the same feelings about Spot. It took a little cajoling, but Dora finally leaped into the carriage and lay down on the floor between the two facing seats. Once we got going, the rhythmic clip-clop of Spot's horseshoed hooves had a soothing effect on Dora. She began to look around and ultimately jumped up onto our seat and took her place between us, staring ahead with a toller's earnest intensity.

Todd's nonstop patter about Philadelphia's past was if nothing else entertaining. Toward the end of our tour we drove past Congress Hall. Todd said that George Washington had delivered his famous Farewell Address in 1796 from the building's balcony. Actually, Washington never delivered the famous speech in public. Instead, it was published in the newspapers in September 1796 so the American people would know ahead of the election that he was not running again for president.

The Farewell Address, ghostwritten by Alexander Hamilton (who

On the corner of Fifth and Chestnut.

was no longer a member of Washington's cabinet), is a masterpiece—
a brilliant expression of Washington's abiding faith in the Union:
"The name of American, which belongs to you in your national ca-
pacity, must always exalt the just pride of patriotism more than any
appellation derived from local discriminations. With slight shades of
difference, you have the same religion, manners, habits, and political
principles." In other words, if this country of different states was going
to stay together, people needed to focus on what they had in common,
not their differences. "There will always be," he said, "reason to distrust the patriotism of those who in any quarter may endeavor to
weaken [the Union's] bands."

What worried Washington more than anything else was what
might happen if a president's chief priority was to divide rather than
unite the American people:

> It serves always to distract the public councils and enfeeble
> the public administration. It agitates the community with
> ill-founded jealousies and false alarms, kindles the ani-
> mosity of one part against another, foments occasionally
> riot and insurrection. It opens the door to foreign influ-
> ence and corruption, which finds a facilitated access to the
> government itself through the channels of party passions.
> Thus the policy and will of one country are subjected to
> the policy and will of another.

As we pulled back into the carriage stand where our tour had begun,
it seemed to me that Washington, with Hamilton's help, had seen
with startling clarity where this country would be in more than 220
years—as in *right now*.

On the way back to the car we stopped at the site of Washington's
Philadelphia White House. The building had long since been demolished, but an archaeological dig of sorts had revealed the original
foundation. The outline of the front door and windows had been
reconstructed and were now part of an outdoor exhibit about George

Washington and slavery. A series of screens showed videos in which interpreters playing Washington's enslaved servants Giles, Paris, Ona Judge, Hercules, and others recounted their experiences. As we continued to the car, their disembodied voices echoed amid the ruins of the former presidential residence, getting the last word.

On the afternoon of Monday, May 20, 2019, we rode the ferry back to Nantucket through the fog. Melissa and I talked about our journey and about George Washington. "He's still a mystery to me," Melissa said. "We followed him every step of the way, but what was he really thinking? He doesn't say much at all in his diary."

The novelist and travel writer Rebecca West once claimed that great leaders are almost invariably without any kind of normal interior life. "The men who excite adoration, who are what is called natural leaders (which means really that people feel an unnatural readiness to follow them) are usually empty." West claimed that Napoleon "gave no outward sign of having any private thoughts or feelings that would give the slightest pleasure to any stranger." Was this Washington?

Certainly, as Melissa had pointed out, he was infuriatingly reticent in his diaries and letters. But that does not mean he was without a robust and often tumultuous inner life. "There must have been within [Washington]," the poet William Carlos Williams writes in *In the American Grain*, "a great country whose wild paths he alone knew and explored in secret and at his leisure." This, I think, is the essence of Washington's hidden, surreptitious self. Most of what he saw and did was never written down. That would have revealed too much. Instead, he reserved it all for the locked vault within. Washington gave his country so much, but he was determined to keep his innermost thoughts to himself. It's not surprising, then, that Martha, who knew him best, burned both his letters to her and her letters to him after his death.

The written evidence may be lacking, but it's clear something was troubling Washington toward the end of his life. His step-grandson remembered how he "would frequently, when sitting with his family, appear absent; his lips would move, his hand be raised, and he would evidently seem under the influence of thoughts, which had nothing to do with the . . . scene around him." There were surely many things on his mind, but I would maintain that Washington, who once admitted that "the unfortunate condition of the persons, whose labor . . . I employed, has been the only unavoidable subject of regret," was struggling with what to do about his enslaved workers.

Less than half of the approximately three hundred enslaved people at Mount Vernon were owned by Washington, while most of the others were the dower slaves owned by Martha's deceased husband's estate. Over the years, the two groups had intermarried, meaning that the emancipation of Washington's slaves would potentially tear those families apart. Washington seems to have explored the possibility of purchasing the dower slaves with the intention of freeing them along with his own slaves. Unfortunately, he didn't have the money to pull it off. At one point he was hopeful that the imminent sale of his lands in the West would provide the necessary funds, but that sale never came through.

Knowing that the emancipation of just his own slaves would inevitably create what he called in his will "insuperable difficulties" at Mount Vernon, Washington reluctantly decided that his slaves' freedom ("earnestly wished by me") must be delayed until after Martha's death. What he failed to anticipate was that instead of making the last years of Martha's life easier, the delay in emancipating his slaves would only add to her anxieties. As Martha explained to her friend Abigail Adams about a year after Washington's death, because she was now the only thing standing between the slaves and their freedom, "she did not feel as though her life was safe in their hands." Her only option was to "set them all free at the close of the year," which she ultimately did.

Life in any age is full of so many competing demands that we're all doomed to fail in one way or another. In this regard, Washington was no different from anyone else. What made him so unique was his place in history as the precedent-setting first president of the United States. It's true that Washington did not have the courage of his convictions and emancipate his slaves in his own lifetime. His relentless pursuit of Ona Judge (even if it was on Martha's behalf) was heartless. But by freeing his slaves after his death, Washington did something that not a single other slaveholding founding father felt obliged to do. For the boy who had become a slaveholder at age eleven, he had come a very long way.

Many white southerners condemned Washington's decision to free his enslaved workers, using the transparent and spurious claim that the enslaved at Mount Vernon were ill prepared for freedom and "succeeded very badly as freemen." In truth, the first free Black community in Fairfax County was composed of, according to contemporary tax records, "General Washington's free negroes."

In the decades after Washington's death, several Quaker abolitionist families from Pennsylvania, New Jersey, and other northern states purchased large tracts of land originally contained within Mount Vernon. Implementing the same scientific farming techniques employed by Washington, these Quaker farmers worked in concert with the preexisting free Black community, creating something that existed nowhere else in the antebellum South. According to the authors of a recent study of this remarkable community, "By making the decision to emancipate his slaves upon his death, George Washington unwittingly created a ripple effect that led to massive cultural change in this small corner of Fairfax County."

In 1835, a visitor to Mount Vernon noticed a work party of eleven African Americans tending the grounds surrounding the president's tomb. The visitor learned that many of the men had been emancipated by Washington's will at the beginning of the century and were volunteering their labor "as the only return in their power to make" to the memory of the man who had granted them their freedom. Washington was imperfect and contradictory and, despite his outward stoicism, uncomfortable to the last about his place in this world. He was a great leader, but he was no empty vessel.

Just as our ferry arrived at the entrance to Nantucket Harbor, the mist began to clear and the sun sparkled on the waves kicked up by the southerly breeze. The island was much greener than it had been at the beginning of the month. It was good to be back and gazing on the same church steeples and houses the old whalers had seen 150 years ago.

John Steinbeck had spent the summer of 1951—the centennial of the publication of *Moby-Dick*—in a little seaside cottage on Nantucket writing *East of Eden*, his generational story about two families in the Salinas Valley of California, where he'd grown up. Steinbeck loved the island, writing to his literary agent, "I feel excited and good. Never knew a place with more energy than here. The air is full of it." Soon after his summer on Nantucket with his new bride, Elaine, Steinbeck bought a place in Sag Harbor, Long Island, another old whaling port. Here he began the journey he chronicled in *Travels with Charley*.

In the early 1990s, when I was in the first stages of moving from being a sailing journalist to a writer of history, I learned that the island was going to be hosting a major literary conference, "Steinbeck and the Environment." Already a big Steinbeck fan, I submitted a proposal for a paper, and much to my surprise it was accepted. The conference's opening reception and dinner were at the Jared Coffin House, the hotel where Herman Melville had stayed during his one and only visit to Nantucket, the year after the publication of *Moby-Dick*.

The conference was a who's who of Steinbeck scholars, but the real celebrity that evening was John Steinbeck's seventy-eight-year-old widow, Elaine, who'd unexpectedly accepted the invitation to return to the island where she and Steinbeck had spent the first summer of their marriage. Elaine, a former actress, was there at the reception surrounded by a crowd of admirers when it came time for dinner. Everyone, of course, wanted to sit with Elaine. The organizers had decided that given the many egos in the room, it was best to go with the local unknowns, meaning that Melissa and I got to sit on either side of Elaine Steinbeck.

She talked of that first summer in the cottage beside the lighthouse and her husband's decision eight years later to drive across the country. By then, Steinbeck's health had begun to deteriorate, and she worried about his traveling alone. "But once John told me he was going to bring Charley," she said, "I knew he was going to be all right."

Steinbeck had traveled the country in search of the meaning of America. What he had discovered—that "Americans are much more American than they are Northerners, Southerners, Westerners, or Easterners"—was exactly what Washington had hoped to accomplish by his own travels. And as Melissa and I could now testify, despite all that had happened in the sixty years since Steinbeck's journey, what he called "the American identity" was still "an exact and provable thing." Whether it was Miguel in Bristol, that Vietnam vet at a restaurant in Northborough, Vaughnette in Savannah, or Melissa, Dora, and I in our Honda Pilot, we were all what Washington had been striving to create: Americans.

Throughout our journey, Melissa, a lifelong knitter, had been purchasing skeins of locally spun wool—from the gift shop at Sturbridge Village, from a knitting store in Charleston—and working on a patchwork blanket. At one point as I watched her knitting in our hotel room, I said she was like Penelope perpetually weaving in anticipation of her husband Odysseus's return. But as Melissa pointed out (after one of her sighs), the comparison didn't work. Yes, we were in the midst of our own odyssey, but unlike Odysseus and Penelope we were traveling together.

The ferry pulled into its slip, and we prepared to disembark. Soon we were walking down the metal ramp to Straight Wharf, with Dora leading the way. Rising over the roofs of the shops were two familiar masts. They belonged to the *Lynx*, the same schooner we'd seen in Annapolis. After a year and a half in pursuit of George Washington, we'd followed that little ship home.

Looking west from the top of Mount Mansfield.

The View from the Mountain

But our travels had not yet ended. I still wanted to retrace Thomas Jefferson and James Madison's journey to the Green Mountains in the late spring of 1791, a trip conducted just as Washington was in the final stages of his southern tour. I also wanted to revisit the place where I had spent all those summers in the foothills of Mount Mansfield, yearning for the waters of Lake Champlain to rise.

On the Sunday of Labor Day weekend 2019, Melissa, Dora, and I stood on the summit of Mount Mansfield looking west. There was Lake Champlain—a narrow riverlike body of water extending more than a hundred miles from north to south in a wide valley of green—with the dark outline of the Adirondack Mountains beyond. Directly below us was the town of Underhill, where my brother, Sam, and I had spent the summers of our youth.

Looking out on the distant waters of Lake Champlain, I tried to imagine that day in May 1791 when a sailboat containing Thomas Jefferson and James Madison tacked back and forth against the stiff northerly breeze, trying to make its way to Burlington. By that point in the journey, Jefferson and Madison had already met with Aaron Burr (who had just unseated Hamilton's father-in-law, Philip Schuyler, in the U.S. Senate), the writer Philip Freneau, and other Anti-Federalists in New York. Still to come would be an informal political conclave in Bennington, Vermont, during their return trip. For now Jefferson and Madison were enjoying the pleasures of sailing—first across the crystalline waters of Lake George and now the more turbid Lake Champlain, churned by the uncooperative wind. They were almost to the deepest portion of the lake at Split Rock when they decided to abandon their hopes of reaching Burlington. "After penetrating into [the lake] about 25 miles," Jefferson wrote to his eighteen-year-old daughter, Martha, "we have been obliged by a head wind and high sea to return, having spent a day and a half in sailing on it." On that very day, Washington arrived in Salem, North Carolina, where the former commander of the Continental army was serenaded by a brass band composed of Moravian pacifists.

Standing on Mount Mansfield at the end of summer, I felt an overwhelming sense of sadness. Our travels with George had come to an end just as the story of the new nation was beginning. Jefferson and Madison would return to Philadelphia and continue to organize the political resistance, confident they were battling the pernicious forces of monarchy and corruption. In the meantime, Hamilton and the Federalists, equally confident in their righteousness, pushed forward the financial programs on which today's economy—with all its excesses and inequalities—is built. In the middle was Washington, a Federalist for sure, but a Federalist who recognized there was another point of view.

What bothered him were not the philosophical differences between his two warring cabinet members but their unwillingness to work cooperatively. "Differences in political opinions are as unavoidable as, to a certain point, they may perhaps be necessary," he wrote to Hamilton. "When matters get to such lengths, the natural inference is that both sides have strained the cords beyond their bearing—and that a middle course would be found the best, until experience shall have pointed out the right mode—or, which is not to be expected, because it is denied to mortals, there shall be some *infallible* rule by which we could *fore* judge events." What both Hamilton and Jefferson needed, Washington seemed to be saying, was a little more humility and self-doubt. Because no one—not even the two most brilliant men of their age—had all the answers.

Unlike Hamilton and Jefferson, Washington didn't need to be right all the time. He just wanted to make things work. He understood that feasible change is not attained by righteous indignation; it's understanding that the road ahead is full of compromises if life is actually going to get better. Not Jefferson. When it came to his beloved French Revolution, he insisted that "rather than it should have failed, I would have seen half the earth desolated. Were there but an Adam and Eve left in every country, and left free, it would be better than it is now." This kind of philosophical dogmatism and melodrama was anathema to Washington. He had spent eight years of his life doing his best to prevent the United States from succumbing to the divisions and violence that were about to consume France. He understood the darkness of self-interest lurking beneath the most high-minded ideals. And yet, despite his inherent skepticism concerning the human condition, he had an abiding faith in the American people. "Although we may be a little wrong now and then," Washington wrote to his former aide-de-camp Jonathan Trumbull Jr., "we shall return to the right path with more avidity." Thomas Jefferson had written the Declaration of Independence, but it had been left to George Washington to translate its words into something real—into something that might one day evolve into what the preamble to the Constitution calls "a more perfect Union."

By subsuming sectional and philosophical interests to the good of the whole, the Union is the antidote to arrogance and self-importance, because there will always be something bigger than a single person, town, city, state, or region—or any single race, religion, sexual orientation, or set of beliefs. The founders never claimed to have created the ideal political system. But no one over the course of the last 244 years has come up with a better form of government. The fact that we are in a position today to find fault with the past is a tribute to what was created by the Declaration of Independence, the Constitution, and the labors of George Washington. If our country is ever going to improve in the future, we need to look the past full in the face today, and there, at the very beginning, is our first president: a slaveholder, a land baron, a general, and a politician, who believed with all his soul in the Union.

To say a lot has happened in the year since we stood on that mountain and gazed upon the waters once plied by Jefferson and Hamilton is an understatement. But that's the way it's always been. A catastrophe of some sort is always just around the corner. And yet things feel different this time. The sinews of this country have been stretched to what feels like the breaking point. If those sinews should ultimately fail and the floodgates of disorder and rage swing open, it won't be Washington's and Jefferson's fault. With the combined gifts of the Declaration of Independence and the Union, they provided the means for future generations to transcend the injustices and inadequacies of their own time. The fault will lie with ourselves.

Beside Route 16 in Holliston, Massachusetts, is the Balancing Rock—a twenty-foot-long, ten-foot-wide, six-foot-thick boulder perched precariously atop an even bigger rock. In 1789, while returning from his New England tour, George Washington passed through Holliston and ordered his carriage to halt beside this weird Stonehenge-like formation. According to local legend, he stepped out of the carriage so that he could, as many people have done since, attempt to push the Balancing Rock off its natural pedestal. The attempt failed, and the president continued on to nearby Uxbridge for the night.

When Melissa, Dora, and I visited Holliston in the winter of 2019, the town historian, Joanne Hulbert, took us to this now famous spot.

At Joanne's urging, I climbed up onto the lower rock and placed my hands against the ancient, lichen-covered boulder and pushed with all my might. Nothing, of course, happened.

Then, just last night, as I was putting the finishing touches on this book, I received an unexpected email from Joanne. "I am saddened to report," she wrote, "that the Balancing Rock in Holliston . . . has for some unknown reason, toppled to the ground." A local police dispatcher theorized that erosion was the culprit. Whatever the cause, the delicately balanced rock that not even George Washington could move had finally fallen.

—Nantucket, September 23, 2020

The Balancing Rock of Holliston.

With George at the National Harbor outlets, Oxon Hill, Maryland.

ACKNOWLEDGMENTS

I'm indebted to the authors of several recent books about Washington's presidential travels: T. H. Breen's *George Washington's Journey: The President Forges a New Nation*; Philip Smucker's *Riding with George: Sportsmanship and Chivalry in the Making of America's First President*; Joanne Grasso's *George Washington's 1790 Grand Tour of Long Island*; Warren Bingham's *George Washington's 1791 Southern Tour*; and Terry Lipscomb's *South Carolina in 1791: George Washington's Southern Tour*. As you can see below, I'm particularly indebted to the many librarians and historical society archivists and volunteers who generously shared documents and insights about George Washington's visit to their town or city. Melissa, Dora, and I ended up visiting many more places than the narrative could possibly accommodate. So our apologies to those who generously gave of their time and did not make it into the book. As a kind of compensation, I'd like to use this space to thank both those who are mentioned in the text and those who are not—all of whom were essential to the writing of this book.

My initial plan had been to start with a journey Washington took in 1784 up the Potomac River and over the Allegheny Mountains to the Monongahela River, where he visited land he owned twenty-five miles south of Pittsburgh (my hometown). I very reluctantly decided this journey through Maryland, Virginia, West Virginia, and Pennsylvania—which took us to some of the most beautiful country we'd ever seen—must be consigned to the cutting room floor. Our thanks nonetheless to Dillard Kirby, Diane Shaw, and Maurice Luker at Lafayette College for the tour of the replica of Lafayette's birthplace, Chavaniac, and the collection of letters written by Lafayette to GW; Marcie Turjan, Sam Clifton, and Ron Howard of the Rolling Rock Hunt Pony Club for the chance to witness a foxhunt; my high school classmate Steve Loevner for the tour of Braddock, Pennsylvania; Mark McCarty of Laurel Highlands River Tours in Ohiopyle, Pennsylvania, for the copy of his father Ralph William McCarty's extremely helpful study of GW's 1784 journey; and Tamara Gibson of the Society of Port Republic Preservationists for taking the time to talk with us about GW's visit to Port Republic even as she prepared for the flooding associated with two successive hurricanes.

Below is a tour-by-tour breakdown of the people who helped us once we started following Washington's presidential travels:

Preinaugural: Mary Thompson, Kevin Butterfield, Susan Schoelwer, and Douglas and Nadine Bradburn (and their dog, Walter), George Washington's Mount Vernon; VanJessica Gladney, Constitutional Walking Tours; Bob and Mary Beth Slivka, Susan Mollica, Bob Belvin, New Brunswick Historical Association; Mayor James Cahill; Mark Nonestied, Indian Queen Tavern, East Jersey Old Town Village; Susan and Lou Luczu, Buccleuch Mansion; Adam Sherry; and Kevin Draper, New York Historical Tours.

New England: Allie Copeland, Rye Historical Association; Michael Jehle and Elizabeth Rose, Fairfield Museum and History Center; Katie McFadden, Stratford Library; Edward Surato, Whitney Library, New Haven Museum; Amy Humphries, Wallingford Public Library; Nancy and Bob Charles (and their poodle, Charley) of the High Meadow Inn in Wallingford; Sierra Dixon, Connecticut Historical Society in Hartford; Amy Kilkenny, Wadsworth Atheneum, also in Hartford; Damien Cregeau and Pamela Hall of Wethersfield and Norwich, Connecticut; Michelle Tom, Windsor Historical Society; the volunteers at the Oliver Ellsworth Homestead; Bill Sullivan, Suffield Academy; Cliff McCarthy and Maggie Humberston, Springfield Museums; Helene O'Connor, Palmer Public Library; Brenda Metterville, Merrick Public Library in Brookfield; Heather Gablaski, Quaboag Historical Society; Ed Londergan of West Brookfield; Wendy Essery, Worcester Historical Museum; Alexander London, Worcester Public Library; Vincent Golden, Mary Lamoureux, and James Moran, American Antiquarian Society; Paula Lupton, Artemas Ward Homestead; Linda Davis, Shrewsbury Historical Society; Priya Rathnam, Shrewsbury Public Library; Teri Evans, Boston by Foot; Sira Dooley Fairchild, Bostonian Society; Nat Sheidley and Jill Conley, Revolutionary Spaces; Matthew Stackpole for the picture of the Christian Gullager sketch at the Massachusetts Historical Society (MHS); Peter Drummey, MHS; Elizabeth Barker, Boston Atheneum; Emily Gonzalez, Cambridge Historical Society; Ethan Lasser, Center for Historical Scientific Instruments at Harvard University; Lauren McCormack, Marblehead Museum; Mary Hviding, Salem Public Library; Bonnie Hurd Smith; Gordon Harris, Ipswich Historical Commission; Giselle Stevens, Sharon Spieldenner, Dana Echelberger, Newburyport Public Library; Molly Moore, Tuck Museum and Hampton Historical Society; Elizabeth Farish, Strawbery Banke Museum in Portsmouth, New Hampshire; Jeff and Molly Bolster; Karen Bouffard, Wentworth Lear Historic Houses; Judy Smart, First Congregational Church at Kittery Point, Maine; James Austin, owner of the Red Cottage; Emma Bray, Independence Museum, Exeter, New Hampshire; Amanda Levy, Haverhill Public Library; Gail Ralston, Phillips Andover Academy; Elaine Cements, Andover Center for History and Culture; Kathy Meagher, Billerica Public Library; Erica McAvoy, Chris Kauffman, Stacey Fraser, and Elizabeth Mubarek, Lexington Historical Society; Kerrianne McQuown, Watertown Free Public Library; Marilynne Roach, Historical Society of Watertown; Gloria Polizzotti Greis, Needham History Center and Museum; Sue Hamilos, Wellesley

Public Library; Betsy Johnson, Sherburne Historical Society; Joanne Hulbert and Ben Clarkson, Holliston Historical Society; Anne Berard, Milford Town Library; Susan Elliott; Phyllis Foley and Andrew Jenrich, Taft Public Library in Mendon, Massachusetts; James and Mary Beauchamp, Uxbridge Historical Society; Peter Emerick, Uxbridge Historical Commission; Joe Iamartino, Mark Snay, Tom Chase, and Stan Swanson, Thompson Historical Society; Roberta Baublitz, Thompson Public Library; Walter and Ann Hinchman, Pomfret Historical Society; Marian and Jasmine Matthews, Henrietta House in Ashford; Lou and Margie Chatey, Westford Hill Distillers; Sheila Siegel; Cindy Lee; Terese Mayer, Babcock Library in Ashford; Ann Galonska, Mansfield Historical Society; Lorraine Stub, Berlin Historical Society; and Richard Platt and Arthur Stowe, Milford Historical Society.

Long Island: Christine Gottsch, Maria Pecorale, Margaret Wulf, and Pamela Van Cott, Sagtikos Manor; Bev Tyler, Three Villages Historical Society; Margot Arceri; Tracy Pfaff and Toby Kissam, Huntington Historical Society; Nomi Dayan, Cold Spring Harbor Whaling Museum; Harriet Gerard Clark and Claire Bellerjeau, Raynham Hall Museum; Phil Roosevelt; and Carol Clarke, Bryant Library, Roslyn, New York.

Rhode Island: Ruth Taylor, Newport Historical Society; Meryle Cawley and Mary Jo Valdes, Touro Synagogue; Norma Artman and Ira Artman, Tree of Life Synagogue; Michelle Farias, Redwood Library; Morgan Grefe, Rick Ring, Dana Signe Munroe, Michelle Chiles, Phoebe Bean, JD Kay, and Scott Alexander, Rhode Island Historical Society; and Jennifer Betts, John Hay Library, Brown University.

South: Warren Bingham for the most helpful advice based on his own travels following GW in the South; Brittany Kemmer and Joseph Macfarland, St. Johns College; B. J. and Charity Armstrong, U.S. Naval Academy; James Cheevers, U.S. Naval Academy Museum; Rod Codfield, Historic London Town and Gardens; Lisa Timmerman, Weems-Botts Museum; Michelle Hamilton, Mary Washington House; Jamie Bosket, William Rasmussen, and Andrew Talkov, Virginia Museum of History and Culture; Jeffrey Nichols and Eric Proebsting,

Thomas Jefferson's Poplar Forest; Frank McMillan, Historic Halifax; Sara and Skip Valentine, Tarboro; Monica Fleming, Edgecombe Community College; Kim Averett, Sheppard Memorial Library, Greenville, North Carolina; John Green, New Bern and Craven County Library; Lindy Cummings and Andy Acasio, Tryon Palace; Richard Stradling, *Raleigh News & Observer*; Robin Triplett; Bernhard Thuersam; Travis Souther, Wilmington Public Library; Alison Dineen, Lower Cape Fear Historical Society at the Latimer House; Wally Zeddun, Rice Museum, Georgetown; David Preston and Tessa Updike, The Citadel; David Ryan, Heyward-Washington House; Dot Glover and Marianne Cawley, Charleston County Public Library; C. J. Cantwell, St. Michael's Church; Hugh Golson and Scott Eisenhart, Solomon's Lodge, Savannah; Stan Deaton, Georgia Historical Society; Mel Galin, Mulberry Grove Foundation; Vaughnette Goode-Walker, Footprints of Savannah; Connie Herndon, Burke County Public Library; Leah Carter, Burke County Museum; Bill Kirby, *Augusta Chronicle*; Tina Monaco, Augusta Public Library; Stephani Roohani, Historic Meadow Garden; Louise Riley and Meade Hendrix, Saluda County Historical Society; Nicholas Doyle, South Carolina Library, University of South Carolina; Rick Wise, Historic Camden; Windy Corbett, Camden Archives and Museum; Wenonah Haire and Kassidy Plyler, Catawba Cultural Preservation Project; Scott Warren, President James K. Polk State Historic Site; Chas Fagan; Thomas Cole, Robinson-Spangler Carolina Room, Charlotte Mecklenburg Library; Gretchen Witt, Rowan County Library; Ed Hall, Thyatira Heritage Museum; Frank Vagnone, Karen Walter, Margaret Krause, and David Joiner, Old Salem Museums and Gardens; Walter and Alice Coles; Bobby and Lucy Conner; Dean Malissa, Steve Bashore, Samantha Snyder, and Dawn Bonner, George Washington's Mount Vernon; David Oleksak, Office of Congressman John Keating; Jean Brown and Doris Crouse, Taneytown History Museum; the staff of the Powel House, Philadelphia; Susan Beegel, the late Wes Tiffney Jr., and Susan Shillinglaw for organizing the "Steinbeck and the Environment" conference on Nantucket back in May 1992.

Jefferson and Madison's Northern Tour: Sam and Sue Philbrick; Peter Gow and Catherine Conover Covert; Robert and Pauline Maguire; Bruce and Lynne Venter; Tyler Resch, Bennington Museum.

Mary Lamoureux for her help in assembling the newspaper coverage; Ben Gambuzza for the research help; Tim Walker, University of Massachusetts Dartmouth, for the contacts, advice, and red wine.

For reading and commenting on the manuscript, I am indebted to Susan Beegel, Warren Bingham, Richard Duncan, Peter Henriques, Mike Hill, Bill Kirby, Peter Panchy, David Preston, Mary Thompson, and family members Ethan Philbrick, Jennie Philbrick McArdle, Melissa Philbrick, Sam Philbrick, Sue Philbrick, and Thomas Philbrick. Special thanks to Peter Gow, who was there chapter by chapter and rewrite by rewrite.

Jenny Pouech was, once again, a huge help in securing permissions for the images in this book. Jeffrey Ward did his usual stellar job with the maps. Thanks to Nate Roberts at Poets Corner Press on Nantucket for all the copying help.

At Viking, my editor, Wendy Wolf, showed me the way during a year like no other. Many thanks, Wendy, for your wisdom, understanding, and persistence. Thanks to Terezia Cicel for her comments on the manuscript and all the other help. Many thanks also to Brian Tart, Andrea Schulz, Bruce Giffords, Randee Marullo, Louise Braverman, Kate Stark, and to Paul Buckley and David Litman for the amazing jacket.

My agent, Stuart Krichevsky, was there for me with this book when I needed him the most; many thanks, Stuart, for the guidance, the insights, and your friendship. Thanks also to his co-workers, Laura Usselman, Aemilia Phillips, Hannah Schwartz, and everyone else at SKLA. Thanks to Rich Green at the Gotham Group for all his support and to Meghan Walker at Tandem Literary for keeping me connected to my readers through my website and social media.

Finally, special thanks to my wife, Melissa, for sharing the journey.

NOTES

Abbreviations

DGW—*The Diaries of George Washington*, edited by Donald Jackson and Dorothy Twohig

PGW—*The Papers of George Washington, Presidential Series*, edited by Dorothy Twohig

I have adjusted the spelling and punctuation of quotations to make them more accessible to a modern audience—something that has already been done by the editors of several collections cited below.

Preface: The Chariot

On John Brown's chariot and the tradition that GW accompanied Brown on a trip to his shipyard in India Point, see Henry Brown's *John Brown of Providence and His Chariot*, pp. 4–8. A transcription of the speech in which Alexander Hamilton paraphrases Governor George Clinton's position at the New York Ratifying Convention as "no general free government can suit" is in founders.archives.gov/documents/Hamilton/01-05-02-0012-0015. Ron Chernow cites Patrick Henry's claim "They'll free your niggers," in *Alexander Hamilton*, p. 267. The account of how GW "unites all hearts" is in the Nov. 10, 1789, *Salem Mercury*. Lafayette's claim "I would never have drawn my sword in the cause of America if I could have conceived that thereby I was founding a land of slavery" is cited in an Oct. 3, 1845, letter from Thomas Clarkson cited in *The Liberty Bell* (1846), p. 64, in en.wikiquote.org/wiki/Gilbert_du_Motier,_Marquis_de_Lafayette. Mary Thompson cites GW's claim that "nothing but the rooting out of slavery can perpetuate the existence of our union, by consolidating it in a common bond of principle," in *"The Only Unavoidable Subject of Regret"* (hereafter cited as *TOUSR*), p. 296.

Chapter 1: Loomings

John Steinbeck's claims "I had to go alone and I had to be self-contained, a kind of casual turtle" and "A dog, particularly an exotic like Charley, is a bond between strangers" are in *Travels with Charley*, pp. 6, 9. Also see "Travelers Who Never Went Alone," in Paul Theroux's *Tao of Travel*, pp. 93–104. On Harry and Bess Truman's travels, see Matthew Algeo's *Harry Truman's Excellent Adventure*. Steinbeck writes, "We do not take a trip; a trip takes us," in *Travels with Charley*, p. 4.

Chapter 2: Mount Vernon

GW writes of bidding "adieu to Mount Vernon, to private life, and to domestic felicity" in *DGW*, 5:445. He writes of feeling like "a culprit who is going to the place of his execution" in an April 1, 1789, letter to Henry Knox, in *PGW*, 2:2. He writes of giving up "all expectations of private happiness in this world" in a May 5, 1789, letter to Edward Rutledge, in *PGW*, 2:217. Mary Thompson cites the statistics about attendance at Graceland and Mount Vernon in *TOUSR*, p. 1. On the history of the Nova Scotia duck-tolling retriever, see Alison Strang and Gail MacMillan's *The Nova Scotia Duck Tolling Retriever*, pp. 1–9, which cites the account by Nicolas Denys, pp. 3–4; the picture of Gunner is on p. 7. For all that is known about the carriage on display at Mount Vernon, known as the Powel coach because it was purchased by Elizabeth Powel at the end of Washington's second term as president, see Elizabeth Jamieson's "Research Report on the Powel Coach at Mount Vernon." GW writes of "those trees which my hands have planted" in a June 2, 1784, letter to Comte de Chastellux, in founders.archives.gov/documents/Washington/04-01-02-0279. For an excellent summary of GW and breeding mules, see the notes to Tobias Lear's May 15, 1791, letter to GW in *PGW*, 8:192–93. GW writes of coming from a "short-lived family" in a Dec. 8, 1784, letter to Lafayette, in founders.archives.gov/documents/Washington/04-02-02-0140. Thompson writes about GW and tooth transplants in *TOUSR*, pp. 199–200; see also, particularly when it comes to GW's dentures, Jennifer Van Horn's "George Washington's Dentures: Disability, Deception, and the Republican Body," pp. 34–38. Ishmael's claim "Not ignoring what is good, I am quick to perceive a horror" is in Herman Melville's *Moby-Dick*, p. 8, as is the claim "all mortal greatness is but disease," p. 82.

Chapter 3: "Wreaths and Chaplets of Flowers"

For information on GW as a Mason, see gwmemorial.org/pages/george-washington -the-mason. GW applied for a loan of five hundred pounds, something he "never expected to be reduced to the necessity of doing," in a March 4, 1789, letter to Richard Conway, in *PGW*, 1:361–62. Alexandria's address to GW, as well as his emotional response, is in *PGW*, 2:59–60. For information on the National Washington-Rochambeau Revolutionary Route Association, see w3r-us.org/. Elkanah Watson compares the terrain between Baltimore and Alexandria in 1785 with "a newly-occupied territory" in *Men and Times of the Revolution*, p. 278. Charles Thomson's description of how his trip from New York to Mount Vernon was "much impeded by tempestuous weather, bad roads, and the many large rivers" is in *PGW*, 2:55. The Philadelphia doctor's description of the brace he made for Billy Lee and GW's characterization of him as his "old faithful servant" are in *PGW*, 2:133–34. The account of GW's march across Gray's Bridge and into Philadelphia comes from "Letter from a Gentleman to His Nephew," which appeared in the April 22, 1789, *Federal Gazette*. Thomas Jefferson describes GW as "the most graceful figure that could be seen on horseback" in a Jan. 2, 1814, letter to Walter Jones, in founders .archives.gov/documents/Jefferson/03-07-02-0052. The article describing GW as "the father, the friend, and the servant of the people" is in the April 22, 1789, *Federal Gazette*. According to a newspaper account cited in *PGW*, 2:102, at 10:00 a.m. "the city troops of light horse paraded, in order to accompany him to Trenton; but his Excellency had left the city before that hour, from a desire to avoid even the appearance of pomp or vain parade." I cite Abigail Adams's observation that GW "possesses a dignity that forbids familiarity" in *In the Hurricane's Eye*, p. 262. Martha refers to "dear little Washington" in a June 8, 1789, letter to Fanny Bassett Washington, marthawashington.us/items/show/436.html. Mary Anna Randolph Custis (the great-granddaughter of Martha Washington) recorded Nelly Custis Lewis's memories of GW in Washington Custis's *Recollections and Memoirs of Washington*, pp. 40–41; my thanks to Mary Thompson for bringing this reference to my attention. GW writes of how "men's minds are as variant as their faces" in a March 9, 1789, letter to Benjamin Harrison, in *PGW*, 1:375. Simon Newman in *Parades and the Politics of the Street* describes GW's reception at Trenton as "one of the most remarkable female rites of the late eighteenth century," p. 48. For information on New Jersey's liberal voting laws in the eighteenth century and how the Anti-Federalist state legislature restricted the right to vote to white males in 1807, see www.nps.gov/articles/voting -rights-in-nj-before-the-15th-and-19th.htm. My account of GW's reception at Trenton comes from the April 29, 1789, issue of the *Gazette of the United States* and from the April 29, 1789, issue of *Freeman's Journal*. On GW's relationship with Catharine Macaulay Graham, see Bob Ruppert's "Catharine Macaulay's Difficult Years, 1778–1787," *Journal of the American Revolution*, allthingsliberty.com/2019/09/catharine -macaulays-difficult-years-1778-1787/. For an account of John Adams and Benjamin Franklin sharing a room at the Indian Queen Tavern, see www.newenglandhis toricalsociety.com/when-john-adams-slept-with-ben-franklin/.

Chapter 4: New York

The fragments of GW's "Undelivered First Inaugural Address" are in *PGW*, 2:158–73, as is the "Final Version," pp. 173–77; for a discussion of the two documents, see pp. 152–58. Unless otherwise indicated, the accounts I've cited of GW's arrival at New York and his inauguration a week later are contained in Phelps Stokes's magisterial compendium *The Iconography of Manhattan Island*, 5:1239–42. GW writes of how all the hoopla on his arrival at New York "filled my mind with sensations as painful (considering the reverse of this scene, which may be the case after all my labors to do good) as they are pleasing" in *DGW*, 5:447. On Captain Philip Freneau and the orangutans' presence during GW's arrival at New York City, see Lewis Leary's *That*

Rascal Freneau, p. 162. For information on the Statue of Liberty, see www.nps.gov /stli/index.htm. For information on the double equestrian statue of Robert E. Lee and Stonewall Jackson in Baltimore, see baltimoreplanning.wixsite.com/monu mentcommission/leeandjacksonmonument. Ray Brighton cites Tobias Lear's account of the evening spent with GW and David Humphreys in *The Checkered Career of Tobias Lear*, p. 60. For information about Federal Hall, see www.nps.gov/feha /index.htm. William Maclay's account of how GW "was agitated and embarrassed more than ever he was by the leveled cannon or pointed musket" is in Maclay's *Diary*, p. 13. When it comes to GW's not freeing his slaves at his inauguration, Jill Lepore writes in *These Truths*, "Few of Washington's decisions would have such lasting and terrible consequences as this one failure to act," p. 134. Philip Morgan, on the other hand, writes in "'To Get Quit of Negroes': George Washington and Slavery," "Nothing and no one—not even George Washington—could have halted the advance of slavery in the United States" during the years of his presidency, pp. 428–29. James Madison's complaint "We are in a wilderness without a single footstep to guide us" is cited by Ron Chernow in *Hamilton*, p. 280. Martha Washington writes of how "our family will be deranged" in an April 20, 1789, letter to John Dandridge, marthawashington.us/items/show/434.html; she writes of how Washy "seemed to be lost in a maze at the great parade that was made for us all the way we come," in a June 8, 1789, letter to Fanny Bassett Washington, marthawashington .us/items/show/436.html. Tobias Lear writes about the oysters and lobsters prepared by Samuel Fraunces in a letter to George Augustine Washington cited by Brighton in *The Checkered Career of Tobias Lear*, p. 62. GW writes of the decisions made in the early days of his presidency having "great and durable consequences, from their having been established at the commencement of a new general government," in a May 10, 1789, letter to John Adams, in *PGW*, 2:245–47. GW's complaint that if he indulges everyone who wants to see him, he will be "unable to attend to any business *whatsoever*" is in *PGW*, 2:248. GW writes of whether it is advisable "to make the tour of the United States" in his May 10, 1789, letter to John Adams, in *PGW*, 2:246. John Adams's May 17, 1789, response is in *PGW*, 2:312–14. GW writes of the "very large and painful tumor" in a July 3, 1789, letter to James McHenry, in *PGW*, 3:112. For an account of GW's illness in the spring of 1789, see James E. Guba's "Anthrax and the President, 1789," gwpapers.virginia.edu/anthrax-and-the-president-1789/, which cites the anecdotal account of the elder Dr. Bard urging his son to cut "deeper" and GW's insistence that "I know that I am in the hands of a good Providence." GW writes of being "able to take exercise in my coach, by having it so contrived, as to extend myself the full length of it," in a July 3, 1789, letter to James McHenry, in *PGW*, 3:112. GW compares his shrunken tumor to the "size of a barley corn" (in the eighteenth century a barley corn was a unit of measure of about three inches) while stating that the lack of exercise will "hasten my departure for that country from whence no traveler returns" in a Sept. 8, 1789, letter to James Craik, in *PGW*, 4:1. GW mentions "a sort of epidemical cold" in New York in his Oct. 12, 1789, letter to his sister Betty Washington Lewis, in *PGW*, 4:161–62. GW announces that "in one word . . . the national government is organized" in an Oct. 13, 1789, letter to Gouverneur Morris, in *PGW*, 4:176–79. GW's Oct. 13, 1789, letter to Thomas Jefferson, in which he offers him the position of secretary of state, is in *PGW*, 4:174–75.

Chapter 5: Dreaming of George Washington

On fainting and dreaming, see Eva Wiseman, "The Unexpected Joys of Fainting," *Guardian*, Feb. 2, 2014, www.theguardian.com/lifeandstyle/2014/feb/02/the-unexpected -joys-of-fainting. For information on N. C. Wyeth's painting *In a Dream I Meet General Washington*, see David Michaelis's *N. C. Wyeth*, pp. 330–33, and collections .brandywine.org/objects/6502/in-a-dream-i-meet-general-washington;jsessionid= F85D4A63047A3A8F3DCAF60409CB02BB?ctx=3cd36318-b113-4d55-9214-917be4 96b158&idx=7. On the Morris-Jumel Mansion, see www.morrisjumel.org/history. Stephen Decatur Jr. in *Private Affairs of George Washington* (hereafter cited as *PAGW*) details the identity and dress of those in GW's "retinue," as well as the carriage, wagon, and horses, pp. 39, 42–43, 54, 78. On John Adams and the presidential title controversy, see www.mountvernon.org/george-washington/facts/washington-stories /a-president-by-any-other-name/. Decatur in *PAGW* details GW's and Martha's levees and how the Anti-Federalist press referred to them as "court-like levees" and "queenly drawing-rooms," pp. 39–41. According to T. H. Breen in *George Washington's Journey*, GW traveled in "an open carriage . . . an older carriage that he had owned since the end of the war," p. 14. On a royal progress, see www.history.com/news/eliza beth-i-royal-progress-expense. On George III's Gold State Coach, see www.regency history.net/2018/05/the-gold-state-coach-at-royal-mews.html. On GW's charger Prescott, see www.mountvernon.org/library/digitalhistory/digital-encyclopedia/arti cle/prescott-horse/. On GW's leopard-skin saddle pad, see historical.ha.com/itm /political/presidential-relics/george-washington-and-british-general-edward- braddock-a-remarkable-leopard-skin-saddle-pad-owned-and-used-by-both- historic-fi/a/6172-43025.s. I cite Abigail Adams's claim that if GW "was really not one of the best-intentioned men in the world, he might be a very dangerous one" in *Bunker Hill*, p. 245. Jacques Pierre Brissot's reference to the road in the vicinity of modern Greenwich, Connecticut, as "nothing but a steep slope of boulders" is cited in *DGW*, 5:462. On the bridge collapse of June 28, 1983, see connecticuthistory.org/mianus -river-bridge-collapses-today-in-history/. GW describes the "rich regalia" of the Connecticut farms and the "handsome cascade" of the waterfall in Stamford in *DGW*, 5:462–64. He writes of the "destructive evidences of British cruelty" in Fairfield in *DGW*, 5:462. Samuel Orcutt in *A History of the Old Town of Stratford and the City of Bridgeport* writes of GW coming across a boat under construction in a field in Stratford, pp. 390–91. Edward Atwater in *History of the City of New Haven* cites Jared Sparks's description of how the citizens of Connecticut "assembled from far and near," p. 86. On the Leverett Hubbard House, I have relied on the account provided by Miss Mary Whiting Deming, contained in a group of clippings at the New Haven Museum.

Chapter 6: "Only a Man"

Martha Washington compares herself with a "state prisoner" in an Oct. 23, 1789, letter to Fanny Bassett Washington, www.mountvernon.org/education/primary-sources -2/article/letter-martha-washington-to-fanny-bassett-washington-october-23- 1789/. Martha's Dec. 26, 1789, letter to Mercy Otis Warren, in which she observes that "the greater part of our happiness or misery depends upon our dispositions, and not upon our circumstances," is in marthawashington.us/items/show/25.html. GW writes of his visit to the Hartford Woolen Manufactory in *DGW*, 5:468–69. He writes of the "very fine" silk thread in Wallingford in *DGW*, 5:467. GW tells of his visit to the card comb manufactory of Giles Richard on Hanover Square in Boston in *DGW*, 5:480; see also Leander Bishop's *History of American Manufactures, 1608–1860*, 1:497. GW promises that "the promotion of domestic manufactures will . . . be among the first consequences . . . to flow from an energetic government" in a letter to the Delaware Society for Promoting Domestic Manufacturers written during his pre-inaugural tour on April 19–20, 1789, in *PGW*, 2:78. John Steele Gordon writes prob-ingly of American attempts to compete against the British textile industry in *An Empire of Wealth*, pp. 88–92. GW describes his visit to the sailcloth (known as duck) manufactory in Boston, which he says is "of public utility and private advantage," in *DGW*, 5:479. Thomas Jefferson claims that manufacturing "suffocates the germ of virtue" in *Notes on the State of Virginia*, pp. 170–71. GW comments on how there is a "great equality in the people" in New England in *DGW*, 5:470, a passage in which he also describes the farms and homes he sees. I cite GW's 1775 description of the New England soldiers in the provincial army as "an exceeding dirty and nasty peo-ple" in *Bunker Hill*, p. 241; I also cite the reference to John Hancock as King Han-cock, p. 121. GW writes of "the grateful sense which I entertain of the honor you intended to confer on me" in an Oct. 22, 1789, letter to John Hancock, in *PGW*, 4:214. GW is referred to as America's "political savior" in the Oct. 29, 1789, edition of the *Massachusetts Spy*. The account of five cannons being fired for the five future states of New England is in the Oct. 26, 1789, issue of *The Boston Gazette*. GW writes that "this ceremony was not to be avoided" in *DGW*, 5:472. An article in the Oct. 26, 1789, *Boston Gazette* describes how New Englanders paid tribute to GW by crowding the sides of the road to "hail him welcome." Elizabeth Ward writes of GW's visit to Shrewsbury in *Old Times in Shrewsbury, Mass.*, pp. 46–47. On Elizabeth Ward and Shrewsbury and the memorializing of Artemas Ward, see www.ameri canantiquarian.org/proceedings/44539558.pdf. The account of the boy saying to GW, "You are nothing but a man," appears in N. Fisher, "Letter Describing Wash-ington's Visit to Salem in 1789," pp. 299–300. The account of GW patting the boy's head and saying, "I am only a *man*," is in George Wingate Chase's *History of Haverhill, Massachusetts*, p. 446. For Samuel Francis Batchelder's *Washington Elm Tradition*, see cambridgehistory.org/research/washington-elm-debate-rages-on-fact-or-legend/. John Hancock writes that "it would have given me pleasure had a residence at my house met with your approbation" in an Oct. 23, 1789, letter to GW, in *PGW*, 4:216.

Chapter 7: Turf Wars

GW refers to the American Revolution as "the dispute with Great Britain" in *DGW*, 5:477. Ray Brighton recounts Tobias Lear's two incidents of "tardiness" in *The Check-ered Career of Tobias Lear*, p. 85. GW writes of the lateness of the militia in Cambridge in *DGW*, 5:473. Ron Chernow writes of how John Adams "committed a major faux pas by snubbing [GW's] invitation" to accompany him on the New England tour in *George Washington*, p. 608. Frederick Gutheim in *The Potomac* cites John Adams's letter to Mercy Otis Warren in which Adams refers to himself as "a morose philosopher and a surly politician," p. 10. Adams refers to the vice presidency as "the most insignificant office that ever the invention of man contrived or his imagination conceived" in a Dec. 18, 1793, letter to Abigail Adams, www.masshist.org/digitaladams /archive/doc?id=L17931219ja. Benjamin Russell's description of the standoff between the Boston selectmen and the state officials is in *PGW*, 4:228–29. The Oct. 29, 1789, edition of the *Massachusetts Spy* tells of how Boston's women watched GW's entrance into the city from the roofs and windows. For the accounts of William Sumner and Isaac Harris, see "Schoolboy Views of President Washington in 1789" in the history blog *Boston1775*, boston1775.blogspot.com/2015/01/schoolboy-views -of-president-washington.html. GW writes of the inscriptions on the triumphal arch and the "vast concourse of people" in *DGW*, 5:475. On cordwainers, see www .thehcc.org/backgrnd.htm. The reference to John Hancock "cast upon a painful couch" is in the Oct. 29, 1789, *Independent Chronicle*. GW writes of how he turned down John Hancock's dinner invitation "under a full persuasion that [Hancock] would have waited upon me so soon as I should have arrived" in *DGW*, 5:475. The story about how GW "unites all hearts" is in the Nov. 10, 1789, *Salem Mercury*, as is the account of the Anti-Federalist who had become one of GW's biggest fans. Even before GW's arrival in Boston, Lucy Cranch wrote to Abigail Adams in an Oct. 23, 1789, letter about the paradoxical behavior of the Anti-Federalists, who "clamour and rave if there is a shadow of power given their rulers and at the same time pay them homage in a manner that would disgrace the subjects of the Grand Turk," in founders.archives.gov/documents/Adams/04-08-02-0230. GW writes of the visit by representatives sent by Governor Hancock in *DGW*, 5:476. Hancock's Oct. 26, 1789, letter to GW, claiming that he "hazards everything as it respects his health" to visit GW at his lodgings is in *PGW*, 4:228. GW writes that Hancock "assured me that indisposition alone had prevented" him from visiting earlier in *DGW*, 5:476. Martha Washington writes of how her two grandchildren have "very bad colds" in her Oct. 23, 1789, letter to Fanny Bassett Washington, www.mountvernon.org/edu cation/primary-sources-2/article/letter-martha-washington-to-fanny-bassett -washington-october-23-1789/. On the Washington influenza, see *DGW*, 5:477. According to Jeremy Belknap, "While GW was in the chapel, Gullager the painter stole a likeness of him from a pew behind the pulpit. . . . Gullager followed GW to Portsmouth where he sat 2.5 hours for him to take his portrait, which he did and obtained a very good likeness," in *PGW*, 4:290. William Maclay's description of GW's gaunt appearance is in a Jan. 20, 1791, entry in his diary, pp. 365–66. The account of Washington's punctual departure from Boston at 8:00 a.m. and his words to Caleb Gibbs appeared in the July 19, 1823, *Columbian Centinel*, cited in boston1775 .blogspot.com/2015/01/president-washington-and-major-gibbs.html. GW's comments about the dilapidated state of Marblehead are in *DGW*, 5:483. The letter from the citizens of Marblehead to GW is in *PGW*, 4:271–72. Samuel Roads Jr. describes GW's visit to the Lee mansion in *The History and Traditions of Marblehead*, pp. 208–11. N. Fisher's account of GW's visit to Salem is in "Letter Describing Washington's Visit to Salem in 1789," pp. 299–300. My account of pillow lace is based on Marta Cotterell Raffel's *Laces of Ipswich: The Art and Economics of an Early American Industry, 1750–1840*, pp. 27–49. Gordon Harris's "President Washington Visits Ipswich" was also very helpful, historicipswich.org/2021/07/17/president-washington-visits-ipswich -october-30-1789/amp/. Jacob Chapman writes of the Philbricks' "natural affection for the sea" in *A Genealogy of the Philbrick and Philbrook Families*, p. 166.

Chapter 8: "A Child of God"

Ray Brighton in *The Checkered Career of Tobias Lear* details GW's reception at Portsmouth, pp. 76–78. GW notes that the women of Portsmouth have "much blacker hair than are usually seen in the Southern States" in *DGW*, 5:490. The account of GW's visit to the home of Tobias Lear's mother and GW's words about the boy sharing his name are in Charles Brewster's *Rambles About Portsmouth*, pp. 254, 266. GW describes the expedition "to view the harbor of Portsmouth" in *DGW*, 5:489. The Nov. 10, 1789, edition of *The Salem Mercury* includes a detailed account of GW's harbor tour: "The serenity of the morning reminds of the following lines; 'Then rose the morning, and the golden sun, with beams refracted, on the ocean shore; clear was the sky, the waves from the murmurs ease, and every ruder wind was hushed in peace.'" Brighton also recounts GW's harbor tour, noting that they ventured "in the vicinity of the modern 2-KR buoy," p. 81; Brighton notes that the first silver dollar wasn't minted until 1794. The tradition surrounding GW landing on the "old stone dock" at Kittery Point is in *DGW*, 5:490. I talked to Judy Smart, a tour guide at the First Congregational Church in Kittery Point, about the tradition surrounding Lady Pepperrell and GW's visit to Kittery Point. The description of the Red Cottage at Kittery Point is listed on the Vrbo website, www.vrbo.com/4087681ha. Stephen Decatur Jr. writes of the "extraordinarily interesting records" he discovered in *PAGW*, p. v. For information about the gundalow *Piscataqua*, see www .gundalow.org/. My account of Ona Judge is based on Erica Armstrong Dunbar's *Never Caught: The Washingtons' Relentless Pursuit of Their Runaway Slave, Ona Judge*, in which Dunbar cites the runaway advertisement about Ona Judge, p. 99, Joseph Whipple's claim that Ona's flight had been motivated by "a thirst for complete freedom," p. 146, as well as GW's response, pp. 148–49, and the reference to the Greenland county clerk Thomas Philbrook, p. 160. Mary Thompson in *TOUSR* writes of three enslaved workers—Tom, Will Shag, and Waggoner Jack—whom GW sold to the sugar plantations in the West Indies, p. 258; Thompson also writes of the time that GW "severely punished" an enslaved worker who repeatedly walked across the grass in front of Mount Vernon, pp. 253–54. For transcripts of the articles based on the two interviews Ona gave late in life about her relationship with the Washingtons and her decision to seek freedom, see www.ushistory.org/presidentshouse /slaves/oneyinterview.php. For another useful discussion of GW's relationship to Ona Judge, see www.huntington.org/verso/2018/08/george-washington-letter-and -runaway-slave.

Chapter 9: The Middle Road Home

GW writes of how "amazingly crooked" the roads are in Massachusetts in *DGW*, 5:494. He observes that Haverhill is in a "beautiful part of the country" in *DGW*, 5:491. Elias Frost writes of seeing GW in Milford, Massachusetts, in "Chronicle of the Frost Family," p. 77. My thanks to Susan Elliott for bringing this unpublished manuscript to my attention and for providing me with a transcription of the relevant passage. George Wingate Chase in *History of Haverhill, Massachusetts* cites the tradition that Washington claimed, "Haverhill is the pleasantest village I have passed through," p. 445. When it comes to the Washington elm phenomenon, John

Batchelder in a 1911 story in the Nov. 10, 1949, *Framingham News*, writes, "Washington must have been of an extremely restful temperament, or a very tired man, as we are informed by various writers that he rested under many of the trees and sought refreshment at most of the taverns between Hartford and Boston. At best, these trees could have been but 25 years of age and hardly large enough to afford shelter for [the president]." On the Amos Wyman House in Billerica, see www.billericahistory .org/amoswymansite.html. James Phinney Munroe explains how he came to write the letter supposedly penned by Sarah Munroe in *The Munroe Clan . . . Together with a Letter from Sarah Munroe to Mary Mason Descriptive of the Visit of the President Washington to Lexington in 1789*, pp. 58–61. Caleb Wall in *Reminiscences of Worcester* recounts how Independence Whipple saw GW's entourage pass by between Uxbridge and Thompson, p. 242. Chase in *History of Haverhill, Massachusetts* tells the story of Bart Pecker's meeting with GW, p. 448. John Currier in *The History of Newburyport, Mass., 1764–1905*, recounts the meeting between GW and Colonel Cotton, pp. 413–14. Hiram Carleton in *Genealogical and Family History of the State of Vermont* recounts the story of GW's chasing after the carriage in Thompson, Connecticut, p. 283. GW complains about how he had to spend a Sunday in Ashford, Connecticut, and "heard very lame discourses from a Mr. Pond" in *DGW*, 5:495. The anecdote about GW at Milford, Connecticut, and the broken pewter spoon is in the WPA's *History of Milford, Connecticut*, p. 65; Richard Platt and Arthur Stowe of the Milford Historical Society also recounted versions of the tradition in two different phone conversations. Ray Brighton in *The Checkered Career of Tobias Lear* cites Lear's letter in which he complains about "very indifferent accommodations," p. 85. GW records finding "Mrs. Washington and the rest of the family all well" in *DGW*, 5:497. Martha Washington tells of how GW's "sensibility has been awakened" by the New England tour in her Dec. 26, 1789, letter to Mercy Otis Warren, marthawashington.us/items /show/25.html.

Chapter 10: The Spies of Long Island

According to Kenn Stryker-Rodda in "George Washington and Long Island," "There are no contemporary newspaper accounts and no hordes of reporters followed his lumbering carriage or cut across fields on fast horses to be present when he arrived at one of his destinations. There is no mention of his visit in the town records of the various localities. There are no extant copies of the speeches of the local dignitaries on these occasions—if any speeches were made," p. 13. Clearly GW had an agenda of his own when he visited western Long Island. On the Culper Spy Ring, see Morton Pennypacker's *General Washington's Spies on Long Island and in New York*, pp. 1–119, and Alexander Rose's *Washington's Spies*, pp. 47–163. On the controversy over Alexander Hamilton's assumption plan, the question of where to locate the federal capital, and the Quaker slavery proposal, I have, among other sources, looked to Ron Chernow's *Washington*, pp. 619–24; Ron Chernow's *Alexander Hamilton*, pp. 304–23; and Norman Risjord's *Chesapeake Politics, 1781–1800*, pp. 343–92. Chernow writes of how the Potomac "formed an institutional tie" that drew GW "ineluctably back to national politics," in *Washington*, p. 500. He cites Maclay's description of Thomas Jefferson's "lounging manner" in *Hamilton*, p. 311. George Clymer's description of GW's "slow fever" is cited in the editorial note to William

Jackson's May 2, 1790, letter to Clement Biddle, in founders.archives.gov/documents/Washington/05-05-02-0253. GW writes of riding in "sight of the sea" in *DGW*, 6:64. Henry Onderdonk in *Revolutionary Incidents of Suffolk and Kings Counties* tells of how GW "good naturedly took two or three turns on the stoop with his hat off," as well as of GW's encounter with the Quaker farmer Jonah Willets, p. 264. Carl Starace in his pamphlet "Sagtikos Manor and George Washington" writes of Isaac Thompson's patriotic sympathies and how GW's tour of western Long Island appears to have been motivated by his interest in visiting Setauket, the epicenter of the Culper Spy Ring. Stryker-Rodda in "George Washington and Long Island" writes of how a boy in Patchogue offered GW a baked potato he'd been roasting beside the road, p. 13. Alex Rose in *Washington's Spies* records the tradition that "Roe was so excited to meet the great warlord he fell off his horse and broke his leg," p. 277. Charles E. Shepard cites Henry Clay Platt's account of GW's visit to Platt's Tavern, an account based on the testimony of "a venerable lady," in "Washington's Tour of Long Island—Day 4," 1927, a newspaper clipping provided by Toby Kissam of the Huntington Historical Society. Shepard also writes of Sarah Mead's memories of GW in Cold Spring Harbor. Another version of Mead's account is in the Jan. 24, 1889, *New-York Tribune*, which cites an article from *The Oyster Bay Pilot*; my thanks to Claire Bellerjeau of the Raynham Hall Museum for bringing this article to my attention. Phil Roosevelt posits the theory that GW stayed with the Youngses while in Oyster Bay as a way to demonstrate the principle of forgiveness in "Youngs Family of Oyster Bay: Talk for the Friends of Sagamore Hill" in the archives of the Raynham Hall Museum. Dard Hunter writes of GW's visit to the Onderdonks and their paper mill in *Papermaking Through Eighteen Centuries*, p. 255. Robert Morris's observation that GW's Long Island tour had allowed him to regain "his looks, his appetite and his health" is cited in the editorial note to William Jackson's May 2, 1790, letter to Clement Biddle, in founders.archives.gov/documents/Washington/05-05-02-0253; my account of GW's illness, along with the comments from William Maclay and Theodore Sedgwick, is based on these same editorial notes.

Chapter 11: Newport

GW writes of having "undergone more and severer sickness than thirty preceding years afflicted me with . . . altogether" in a June 15, 1790, letter to David Stuart, in *PGW*, 5:523–27. Lafayette admonishes GW to "take care of your health" in an Aug. 23, 1790, letter in *PGW*, 6:316. Ron Chernow cites Jefferson's claim that the disputes over assumption and the residency bills created "the most bitter and angry contest ever known in Congress before or since the union of the states" in *Alexander Hamilton*, p. 321. Norman Risjord cites the reference to the Senate adjourning "amid furious uproar" in *Chesapeake Politics, 1781–1800*, p. 583; Risjord also writes of how William Jackson took a leading role in the behind-the-scenes politicking for the bill, p. 375, and Jefferson's struggles with migraines before moving into his quarters on Maiden Lane, p. 382. Chernow cites Jefferson's account of the famous dinner with Hamilton and Madison in *Alexander Hamilton*, p. 328. Thomas Jefferson writes of the need "to give as well as take in a government like ours" in a June 13, 1790, letter to George Mason, in founders.archives.gov/documents/Jefferson/01-16-02-0295. Jefferson complained of being "duped into it by the secretary of the treasury" in a

Sept. 9, 1792, letter to GW, in founders.archives.gov/documents/Jefferson/01-24-02
-0330. Risjord writes of how the coining of the name "Republican" by the Anti-
Federalists was a "standing rebuke" to GW's presidency in *Chesapeake Politics, 1781–
1800*, p. 343. GW writes of how "I feel myself supported by able co-adjutors, who
harmonize extremely well together," in a June 3, 1790, letter to Lafayette, in *PGW*,
5:468–69. Jefferson writes of the hope that nothing "so generative of dissension can
arise again" in an Aug. 14, 1790, letter to Thomas Mann Randolph, in founders
.archives.gov/documents/Jefferson/01-17-02-0102. On the arrival of coyotes on
Naushon Island, see movies2.nytimes.com/library/national/science/010597sci-animal
-coyote.html. The references to GW's "agreeable passage" to Newport and the
"considerable concourse" of people they encountered are cited in the notes to GW's
Aug. 18, 1790, letter to the Clergy of Newport, Rhode Island, in *PGW*, 6:280. I'm
indebted to Ruth Taylor of the Newport Historical Society for her remarks about
how Rhode Island's laws granting all "persons" religious liberty allowed wives to
sue their husbands for the right to worship as they pleased. On Newport and the
slave trade, see newportmiddlepassage.org/hello-world/. The toast "May the last be
the first" and the description of how the citizens of Newport looked "with unceasing pleasure on THE MAN" are in the Aug. 19, 1790, *Newport Herald*. GW's reply
to the Hebrew Congregation in Newport is in *PGW*, 6:286. For information on the
design and building of the Touro Synagogue, I have consulted Theodore Lewis's
"Touro Synagogue—National Historic Site," pp. 281–311; see also www.chabad
.org/library/article_cdo/aid/3000446/jewish/The-History-of-Jewish-Newport
-Rhode-Island.htm.

Chapter 12: Providence

My description of GW's arrival and first night in Providence is based on the account
in the Aug. 23, 1790, *Newport Mercury* as well as the journal of William L. Smith,
which is excerpted in *PGW*, 6:301–2. On the statue of Roger Williams at Prospect
Terrace, see www.nps.gov/rowi/learn/historyculture/prospect-park.htm. William
Smith writes of GW's nighttime visit to Rhode Island College in his journal, excerpted in *PGW*, 6:303. The authors of the Report of the Brown University Steering
Committee on Slavery and Justice, *Slavery and Justice*, write of the Brown family's
connection to what was then Rhode Island College and the voyage of the slave ship
Sally; they also discuss the newspaper war between the brothers John and Moses
Brown as well as Rhode Island's intimate connection to slavery in www.brown.edu
/about/administration/institutional-diversity/resources-initiatives/slavery-justice
-report. See also Charles Rappleye's *Sons of Providence: The Brown Brothers, the Slave
Trade, and the American Revolution*, pp. 53–293. On John Brown's chariot and the
tradition that GW accompanied Brown on a trip to India Point, I am indebted to
Henry Brown's *John Brown of Providence and His Chariot*, pp. 4–8, as well as my conversation with Morgan Grefe of the Rhode Island Historical Society, who spoke of
John Brown's obsession with GW. On GW's mention in 1794 of the petition put
forward by Rhode Island Quakers concerning the slave trade, see Rappleye's *Sons of
Providence*, pp. 297–99. On the Brown Slavery Memorial, see www.brown.edu/about
/public-art/martin-puryear-slavery-memorial. William Smith writes of how GW's
four-hour walkabout to Rhode Island College and India Point left his entourage

"completely fatigued" in *PGW*, 6:303–4. The newspaper accounts describing GW's final dinner and departure from Providence, as well as the judgment that after GW's visit Rhode Islanders "must now feel a confidence in the administration of one who possesses their universal esteem," are cited in *PGW*, 6:304–5.

Chapter 13: Terra Incognita

Benjamin Hawkins writes of how "some of the Antifederal gentlemen" in North Carolina "are as violent, or more so than ever," as well as of Willie Jones's refusal to entertain President Washington, in an April 5, 1791, letter to GW, in *PGW*, 8:66. James Iredell's memo to GW in which he describes the bad roads and "very wretched" accommodations in the South is in *PGW*, 7:480–81. According to Stephen Decatur Jr., in *PAGW*, Washington's new "chariot," built by David and F. Clark of Philadelphia, was "in reality a light traveling coach," with two facing seats, p. 202. For a definitive account of the carriages owned by GW throughout his lifetime, see Elizabeth Jamieson's "Research Report on the Powel Coach at Mount Vernon." Thomas Jefferson writes of "lowering the hang" of GW's carriage in *PGW*, 8:13. In a March 24, 1791, letter, Henry Lee warns GW of the "pestilential effects of the southern sun in the hot season," in *PGW*, 8:5. GW writes of how he devised his "line of march" for the southern tour in a June 13, 1791, letter to Alexander Hamilton, in *PGW*, 8:264. GW writes of how he had informed his cabinet that he would "return immediately" from his southern tour in case of an emergency in *DGW*, 6:106. GW describes his enslaved servant Paris as "self-willed and impudent" in a June 19, 1791, letter to Tobias Lear, in *PGW*, 8:277. GW describes his ill-fated crossing of the Chesapeake in a March 25, 1791, entry in *DGW*, 6:100–101. GW comments on the Maryland statehouse being "much out of repair" in a March 26, 1791, entry in *DGW*, 6:101. Ron Chernow cites John Adams's claim that GW's family profited "a thousand percent" from the decision to build the nation's capital on the Potomac and writes of how the deal "shattered some magic spell" in *Washington*, p. 631. On GW's 1754 canoe trip down the Potomac, see Robert Kapsch's *Potomac Canal: George Washington and the Waterway West*, pp. 10–15. Kenneth Bowling in *The Creation of Washington, D.C.* cites Representative William Smith's observation that "almost all men form their opinions by their interest without always knowing the governing principle of their motives or actions," p. 213. Bowling also defines "Potomac Fever" as "a delusion-inducing obsession with the grandeur and commercial future of the Potomac River," p. 106. GW's argument that the capital of the United States needed to be bigger than the capital of a state, such as Philadelphia, is in a May 7, 1791, letter to the Commissioners for the Federal District, in *PGW*, 8:159. GW writes of how the landowners came to the realization that "whilst they were contending for the shadow they might lose the substance" in a March 30, 1791, entry in *DGW*, 6:105.

Chapter 14: The Fellowship of the Past

GW recounts the accident on the Occoquan River in an April 7, 1791, entry in *DGW*, 6:107. Michelle Hamilton at the Mary Ball Washington House spoke of Mary's words to GW during our May 11, 2019, visit to Fredericksburg. Betty Lewis's July 24, 1789, letter in which she writes of how their mother "will not believe you are

well till she has it from under your hand" is in *PGW*, 3:301. Michelle Hamilton recounted how it was said you could "set your watch" to Mary Washington's delivery
of gingerbread to her grandchildren during our visit to Fredericksburg. Samuel
Eliot Morison's 1932 essay "The Young Washington" contains the reference to
Mary Washington's opposing anything he ever did "for the public good," www
.historyaccess.com/theyoungmanwashi.html. Peter Henriques cites GW's cousin's
account of how Mary Ball Washington "awed me in the midst of her kindness," in
www.colonialwilliamsburg.com/learn/trend-and-tradition-magazine/trend-and
-tradition-winter-2019/complicated-very-complicated. Hamilton's description of Jefferson as "a man of sublimated and paradoxical imagination" is in founders.archives
.gov/documents/Hamilton/01-12-02-0396. Jefferson's description of Hamilton as
"not only a monarchist, but for a monarchy bottomed on corruption" is in www
.mountvernon.org/george-washington/the-first-president/washingtons
-presidential-cabinet/jefferson-and-hamilton-political-rivals/. On Jefferson's comment that he and Hamilton were "opposed in death as in life," see www.monticello
.org/site/research-and-collections/alexander-hamilton-bust-sculpture. On the new
evidence about Alexander Hamilton and slavery, see www.smithsonianmag.com
/history/new-research-alexander-hamilton-slave-owner-180976260/. On the removal
of the statue of Jefferson Davis in Richmond, see www.nytimes.com/2020/06/11/us
/Jefferson-Davis-Statue-Richmond.html. The protester's claim that "if anyone's
going to lead by example, it needs to be us" is in a story by Ryan Miller, Ledyard
King, and Sarah Elbeshbishi in the *Cape Cod Times*, June 6, 2020. On the destruction
of the monument that once stood in New York City's Bowling Green, see Krystal
D'Costa's "History Behind the King George III Statue Meme," blogs.scientificameri
can.com/anthropology-in-practice/the-history-behind-the-king-george-iii-statue
-meme/. Kevin Draper of New York Historical Tours spoke to Melissa and me about
the wrought-iron fence at the Bowling Green, which is now the city's oldest surviving fence. Thomas Jefferson's Nov. 6, 1801, circular to his cabinet, in which he
describes how GW organized the paper flow in his cabinet, is cited in the notes of
PGW, 5:302–3. Richard Venable was the Virginia lawyer who recorded "Strange is
that impulse which is felt by almost every breast to see the face of a great gentleman"
in his diary around the time GW visited Charlotte Courthouse, MSS 5:1 V5506,
Virginia Museum of History and Culture. For GW's Farewell Address, see www
.ourdocuments.gov/doc.php?flash=false&doc=15&page=transcript. For Thomas Jefferson's notes of a conversation with GW's attorney general, Edmund Randolph, in
which Randolph claimed that GW had told him that in the event the Union broke
into two sections over the issue of slavery, he "had made up his mind to remove and
be of the Northern [portion]," see founders.archives.gov/documents/Jefferson/01
-28-02-0441. Although Melissa and I weren't aware of it during our visit to Richmond, we subsequently learned that the sculptor Edward Valentine (brother of the
founder of the museum that bears the family's name and where Melissa interned in
the fall of 1979) had sculpted the statues of both Jefferson Davis on Monument
Avenue and Thomas Jefferson at the Jefferson Hotel; for a story about how the
Valentine Museum hopes to display the Davis statue "not in its former glory, but
tipped over, dented and covered with paint from protesters," see www.washington
post.com/local/virginia-politics/richmond-sculptor-edward-valentine-created
-many-of-the-statues-that-defined-lost-cause-mythology-now-his-familys

-museum-is-confronting-the-legacy/2020/12/31/e9ed90c0-4b7b-11eb-a9d9-
1e3ec4a928b9_story.html?utm_campaign=wp_post_most&utm_medium=email&
utm_source=newsletter&wpisrc=nl_most&carta-url=https%3A%2F%2Fs2.wash
ingtonpost.com%2Fcar-ln-tr%2F2e0ce3f%2F5ff0a45e9d2fda0efb9c5b3f%
2F59739002ae7e8a1cf4bb8c98%2F52%2F66%2F5ff0a45e9d2fda0efb9c5b3f. GW in-
structs Tobias Lear to attempt to get the enslaved members of his staff out of Pennsylvania "under pretext that may deceive both them and the public" in an April 12,
1791, letter, in *PGW*, 8:84–86. Lear writes to GW that his willingness to participate
in the plan is predicated on his assumption that GW's enslaved servants "will at
some future period be liberated" in an April 24, 1791, letter, in *PGW*, 8:129–33. William Loughton Smith's claim that the Potomac site for the Federal City "unites more
advantages for the place intended than any spot I have seen in America" is in his
Journal, p. 49; Smith recounts overhearing a conversation about the federal government while staying at a tavern in southern Virginia in his *Journal*, pp. 54–55. GW
records Edward Carrington's claim that the tax on whiskey "may be executed without difficulty" in *DGW*, 6:110. GW chronicles his journey to Halifax, North Carolina, in the April 16, 1791, entry of *DGW*, 6:112–13. Samuel Johnston's letter in
which he says "the reception of the president at Halifax was not such as we could
wish" is in *DGW*, 6:114. GW writes of his reception in Tarboro in *DGW*, 6:114. GW
describes Greenville as a "trifling place" in *DGW*, 6:115. For information on the
longleaf pine, I have looked to Lawrence Early's *Looking for Longleaf*, pp. 76–96. GW
describes his mixed reaction to the longleaf pine forests of North Carolina in *DGW*,
6:118–19. Early in *Looking for Longleaf* writes of the possible sources for the term "Tar
Heel," p. 96. The story of GW's breakfast at John Allen's house is told by W. Keats
Sparrow in "George Washington's 1791 Visit to Pitt County," pp. 72–75. GW writes
of his mistaken impression that he was dining at a tavern instead of a private home
in *DGW*, 6:115. Archibald Henderson in *Washington's Southern Tour* (hereafter cited
as *WST*) tells the story of GW and Lal Dorsey, the man who had not drunk water
in forty years, pp. 115–16. The story of how a boy cutting his face on a tree led to
the discovery of a GW monument at a park in Wilmington, North Carolina, is from
a July 2, 1949, newspaper clipping in the files of the New Hanover County Public
Library in Wilmington.

Chapter 15: "Follow the Yellow Brick Road"

On the Withers family and the history of Myrtle Beach, see A. Goff Bedford, *The
Independent Republic*, p. 58. For GW's time in the area, Terry Lipscomb provides a
helpful account of GW's travels through the region in *South Carolina in 1791*, pp.
8–11. GW writes of his journey across what is now Myrtle Beach in *DGW*, 6:122.
The description of the rice fields in early spring is by St. Julien Ravenel and cited by
Archibald Henderson in *WST*; Henderson also quotes GW's reference to the low-
country rice fields as a "fairyland," pp. 126–27. For information about slavery in
South Carolina in the eighteenth century, I have relied on Philip Morgan's *Slave
Counterpoint: Black Culture in the Eighteenth-Century Chesapeake and Lowcountry*; Morgan
cites George Ogilvie's comparison of himself with "the tyrant of some Asiatic Isle,
the only free man on an island of slaves," pp. 30–101. The sketch of the planters drinking around a table late at night was drawn around 1760 by George Roupell; it depicts

the low-country plantation owner Peter Manigault and friends and is at the Museum of Early Southern Decorative Arts in Winston-Salem, North Carolina; see mesda.org/exhibit/mr-peter-manigault-1731-1773-and-his-friends/. For information about Hampton Plantation, I have looked to Archibald Rutledge's "When Washington Visited My Home," pp. 4–7, and his *Home by the River*, pp. 18–54. Henderson cites Eliza Pinckney's letter in which she says, "I look . . . upon an old oak with the reverential esteem of a Druid, it staggered my philosophy to bear with patience the cutting down of one remarkably fine tree," *WST*, p. 140. Adam Nicolson in *The Gentry* cites the account in which GW proclaims that "an oak is a thing no man can make," p. 273. Sue Alston's quotation about the enduring legacy of slavery at Hampton Plantation is cited on an exhibit panel in the house. Rutledge writes of St. James Santee Episcopal Church in *Home by the River*, pp. 33–34. GW complains of having not been "allowed . . . a moment that I could call my own" in Charleston in *PGW*, 8:183–84. Lipscomb in *South Carolina in 1791* cites the account of GW working the room during the concert at the Exchange, p. 36. GW writes of "the beauty of the prospect" from the tower of St. Michael's Church in *DGW*, 6:131–32. For the interview in which two former Charleston librarians talk about Martha Koopman, see www.libsci.sc.edu/histories/oralhistory/Mosimann/mosimann.html. The letter in which the landowners claim that the contract GW wants them to sign "goes far beyond our idea of what was the spirit of the agreement" is in *PGW*, 8:97. GW writes of the "pain which this occurrence occasions me" in a May 7, 1791, letter to the Commissioners for the Federal District, in *PGW*, 8:158. Lipscomb writes about GW, Trumbull, and the painting of GW at Charleston in *South Carolina in 1791*, pp. 39–40; also see Robert Behre's "What's with the Horse in George Washington's Charleston Portrait? 'Just Look at It,'" *Charleston Post and Courier*, Nov. 10, 2018. Rutledge writes of how there is "no earthly loneliness like that created by man's abandonment of what he once . . . considered secure and permanent," in *Home by the River*, pp. 19–20. GW writes of being "kindly and hospitably entertained" at the plantation of Judge Heyward in *DGW*, 6:134.

Chapter 16: "Eleven O'Clock Sunday Morning"

For Peter Gordon's "A view of Savannah as it stood the 29th of March 1734," see www.loc.gov/resource/g3924s.pm001305/. GW describes the "bower" constructed on the edge of the Savannah River, where he had views of the "rice lands both above and below the town," in *DGW*, 6:138. Archibald Henderson in *WST* cites the story from *The Georgia Gazette* describing GW's "unaffected ease and dignity," p. 232. Kwesi DeGraft-Hanson cites the *New-York Tribune* reporter's account of the auction of the enslaved workers owned by Pierce Mease Butler in "Unearthing the Weeping Time: Savannah's Ten Broeck Race Course and 1859 Slave Sale," southernspaces .org/2010/unearthing-weeping-time-savannahs-ten-broeck-race-course-and -1859-slave-sale/. On Charles Augustus Lafayette Lamar and the *Wanderer*, see Tom Henderson Wells, "Charles Augustus Lafayette Lamar: Gentleman Slave Trader," pp. 158–68, and www.oldsaltblog.com/2017/09/tbt-repost-wanderer-slave-ship-flying -new-york-yacht-club-burgee/. Chuck Mobley writes of the history of Mulberry Grove and quotes the local historian's claim that "the president made his companions wait outside" in "Two Prominent Savannah River Plantations Share Common

Heritage and Classic Oak-Lined Avenue," *Savannah Morning News*, March 1, 2008, www.savannahnow.com/article/20080301/NEWS/303019861. John Stegeman and Janet Stegeman in *Caty: A Biography of Catharine Littlefield Greene* cite Caty's daughter Cornelia's claim that her mother possessed "the most remarkable combination of intellectual power and physical beauty I have personally encountered in woman-hood," as well as Nathanael Greene's comment "Her flowing tongue and cheerful countenance quite triumph over my grave face," pp. 95, 111. Terry Lipscomb cites the claim by the citizens of Piney Woods, South Carolina, that the tax on whiskey was "repugnant to the condition and liberties of a free people" in *South Carolina in 1791*, p. 59. GW writes of his fears the speculators in Georgia's Yazoo lands might one day "involve the country in trouble, perhaps in blood" in *DGW*, 6:155. The description of GW's heart being "as tender as a woman's" on the death of the grey-hound Cornwallis is in the April 1, 1892, edition of *The Augusta Chronicle*. On the death of Cornwallis, also see scratchofthequill.wordpress.com/2013/04/27/wash ington-and-the-death-of-cornwallis/. On the Savannah River Site, see Doug Pardue's "Deadly Legacy: Savannah River Site near Aiken One of the Most Contaminated Places on Earth," *Post and Courier*, May 21, 2017, www.postandcourier.com/news /deadly-legacy-savannah-river-site-near-aiken-one-of-the-most-contaminated -places-on-earth/article_d325f494-12ff-11e7-9579-6b0721ccae53.html. GW describes the road between Augusta and Columbia as "a pine barren of the worst sort" in *DGW*, 6:145. Lipscomb in *South Carolina in 1791* writes of the sycamore at which GW stopped to tend to his foundered horse as well as Columbia's new statehouse de-signed by James Hoban, pp. 63–64. Lottie Joiner writes of Bree Newsome taking down the Confederate flag at the statehouse in Columbia in the June 27, 2017, issue of *Vox*, www.vox.com/identities/2017/6/27/15880052/bree-newsome-south-carolinas -confederate-flag. Henderson in *WST* cites Washington Custis's account of GW's punctuality during the second half of the southern tour, p. 292.

Chapter 17: "A Cat May Look on a King"

On the story of GW's leaving half a Spanish peso at the Barr tavern, see Terry Lips-comb's *South Carolina in 1791*, p. 78. On the Carolina Piedmont, see southernspaces .org/2004/carolina-piedmont. James Merrell cites the reference to the Catawba being "the bravest fellows on the continent" in *The Catawbas*, p. 47. Lipscomb cites the account of the Methodist minister's meeting with the Catawba in *South Carolina in 1791*, pp. 79–80. On Chas Fagan's statues of King Hagler and Thomas Spratt, see charlottetrailofhistory.org/portfolio/thomas-spratt-king-haigler. On GW's Native name of Conotocarious, see www.mountvernon.org/library/digitalhistory/digital -encyclopedia/article/conotocarious/. In *Recollections and Private Memoirs of Washing-ton*, Washy Custis claims that GW's unique way of walking was derived from his experiences with Native people on the frontier, pp. 11, 39; see also my *Valiant Ambi-tion*, p. 68. On the traditions surrounding the Wampanoag Simeon Simons serving in GW's Life Guards, see E. B. Dimock's "Story of Simons from an Old Newspaper," p. 111. My account of the tradition regarding Simons also benefited from a conver-sation with William Guy, sagamore of the Pokanoket tribe of the Wampanoag, who is a direct descendant of Simons. Handsome Lake's vision of GW and the dog in the celestial house appears in Section 92 of *The Code of Handsome Lake, the Seneca*

Prophet, compiled by Arthur C. Parker in 1913; see www.sacred-texts.com/nam/iro /parker/index.htm. My thanks to Mary Thompson for bringing this account to my attention. Colin Calloway in *The Indian World of George Washington* writes of Ely Parker and the peace medal given to his ancestor by GW, pp. 489–90. Charles Caldwell writes of seeing GW riding Prescott near the North Carolina border in his *Autobiography*, pp. 281–82. Lipscomb in *South Carolina in 1791* cites GW's letter to David Humphreys in which GW reports that he has enjoyed "very good health during my journey and have rather gained flesh upon it," p. 81. Archibald Henderson writes of the tradition surrounding GW's visit to the home of Betsy Brandon in *WST*, pp. 295–96; on the evidence indicating the tradition may not in fact be true, see www.salisburypost.com/2015/05/10/newspaper-find-gives-more-details-on -washingtons-1791-visit-to-salisbury/. Henderson recounts how GW claimed he was "only an old gray-haired man" while in Salisbury as well as the claim GW was "more pleased with the plain, frank earnest welcome of Salisbury than the gaudy and fantastic reception at Charleston" in *WST*, pp. 305, 307. The address from the citizens of Salisbury is in *PGW*, 8:225–26. In a July 20, 1791, letter to David Humphreys, GW claims, "At the time of passing a law imposing a duty on home made spirits, it was vehemently affirmed by many, that such a law could never be executed in the southern States, particularly in Virginia and North Carolina. As this law came in force only on the first of this month little can be said of its effects from experience; but from the best information I could get on my journey respecting its operation on the minds of the people (and I took some pains to obtain information on this point) there remains no doubt but it will be carried into effect not only without opposition, but with very general approbation in those very parts where it was foretold that it would never be submitted to by any one," in *PGW*, 8:358. Lipscomb in *South Carolina in 1791* writes of how the tax on whiskey was received in the Carolinas in the years after GW's southern tour; in 1792, two South Carolina counties bordering the Blue Ridge Mountains became "the scene of 'menaces so violent and serious as to occasion the Collector to refrain from the execution of his duty'"; the opposition subsided, and the following year it was reported by Congressman William Loughton Smith that the "people were becoming reconciled to the tax," with the amount of revenue collected by the tax increasing with each successive year, p. 83. The proverbs "As you make your bed so you must lie" and "A cat may look on a king" appear in Noah Webster's *American Spelling Book*, p. 62. In a June 1, 1791, letter to Abraham Steiner, Samuel Kramsch writes, "Our illustrious president will go from here to the battleground of Guilford tomorrow morning. . . . This forenoon he visited the public buildings and came also in my school. We had . . . English reading school out of Noah Websters' *American Spelling Book* and as one boy was called up for reading it happened that he read the following words: 'A cat may look on a King,' whereupon he said to me, that, they think it now also. This day about 2 pm he received our humble address and gave an excellent answer," in *PGW*, 8:226–27. For a description of the Tavern Room of Reflection and Meditation, see www.oldsalem.org/out-of-bounds-sounds-of-hidden-town/. At some point during GW's visit to Salem, he attended a performance by a young woman playing a spinet. According to the tale recorded by Henderson in *WST*, once the girl had finished, she waited expectantly for the president to "compliment her upon her skill." Unfortunately for the girl, GW had noticed she had a wart on one of her hands. So instead of telling her what a great performance she had just given, he provided her with a formula for wart removal, p. 315. GW records his impressions of Nathanael Greene's strategy at Guilford Courthouse as well as his instructions to the governor to dismiss his cavalry escort in *DGW*, 6:154–55. GW records his overall impressions of the southern tour in *DGW*, 6:156–59.

Chapter 18: Muddy Freshets

Archibald Henderson in *WST* cites the tradition about the member of the Coles household remembering that GW had *"praised the pudding,"* p. 328. Walter Coles is quoted as saying a uranium mine on his property would be "the engine of economic growth" in a story by Gregory Schneider and Robert Barnes, "Supreme Court to Consider Virginia Uranium Case That Divides a Rural County," *Washington Post*, Nov. 4, 2018. For the Supreme Court's decision regarding the state of Virginia's moratorium on uranium mining, see www.supremecourt.gov/opinions/18pdf/16 -1275_7lho.pdf. Thomas Jefferson's May 8, 1791, letter to GW in which he mentions his reference to "the political heresies which have sprung up among us" in the foreword to a new edition of Thomas Paine's *The Rights of Man* and how he is "sincerely mortified to be thus brought forward on the public stage" is in *PGW*, 8:163–65. On the controversy ignited by the incident, see the editorial note concerning the "Contest of Burke and Paine in America," in *The Papers of Thomas Jefferson*, 20:268–90. According to the editors, "It is difficult to escape the conclusion that the deterioration of the bonds of friendship, trust, and affection that once existed between the central figure of the Revolution [GW] and the preeminent spokesman for its moral and philosophical propositions [Jefferson] had its origin in the unauthorized publication of Jefferson's letter to Jonathan Bayard Smith [in Paine's *The Rights of Man*]," p. 289. The editors cite John Adams's comment "It is thought rather early for electioneering," p. 278, as well as GW's response of "icy silence" to Jefferson's May 8 letter of explanation, p. 288. Henderson in *WST* cites the Anti-Federalist criticisms of the addresses and the "adulation" associated with GW's southern tour, as well as Jefferson's complaint that "the people will support him in whatever he will do or will not do, without appealing to their own reason," p. xxiii. Jefferson writes of his imminent departure on a trip with Hamilton to Vermont in a May 15, 1791, letter to GW, in *PGW*, 8:185–86. Robert Troup writes of Jefferson's and Hamilton's "passionate courtship" of Anti-Federalist figures in New York during their northern tour in a June 15, 1791, letter to Alexander Hamilton, in founders.archives.gov/documents /Hamilton/01-08-02-0407. In an Aug. 26, 1792, letter to Hamilton, GW pleads for "more charity in deciding on the opinions and actions of one another," in founders .archives.gov/documents/Hamilton/01-12-02-0206. On Jefferson's hiring of Philip Freneau and Freneau's editorship of the *National Gazette* and "the accusation that he had betrayed a public trust by an improper use of patronage," see the editorial note, "Jefferson, Freneau, and the Founding of the *National Gazette*," in *Papers of Thomas Jefferson*, 20:718–54. Ron Chernow cites Jefferson's account of the cabinet meeting in which an irate GW proclaimed, "He had rather be in his grave . . . than to be made *emperor of the world*," in *George Washington*, p. 696. When it comes to the overused phrase "Washington slept here," there is even a 1942 comedy titled *George Washington Slept Here*. Starring Jack Benny and Ann Sheridan and based on a play by Moss Hart and George S. Kaufman, the movie is, I must admit, pretty funny. A young couple moves into a dilapidated house in rural Bucks County, Pennsylvania, with the understanding that the property once served as Washington's military headquarters, only to discover that the Revolutionary War general who actually slept in the house was not Washington but the traitor Benedict Arnold. On the creation of Lake Anna, see www.stateparks.com/lake_anna_state_park_in_virginia.html. In a June 13, 1791, letter to Alexander Hamilton, GW writes of finishing the southern tour more than a week ahead of schedule, in *PGW*, 8:265. Terry Lipscomb writes of how "the slave Paris had become too sick to travel and had remained in Wilmington under the temporary care of a physician," in *South Carolina in 1791*, p. 7. In a June 5, 1791, letter to GW, Tobias Lear writes of how Hercules was "mortified to the last degree to think a suspicion could be entertained of his fidelity or attachment to you," in *PGW*, 8:231–35. On Hercules's eventual escape from Mount Vernon and his daughter's insistence that "I am very glad, because he is free now!," see www.mountvernon.org /library/digitalhistory/digital-encyclopedia/article/hercules/. Frank Vagnone and Deborah Ryan write of their desire "to elevate emotive experience to a standing equal with historical exactitude" in *Anarchist's Guide to Historic House Museums*, p. 37. On GW's intentional dismemberment of Mount Vernon, see Robert Dalzell and Lee Dalzell's opinion piece in the Nov. 21, 1999, *Atlanta Journal-Constitution*: "It is hard not to believe that he foresaw full well the future that awaited it in the slow, steady slide into decay that would carry his once-grand home to the brink of ruin over the next 50 years. Yet that was the future he envisioned; it was also a future of his own making. Leaving his slaves in bondage, keeping his assets intact, not dividing Mount Vernon, and settling it all onto one or two heirs would have produced a very different outcome. . . . Washington chose to do none of those things, however. He had built Mount Vernon, and now he was apparently decreeing, all but literally, its destruction. . . . [P]iece by piece Mount Vernon was to be taken apart, its contents scattered, its lands divided, its slaves freed, and the house itself left to slip into decrepitude. . . . Now, with nature alone to point the way, his creation would soon enough fade into the bower of greenery he had caused to grow around it," from a newspaper clipping provided by Bill Kirby of *The Augusta Chronicle*. The character Gloria insists, "There's no beauty without poignancy and there's no poignancy without the feeling that it's going, men, names, books, houses—bound for dust—mortal," in F. Scott Fitzgerald's *The Beautiful and Damned*, pp. 166–67.

Chapter 19: "The Devil's Own Roads"

GW writes of "the consequences of delay in this business" in *DGW*, 6:164. On Benjamin Banneker and the surveying of the Federal City, see Fergus Bordewich's *Washington: The Making of the American Capital*, pp. 67–72; Bordewich cites the *Georgetown Weekly Ledger*'s mention of "an Ethiopian, whose abilities, as a surveyor and an astronomer, clearly prove that Mr. Jefferson's concluding that race of men were void of mental endowments was without foundation," p. 71. For Banneker's Aug. 19, 1791, letter to Thomas Jefferson, see founders.archives.gov/documents/Jefferson /01-22-02-0049. For Jefferson's Aug. 30, 1791, reply, see founders.archives.gov/docu ments/Jefferson/01-22-02-0091. Jefferson complains that Andrew Ellicott "never missed an opportunity of puffing [Banneker]" in an Oct. 8, 1809, letter to Joel

Barlow, in founders.archives.gov/documents/Jefferson/03-01-02-0461. L'Enfant writes of the hill on which the Capitol would ultimately be built as a "pedestal waiting for a monument" in his June 22, 1791, letter to GW, in *PGW*, 8:287–93. Adam Costanzo in *George Washington's Washington* cites L'Enfant's vision of the United States as "a grand empire . . . over whose progress the eyes of every other nation envying the opportunity denied them will stand judge," p. 28. Bordewich cites Ellicott's disparaging comparison of the lands around the Potomac to a "stall-fed Ox" in *Washington: The Making of the American Capital*, p. 82. GW speaks of the landowners' "general approbation of the measure" in *DGW*, 6:165. Mary Thompson in *TOUSR* cites the claim that Washington Custis fathered forty mulatto children in the Washington, D.C., area, p. 146; see www.newspapers.com/clip/5669086/cleveland -daily-leader/ for the article in the Sept. 26, 1865, *Cleveland Daily Leader* that makes the claim concerning the "forty half-brothers and sisters" of "Mrs. General Lee." On Abraham Lincoln's speech in Trenton in which he cited his childhood reverence for GW, see Ted Widmer's *Lincoln on the Verge*, pp. 364–69. F. Scott Fitzgerald writes of Washington, D.C.'s "harsh repellent light" in *The Beautiful and Damned*, p. 166. On GW's plans to be buried in a tomb beneath the Capitol rotunda, see C. M. Harris's "Washington's Gamble, L'Enfant's Dream: Politics, Design, and the Founding of the National Capital," pp. 559–64. On the relationship between GW and James Monroe, which cites GW's outraged marginalia, as well as Monroe's memory of GW during the retreat across New Jersey in 1776, see Peter Henriques's *First and Always*, pp. 91–96. Tim McGrath cites Monroe's pronouncement that a president "ought not to be head of a party, but of the nation itself," in *James Monroe*, p. 377; McGrath also chronicles Monroe's own presidential tour in 1817 and cites Abigail Adams's praise of Monroe's "agreeable affability and unassuming manners," pp. 379–98. Archibald Henderson cites Washington Custis's account of John Fagan's reference to "the devil's own roads," in *WST*, p. 19. After GW's death, Washington Custis would end up with GW's chariot, which was eventually sold to Bishop William Meade. Meade made the decision to break the by then decrepit carriage into pieces for "those who delight in relics . . . , converting the fragments into walking sticks, picture frames, and snuff-boxes. . . . Besides other mementos of it, I have in my study, in the form of a sofa, the hind-seat on which the General and his lady were wont to sit," cited in Elizabeth Jamieson's "Research Report on the Powel Coach at Mount Vernon," p. 18. For GW's Farewell Address, see www.ourdocuments .gov/doc.php?flash=false&doc=15&page=transcript. Rebecca West writes of how "natural leaders . . . are usually empty," in *Survivors in Mexico*, p. 20, a reference that was brought to my attention by Paul Theroux's *On the Plain of Snakes: A Mexican Journey*. William Carlos Williams writes of the "great country" within GW in *In the American Grain*, p. 141. Washington Custis writes of how GW would frequently "appear absent" when with his family in *Recollections and Private Memories of George Washington*, p. 8. In addition to citing GW's confession that "the unfortunate condition of the persons, whose labor . . . I employed, has been the only unavoidable subject of regret," Mary Thompson discusses GW's unsuccessful attempts to shield Martha from the "insuperable difficulties" associated with freeing his slaves as well as the negative reaction to GW's decision to free his enslaved workers and how they formed the first free Black community in Fairfax County, in *TOUSR*, pp. 309–11, 314–17, 322. Susan Hellman and Maddy McCoy cite the tax records referring to "General

Washington's free negroes" in "Soil Tilled by Free Men: The Formation of a Free Black Community in Fairfax County, Virginia," p. 44. Hellman and McCoy also write of how that community became "racially diverse and harmonious" and of the "ripple effect" of GW's decision to free his slaves, pp. 39, 64. Mary Thompson recounts the story of the African American volunteers tending to GW's tomb "as the only return in their power to make" in *TOUSR*, p. 323. I cite John Steinbeck's rhapsodic description of Nantucket as well as his insistence that "Americans are much more American than they are Northerners, Southerners, Westerners, or Easterners" in "At Sea in the Tide Pool: The Whaling Town and America in Steinbeck's *The Winter of Our Discontent* and *Travels with Charley*," pp. 229–42.

Epilogue: The View from the Mountain

On Jefferson and Madison's northern tour, see "Editorial Note: The Northern Journey of Jefferson and Madison," founders.archives.gov/documents/Jefferson/01-20 -02-0173-0001, Willard Sterne Randall's "Thomas Jefferson Takes a Vacation," *American Heritage*, July/Aug. 1996, www.americanheritage.com/thomas-jefferson -takes-vacation, and Sydney Stokes Jr., "A Visit to Vermont," pp. 4–13. For Jefferson's May 31, 1791, letter to his daughter Martha Jefferson Randolph, in which he writes of his sail up Lake Champlain, see founders.archives.gov/documents/Jefferson/01 -30-02-0271. GW writes of the necessity of finding "a middle course" in an Aug. 26, 1792, letter to Hamilton, in founders.archives.gov/documents/Hamilton/01-12-02 -0206. Jefferson claims that a revolution that leaves "half the earth desolated . . . would be better than it is now" in a Jan. 3, 1793, letter to William Short, in founders .archives.gov/documents/Jefferson/01-25-02-0016. GW writes of his confidence that the American people "shall return to the right path with more avidity" in a March 3, 1797, letter to Jonathan Trumbull Jr., in founders.archives.gov/documents /Washington/99-01-02-00393. For an account of the fall of the Balancing Rock of Holliston, Massachusetts, see www.milforddailynews.com/news/20200922/balancing -rock-of-holliston-has-toppled-george-washington-once-tried-to-knock-it-down.

BIBLIOGRAPHY

Agee, James. *Let Us Now Praise Famous Men*. New York: Houghton Mifflin, 2001.

Algeo, Matthew. *Harry Truman's Excellent Adventure: The True Story of a Great American Road Trip*. Chicago: Chicago Review Press, 2011.

Asch, Chris Myers, and George Derek Musgrove. *Chocolate City: A History of Race and Democracy in the Nation's Capital*. Chapel Hill: University of North Carolina Press, 2017.

Atwater, Edward. *History of the City of New Haven*. New York: Edward Munsell, 1887.

Bageant, Joe. *Deer Hunting with Jesus: Dispatches from America's Class War*. New York: Broadway Books, 2008.

Baker, William Spohn. *Washington After the Revolution, 1784–1799*. Philadelphia: 1897.

Bales, Kevin. *Disposable People: New Slavery in the Global Economy*. Berkeley: University of California Press, 1999.

Bartram, William. *Travels of William Bartram*. Edited by Mark Van Doren. New York: Dover, 1955.

Beall, Mary Stevens. *The Story of the Washington Coachee and of the Powel Coach Which Is Now at Mount Vernon*. Washington, D.C.: Neale, 1908.

Bedford, A. Goff. *The Independent Republic: A Survey History of Horry County, South Carolina*. Conway, S.C.: Horry County Historical Society, 1989.

Berkin, Carol. *A Sovereign People: The Crises of the 1790s and the Birth of American Nationalism*. New York: Basic Books, 2017.

Bernard, John. *Retrospections of America, 1797–1811*. New York: Harper and Bros., 1887.

Bingham, Warren L. *George Washington's 1791 Southern Tour*. Charleston, S.C.: History Press, 2016.

Bishop, J. Leander. *A History of American Manufactures, 1608–1860*. Vol. 1. Philadelphia: Edward Young, 1861.

Blight, David W. *Frederick Douglass: Prophet of Freedom*. New York: Simon & Schuster, 2018.

Blumer, Thomas J. *Catawba Nation: Treasures in History*. Charleston, S.C.: History Press, 2007.

Blythe, LeGette, and Charles Raven Brockman. *Hornet's Nest: The Story of Charlotte and Mecklenburg County*. Charlotte, N.C.: Public Library of Charlotte and Mecklenburg County, 1961.

Bordewich, Fergus M. *The First Congress: How James Madison, George Washington, and a Group of Extraordinary Men Invented the Government*. New York: Simon & Schuster, 2017.

———. *Washington: The Making of the American Capital*. New York: HarperCollins, 2009.

Boutell, Henry Sherman. *A Deserted Village*. 1894. Reprint, Cedar Rapids, Iowa: Torch Press, 1943.

Bowen, Clarence Winthrop. *The Centennial Celebration of the Inauguration of George Washington*. New York: Committee on the Centennial of Washington's Inauguration, 1889.

Bowling, Kenneth. *The Creation of Washington, D.C.: The Idea and Location of the American Capital*. Fairfax, Va.: George Mason University Press, 1991.

Breen, T. H. *George Washington's Journey: The President Forges a New Nation*. New York: Simon & Schuster, 2016.

Brewster, Charles W. *Rambles About Portsmouth*. Portsmouth: New Hampshire Publishing Company, 1972.

Brighton, Ray. *The Checkered Career of Tobias Lear*. Portsmouth, N.H.: Portsmouth Marine Society, 1985.

Brower, Marion Willetts. *The Story of the Roslyn Grist Mill*. Roslyn, N.Y.: Roslyn Grist Mill, 1953.

Brown, Henry A. L. *John Brown of Providence and His Chariot*. Providence: Webster Press, 1989.

Brown, Stuart E. *Virginia Baron: The Story of Thomas 6th Lord Fairfax*. Berryville, Va.: Chesapeake Book Company, 1965.

Brox, Jane. *Brilliant: The Evolution of Artificial Light*. Boston: Mariner Books, 2011.

———. *Silence: A Social History of One of the Least Understood Elements of Our Lives*. Boston: Houghton Mifflin Harcourt, 2019.

Burrows, Edwin G., and Mike Wallace. *Gotham: A History of New York City to 1898*. New York: Oxford University Press, 2000.

Burt, Nathaniel. *Address of Nathaniel Burt, February 12, 1875, on the Washington Mansion in Philadelphia*. Philadelphia: James A. Moore, 1875.

Caldwell, Charles. *Autobiography of Charles Caldwell*. Philadelphia: Lippincott, Grambo, 1855.

Caldwell, Erskine. *Tobacco Road*. Athens: University of Georgia Press, 1995.

Calloway, Colin G. *The Indian World of George Washington: The First President, the First Americans, and the Birth of the Nation*. New York: Oxford University Press, 2018.

Calonius, Erik. *The Wanderer: The Last American Slave Ship and the Conspiracy That Set Its Sails*. New York: St. Martin's Press, 2006.

Carleton, Hiram. *Genealogical and Family History of the State of Vermont*. New York: Lewis, 1903.

Carney, Judith A. *Black Rice: The African Origins of Rice Cultivation in the Americas*. Cambridge, Mass.: Harvard University Press, 2001.

Carraway, Gertrude S. *Years of Light: History of St. John's Lodge, No. 3, New Bern, North Carolina, 1772–1944*. New Bern, S.C.: Owen G. Dunn, 1944.

Carrington-Farmer, Charlotte. "The Rise and Fall of the Narragansett Pacer." *Rhode Island History* 76, no. 1 (Winter/Spring 2018): 1–38.

Cashin, Edward J. *The Story of Augusta*. Augusta, Ga.: Richmond County Board of Education, 1980.

Chapman, Jacob. *A Genealogy of the Philbrick and Philbrook Families*. Exeter, N.H.: Exeter Gazette, 1886.

Chase, George Wingate. *History of Haverhill, Massachusetts*. Haverhill, Mass.: by the author, 1861.

Chernow, Ron. *Alexander Hamilton*. New York: Penguin Press, 2004.

———. *Washington: A Life*. New York: Penguin Press, 2010.

Clotworthy, William G. *In the Footsteps of George Washington*. Blacksburg, Va.: McDonald and Woodward, 2002.

Colles, Christopher. *A Survey of the Roads of the United States of America, 1789*. Edited by Walter W. Ristow. Cambridge, Mass.: Belknap Press, 1961.

Cook, Kenneth. "Washington Passes Through Halifax." A talk given to the United Daughters of the Confederacy, April 2, 1976. www.oldhalifax.com/county/Geo Washington.htm.

Costanzo, Adam. *George Washington's Washington: Visions for the National Capital in the Early American Republic*. Athens: University of Georgia Press, 2018.

Crofut, Florence S. Marcy. *Guide to the History and the Historic Sites of Connecticut*. Vol. 1. New Haven, Conn.: Yale University Press, 1937.

Currier, John. *The History of Newburyport, Mass., 1764–1905*. Newburyport, Mass.: published by the author, 1906.

Custis, George Washington Parke. *Recollections and Private Memoirs of Washington*. Washington, D.C.: William H. Moore, 1859.

Dalzell, Robert F., and Lee Baldwin Dalzell. *George Washington's Mount Vernon: At Home in Revolutionary America*. New York: Oxford University Press, 1999.

Damrosch, Leo. *Tocqueville's Discovery of America*. New York: Farrar, Straus and Giroux, 2010.

Decatur, Stephen, Jr. *Private Affairs of George Washington: From the Records and Accounts of Tobias Lear, Esquire, His Secretary*. Boston: Houghton Mifflin, 1933.

DeGraft-Hanson, Kwesi. "Unearthing the Weeping Time: Savannah's Ten Broeck Race Course and 1859 Slave Sale." southernspaces.org/2010/unearthing-weeping -time-savannahs-ten-broeck-race-course-and-1859-slave-sale/.

Delbanco, Andrew. *The War Before the War: Fugitive Slaves and the Struggle for America's Soul from the Revolution to the Civil War*. New York: Penguin Press, 2018.

Denenberg, Thomas Andrew. *Wallace Nutting and the Invention of Old America*. New Haven, Conn.: Yale University Press, 2003.

Destler, Chester McArthur. "The Hartford Woolen Manufactory: The Story of a Failure." *Connecticut History Review*, no. 14 (June 1974): 8–32.

Dickey, J. D. *Empire of Mud: The Secret History of Washington, D.C.* Guilford, Conn.: Lyons Press, 2016.

Dimock, E. B. "The Story of Simons from an Old Newspaper: Washington—His Life Guardsman a Pachaug Soldier." *Narragansett Dawn* 1, no. 5 (September 1935): 110–11.

Dobson, Meade. "George Washington's Presidential Tour of Long Island Retraced over His Route of 1790." *Quarterly Journal of the New York State Historical Association* 8, no. 3 (July 1927): 246–51.

Dumbauld, Edward. *Thomas Jefferson American Tourist: Being an Account of His Journeys in the United States of America, England, France, Italy, the Low Countries, and Germany.* Norman: University of Oklahoma Press, 1976.

Dunbar, Erica Armstrong. *Never Caught: The Washingtons' Relentless Pursuit of Their Runaway Slave, Ona Judge.* New York: Atria, 2017.

Durnin, Richard G. *George Washington in Middlesex County, New Jersey.* North Brunswick, N.J.: Middlesex County and Heritage Commission, 1989.

Early, Lawrence S. *Looking for Longleaf: The Fall and Rise of an American Forest.* Chapel Hill: University of North Carolina Press, 2004.

Ellis, Edward Robb. *The Epic of New York City: A Narrative History.* New York: Basic Books, 2001.

Ellis, Joseph J. *His Excellency George Washington.* New York: Vintage Books, 2005.

Ellis, Richard J. *Presidential Travel: The Journey from George Washington to George W. Bush.* Lawrence: University Press of Kansas, 2008.

Erickson, Carolly. *The First Elizabeth.* New York: St. Martin's Griffin, 1983.

Estes, J. Worth, and Billy G. Smith, eds. *A Melancholy Scene of Devastation: The Public Response to the 1793 Philadelphia Yellow Fever Epidemic.* Philadelphia: Science History Publications, 1997.

Evans, Eli N. *An American Experience: Adeline Moses Loeb and Her Early American Jewish Ancestors.* New York: Sons of the Revolution in the State of New York, 2009.

Farrow, Anne, Joel Lang, and Jenifer Frank. *Complicity: How the North Promoted, Prolonged, and Profited from Slavery.* New York: Ballantine Books, 2006.

Favretti, Rudy J. *Mansfield Four Corners: What It Used to Be and What George Washington Didn't See.* Storrs, Conn.: 2003.

Feeser, Andrea. *Red, White, and Black Make Blue: Indigo in the Fabric of South Carolina.* Athens: University of Georgia Press, 2013.

Ferling, John. *The Ascent of George Washington: The Hidden Political Genius of an American Icon.* New York: Bloomsbury Press, 2010.

———. *A Leap in the Dark: The Struggle to Create the American Republic.* New York: Oxford University Press, 2003.

Fischer, David Hackett. *Albion's Seed: Four British Folkways in America.* New York: Oxford University Press, 1989.

Fisher, Leonard Everett. *To Bigotry No Sanction: The Story of the Oldest Synagogue in America.* New York: Holiday House, 1998.

Fisher, N. "Letter Describing Washington's Visit to Salem in 1789." (From N. Fisher, a woman writer to her brother.) *Historical Collections of the Essex Institute* 67 (1931): 299–300.

Fitzgerald, F. Scott. *The Beautiful and Damned.* New York: Charles Scribner's Sons, 1922.

Flexner, James Thomas. *George Washington and the New Nation (1783–1793)*. Boston: Little, Brown, 1970.

———. *George Washington: Anguish and Farewell (1793–1799)*. Boston: Little, Brown, 1972.

———. *Washington: The Indispensable Man*. New York: Little, Brown, 1974.

Fort, Karen Gerhardt Britton. *Bale o' Cotton: The Mechanical Art of Cotton Ginning*. College Station: Texas A&M University Press, 1992.

Foster, Hanna W. *The Coquette*. 1797. Reprint, New York: Oxford University Press, 1986.

Fraser, Flora. *The Washingtons: George and Martha "Join'd by Friendship, Crown'd by Love."* New York: Knopf, 2015.

Frazier, Herb, Bernard Edward Powers Jr., and Marjory Wentworth. *We Are Charleston: Tragedy and Triumph at Mother Emanuel*. Nashville: Thomas Nelson Press, 2016.

Freeman, Douglas Southall. *George Washington: Patriot and President*. New York: Scribner's, 1954.

Frost, Elias. "Chronicle of the Frost Family: With Anecdotes and Notices Illustrative of Individual Characters." Transcribed by Susan Elliott. Unpublished manuscript, Rauner Library, Dartmouth College.

Gallay, Alan. *The Indian Slave Trade: The Rise of the English Empire in the American South, 1670–1717*. New Haven, Conn.: Yale University Press, 2002.

Garrett, Wilbur E. "The Patowmack Canal: Waterway That Led to the Constitution." *National Geographic*, June 1987, 716–53.

Gilje, Paul A., and William Pencak, eds. *New York in the Age of the Constitution, 1775–1800*. Rutherford, N.J.: Farleigh Dickinson University Press, 1992.

Glatthaar, Joseph T. *The March to the Sea and Beyond: Sherman's Troops in the Savannah and Carolinas Campaigns*. Baton Rouge: Louisiana State University Press, 1985.

Goler, Robert I. *Capital City: New York After the Revolution*. New York: Fraunces Tavern Museum, 1987.

Goodwin, George M., and Ellen Smith, eds. *The Jews of Rhode Island*. Waltham, Mass.: Brandeis University Press, 2004.

Gordon, John Steele. *An Empire of Wealth: The Epic History of American Economic Power*. New York: Harper Perennial, 2005.

———. "Technology Transfer." *American Heritage*, Feb. 1990. www.americanheritage.com/technology-transfer.

———. *Washington's Monument: And the Fascinating History of the Obelisk*. New York: Bloomsbury, 2016.

Gordon-Reed, Annette. *The Hemingses of Monticello: An American Family*. New York: Norton, 2008.

Grasso, Joanne S. *George Washington's 1790 Grand Tour of Long Island*. Charleston, S.C.: History Press, 2018.

Gutheim, Frederick. *The Potomac*. Baltimore: Johns Hopkins University Press, 1986.

Hagedorn, Herman. *The Roosevelt Family of Sagamore Hill*. New York: Macmillan, 1954.

Hammond, John E. *Oyster Bay Remembered*. Huntington, N.Y.: Maple Hill Press, 2002.

Harris, C. M. "Washington's Gamble, L'Enfant's Dream: Politics, Design, and the Founding of the National Capital." *William and Mary Quarterly* 56 (1999): 527–64.

Hayes, Kevin F. *George Washington: A Life in Books*. New York: Oxford University Press, 2017.

Hellman, Susan, and Maddy McCoy. "Soil Tilled by Free Men: The Formation of a Free Black Community in Fairfax County, Virginia." *Virginia Magazine of History and Biography* 125, no. 1 (January 2017): 38–67.

Henderson, Archibald. *Washington's Southern Tour, 1791*. Boston: Houghton Mifflin, 1923.

Henriques, Peter R. *First and Always: A New Portrait of George Washington*. Charlottesville: University of Virginia Press, 2020.

———. *Realistic Visionary: A Portrait of George Washington*. Charlottesville: University of Virginia Press, 2008.

Herman, Bernard L. *Town House: Architecture and Material Life in the Early American City, 1780–1830*. Chapel Hill: University of North Carolina Press, 2005.

Hessel, Mary Stanley. *Profile of a Patriot: John Wright Stanly, Revolutionary War Privateer*. New Bern, N.C.: Tryon Palace Commission, 1983.

Higginbotham, Don. *George Washington: Uniting a Nation*. Lanham, Md.: Rowman and Littlefield, 2004.

———, ed. *George Washington Reconsidered*. Charlottesville: University Press of Virginia, 2001.

Hirschfeld, Fritz. *George Washington and the Jews*. Newark: University of Delaware Press, 2005.

Hogeland, William. *The Whiskey Rebellion: George Washington, Alexander Hamilton, and the Frontier Rebels Who Challenged America's Newfound Sovereignty*. New York: Simon & Schuster, 2010.

Horn, Jonathan. *The Man Who Would Not Be Washington: Robert E. Lee's Civil War and His Decision That Changed American History*. New York: Scribner, 2015.

Horry, Harriott Pinckney. *A Colonial Plantation Cookbook: The Receipt Book of Harriott Pinckney Horry, 1770*. Edited by Richard J. Hooker. Columbia: University of South Carolina Press, 1984.

Horton, James Oliver, and Lois E. Horton, eds. *Slavery and Public History: The Tough Stuff of American Memory*. Chapel Hill: University of North Carolina Press, 2006.

Howard, Hugh. *The Painter's Chair: George Washington and the Making of American Art*. New York: Bloomsbury Press, 2009.

Howard, John Tasker. *The Music of George Washington's Time*. Washington, D.C.: United States George Washington Bicentennial Commission, 1931.

Hunter, Dard. *Papermaking Through Eighteen Centuries*. New York: William Edwin Rudge, 1930.

Irving, Washington. *Life of George Washington*. 5 vols. New York: Putnam, 1859.

Isenberg, Nancy. *White Trash: The 400-Year History of Class in America*. New York: Penguin Books, 2017.

Jackson, Kenneth T. *Crabgrass Frontier: The Suburbanization of the United States*. New York: Oxford University Press, 1985.

Jamieson, Elizabeth. "Research Report on the Powel Coach at Mount Vernon." A forty-seven-page document commissioned by the curatorial staff at George Washington's Mount Vernon, May 2017.

Jefferson, Thomas. *Notes on the State of Virginia*. 1785. New York: Penguin Books, 1999.

———. *The Papers of Thomas Jefferson*. Vol. 20. Edited by Julian Boyd. Princeton, N.J.: Princeton University Press, 1982.

Johnson, Cynthia Mestad. *James DeWolf and the Rhode Island Slave Trade*. Charleston, S.C.: History Press, 2014.

Johnson, Victoria. *American Eden: David Hosack, Botany, and Medicine in the Garden of the Early Republic*. New York: Liveright, 2018.

Johnson, Worthington B. *Black Savannah, 1788–1864*. Fayetteville: University of Arkansas Press, 1996.

Kaminski, John P., and Jill Adair McCaughan, eds. *A Great and Good Man: George Washington in the Eyes of His Contemporaries*. Lanham, Md.: Rowman and Littlefield, 2008.

Kapsch, Robert J. *The Potomac Canal: George Washington and the Waterway West*. Morgantown: West Virginia University Press, 2007.

Karasick, Gary. *New Brunswick and Middlesex County*. Northbridge, Calif.: Windsor, 1986.

Kemble, Frances Anne. *Journal of a Residence on a Georgian Plantation in 1838–1839*. Athens: University of Georgia Press, 1984.

Kidder, William L. *Crossroads of the Revolution: Trenton, 1774–1783*. Lawrence Township, N.J.: Knox Press, 2017.

King, Charles K. *The Life and Correspondence of Rufus King*. New York: Putnam's, 1894.

King, Henry. *Sketches of Pitt County, 1704–1910*. Greenville, N.C.: Era Press, 1976.

Larned, Ellen D. *History of Windham County, Connecticut*. Vol. 2. Worcester, Mass.: Charles Hamilton, 1880.

Lasser, Ethan W. *The Philosophy Chamber: Art and Science in Harvard's Teaching Cabinet, 1766–1820*. Cambridge, Mass.: Harvard Art Museums, 2017.

Latham, Den. *Painting the Landscape with Fire: Longleaf Pines and Fire Ecology*. Columbia: University of South Carolina Press, 2013.

Leary, Lewis. *That Rascal Freneau: A Study in Literary Failure*. New Brunswick, N.J.: Rutgers University Press, 1941.

Lengel, Edward G. *First Entrepreneur: How George Washington Built His—and the Nation's—Prosperity*. New York: Da Capo Books, 2016.

———, ed. *A Companion to George Washington*. Malden, Mass.: Blackwell, 2012.

Lepore, Jill. *These Truths: A History of the United States*. New York: Norton, 2018.

Levasseur, Auguste. *Lafayette in America in 1824 and 1825*. Translated by Alan R. Hoffman. Manchester, N.H.: Lafayette Press, 2006.

Lévy, Bernard-Henri. *American Vertigo: Traveling America in the Footsteps of Tocqueville*. New York: Random House, 2006.

Levy, Philip. *Fellow Travelers: Indians and Europeans Contesting the Early American Trail*. Gainesville: University Press of Florida, 2007.

———. *George Washington Written upon the Land: Nature, Memory, Myth, and Landscape*. Morgantown: West Virginia University Press, 2015.

———. "Washington and Judaism." *Washington Papers* (Winter 2018): 9.

———. *Where the Cherry Tree Grew: The Story of Ferry Farm, George Washington's Boyhood Home*. New York: St. Martin's Press, 2013.

Lewis, Theodore. "Touro Synagogue—National Historic Site." *Newport History* 159, no. 48, pt. 3 (Summer 1975): 281–320.

Lewis, Tom. *Divided Highways: Building the Interstate Highways, Transforming American Life*. New York: Viking, 1997.

Lipscomb, Terry W. *South Carolina in 1791: George Washington's Southern Tour*. Columbia: South Carolina Department of Archives and History, 1993.

Maass, John. *George Washington's Virginia*. Charleston, S.C.: History Press, 2017.

Maclay, William. *The Diary of William Maclay and Other Notes on Senate Debates, March 4, 1789–March 3, 1791*. Edited by Kenneth Bowling and Helen Veit. Baltimore: Johns Hopkins University Press, 1988.

Madison, James. *Notes of Debates in the Federal Convention of 1787*. Athens: Ohio University Press, 1985.

Madison, James, Alexander Hamilton, and John Jay. *The Federalist Papers*. Edited by Isaac Kramnick. New York: Penguin Books, 1987.

Maguire, J. Robert, ed. *The Tour to the Northern Lakes of James Madison and Thomas Jefferson, May–June 1791*. Ticonderoga, N.Y.: Fort Ticonderoga, 1995.

Maier, Pauline. *Ratification: The People Debate the Constitution, 1787–1788*. New York: Simon & Schuster, 2011.

Manca, Joseph. *George Washington's Eye: Landscape, Architecture, and Design at Mount Vernon*. Baltimore: Johns Hopkins University Press, 2012.

Marling, Karal Ann. *George Washington Slept Here: Colonial Revivals and American Culture, 1876–1986*. Cambridge, Mass.: Harvard University Press, 1988.

Martin, Lawrence, ed. *The George Washington Atlas*. Washington, D.C.: United States George Washington Bicentennial Commission, 1932.

Marx, Leo. *The Machine in the Garden: Technology and the Pastoral Ideal in America*. New York: Oxford University Press, 1976.

McCarty, Ralph William. *George Washington and the Constitutional Convention: An Account of Affairs and Circumstances Preceding and Including the Convention at Philadelphia*. Ohiopyle, Pa.: Mountain Streams and Trails Outfitters, 1987.

McGrath, Charles. "A Reality Check for Steinbeck and Charley." *New York Times*, April 3, 2011.

McGrath, Tim. *James Monroe: A Life*. New York: Dutton, 2020.

McLeod, Stephen A., ed. *Dining with the Washingtons: Historic Recipes, Entertaining, and Hospitality from Mount Vernon*. Mount Vernon, Va.: Mount Vernon Ladies' Association, 2011.

Meacham, Jon. *American Lion: Andrew Jackson in the White House*. New York: Random House, 2008.

———. *Thomas Jefferson: The Art of Power*. New York: Random House, 2013.

Melville, Herman. *Moby-Dick; or, The Whale*. New York: Penguin, 2009.

Merrell, James H. *The Catawbas*. New York: Chelsea House, 1989.

———. "The Indians' New World: The Catawba Experience." *William and Mary Quarterly*, 3rd ser., 41, no. 4 (1984): 537–65.

Michaelis, David. *N. C. Wyeth: A Biography*. New York: Perennial, 2003.

Moore, Peter. *Endeavour: The Ship That Changed the World*. New York: Farrar, Straus and Giroux, 2018.

Morgan, Philip D. *Slave Counterpoint: Black Culture in the Eighteenth-Century Chesapeake and Lowcountry*. Chapel Hill: University of North Carolina Press, 1998.

———. "'To Get Quit of Negroes': George Washington and Slavery." *Journal of American Studies* 36, no. 3 (December 2005): 403–29.

Munroe, James Phinney. *The Munroe Clan . . . Together with a Letter from Sarah Munroe to Mary Mason Descriptive of the Visit of the President Washington to Lexington in 1789*. Boston: George Ellis, 1900.

Nelson, John. *Worcester County: A Narrative History*. New York: American Historical Society, 1934.

Newman, Simon P. *Parades and the Politics of the Street: Festive Culture in the Early American Republic*. Philadelphia: University of Pennsylvania Press, 1997.

Nicolson, Adam. *The Gentry: Stories of the English*. London: HarperPress, 2011.

Northington, Oscar R., Jr. "The Taverns of Old Petersburg, Virginia." *William and Mary Quarterly* 16, no. 3 (July 1936): 339–46.

Onderdonk, Henry. *Revolutionary Incidents of Suffolk and Kings Counties*. Port Washington, N.Y.: Kennikat Press, 1970.

Orcutt, Samuel. *A History of the Old Town of Stratford and the City of Bridgeport*. Fairfield, Conn.: Fairfield Historical Society, 1886.

Page, Elwin L. *George Washington in New Hampshire*. Cambridge, Mass.: Riverside Press, 1932.

Peck, Garrett. *The Potomac River: A History and Guide*. Charleston, S.C.: History Press, 2012.

Pennypacker, Morton. *General Washington's Spies on Long Island and in New York*. Brooklyn: Long Island Historical Society, 1939.

Perrier, Dianne. *Interstate 95: The Road to Sun and Sand*. Gainesville: University Press of Florida, 2010.

Peucker, Paul. *A Time of Sifting: Mystical Marriage and the Crisis of Moravian Piety in the Eighteenth Century*. University Park: Pennsylvania State University Press, 2015.

Philbrick, Nathaniel. "At Sea in the Tide Pool: The Whaling Town and America in Steinbeck's *The Winter of Our Discontent* and *Travels with Charley*." In *Steinbeck and the Environment: Interdisciplinary Approaches*, edited by Susan Beegel, Susan Shillinglaw, and Wesley Tiffney Jr., 229–42. Tuscaloosa: University of Alabama Press, 1997.

———. *Bunker Hill: A City, a Siege, a Revolution*. New York: Penguin Books, 2014.

———. *In the Hurricane's Eye: George Washington and the Victory at Yorktown*. New York: Penguin Books, 2019.

———. *Valiant Ambition: George Washington, Benedict Arnold, and the Fate of the American Revolution*. New York: Penguin Books, 2017.

Phillips, Harriet Lauren. "A Landscape Analysis and Cultural Resource Inventory of Troublesome Creek Ironworks: A Geographical and Archaeological Approach." Master's thesis, University of North Carolina at Greensboro, 2011.

Pinckney, Eliza Lucas. *The Letter Book of Eliza Lucas Pinckney, 1739–1762*. Edited by Elise Pinckney. Columbia: University of South Carolina Press, 1997.

Poole, Robert M. *On Hallowed Ground: The Story of Arlington National Cemetery*. New York: Bloomsbury, 2010.

Post, Lydia Minturn. *Personal Recollections of the American Revolution*. Edited by Sidney Barclay. New York: Rudd and Carlton, 1859.

Raffel, Marta Cotterell. *The Laces of Ipswich: The Art and Economics of an Early American Industry, 1750–1840*. Hanover, N.H.: University Press of New England, 2003.

Ramsey, William. *The Yamasee War: A Study of Culture, Economy, and Conflict in the Colonial South*. Lincoln: University of Nebraska Press, 2008.

Randall, Willard Sterne. "Thomas Jefferson Takes a Vacation." *American Heritage*, July/August 1996. www.americanheritage.com/thomas-jefferson-takes-vacation.

Rappleye, Charles. *Sons of Providence: The Brown Brothers, the Slave Trade, and the American Revolution*. New York: Simon & Schuster, 2006.

Rice, James D. *Nature and History in the Potomac Country: From Hunter-Gatherers to the Age of Jefferson*. Baltimore: Johns Hopkins University Press, 2009.

Risjord, Norman K. *Chesapeake Politics, 1781–1800*. New York: Columbia University Press, 1978.

Roads, Samuel, Jr. *The History and Traditions of Marblehead*. Boston: Houghton, 1880.

Rogers, George C. *Charleston in the Age of the Pinckneys*. Columbia: University of South Carolina Press, 1980.

———. *Evolution of a Federalist: William Loughton Smith of Charleston*. Columbia: University of South Carolina Press, 1962.

Roosevelt, Phil. "Youngs Family of Oyster Bay: Talk for Friends of Sagamore Hill," April 25, 2006. Manuscript in the Archives of the Raynham Hall Museum.

Rose, Alexander. *Washington's Spies: The Story of America's First Spy Ring*. New York: Bantam Dell, 2007.

Rose, Lisle A. *Prologue to Democracy: The Federalists in the South, 1789–1800*. Lexington: University of Kentucky Press, 1968.

Rosenfeld, Richard N. *American Aurora: A Democratic-Republican Returns: The Suppressed History of Our Nation's Beginnings*. New York: St. Martin's Press, 1997.

Rumple, Jethro. *A History of Rowan County, North Carolina*. Salisbury, N.C.: J. J. Bruner, 1881.

Rutledge, Archibald. *God's Children*. Charleston, S.C.: History Press, 2009.

———. *Home by the River*. Orangeburg, S.C.: Sandlapper, 1983.

———. *Hunting and Home in the Southern Heartland: The Best of Archibald Rutledge*. Edited by Jim Casada. Columbia: University of South Carolina Press, 1992.

———. "When Washington Visited My Home." *South Carolina Magazine*, September 1958, 4–7, 26–29.

Salinger, Sharon V. *Taverns and Drinking in Early America*. Baltimore: Johns Hopkins University Press, 2002.

Salley, A. S. *President Washington's Tour Through South Carolina in 1791*. Bulletins of the Historical Commission of South Carolina, no. 12. Columbia, S.C.: State Company, 1932.

Sanders, Brad. *Guide to William Bartram's Travels: Following the Trail of America's First Great Naturalist*. Athens, Ga.: Fevertree Press, 2002.

Sandoval-Strausz, A. K. *Hotel: An American History*. New Haven, Conn.: Yale University Press, 2018.

———. "A Public House for a New Republic: The Architecture of Accommodation and the American State, 1789–1809." In *Perspectives in Vernacular Architecture*. Vol. 9, *Constructing Image, Identity, and Place*, edited by Alison K. Hoagland and Kenneth A. Breisch, 54–70. Knoxville: University of Tennessee Press, 2003.

Saxton, Martha. *The Widow Washington: The Life of Mary Washington*. New York: Farrar, Straus and Giroux, 2019.

Schecter, Barnet. *George Washington's America: A Biography Through His Maps*. New York: Walker, 2010.

Schulze, Richard. *Carolina Gold Rice: The Ebb and Flow History of a Lowcountry Cash Crop*. Charleston, S.C.: History Press, 2012.

Seo, Sarah A. *Policing the Open Road: How Cars Transformed American Freedom.* Cambridge, Mass.: Harvard University Press, 2019.

Shackelford, George Green. *Thomas Jefferson's Travels in Europe, 1784–1789.* Baltimore: Johns Hopkins University Press, 1995.

Shepard, Charles E. "Washington's Tour of Long Island—Day 4," 1927, clipping provided by Toby Kissam, Huntington Historical Society.

Shirley, Craig. *Mary Ball Washington: The Untold Story of George Washington's Mother.* New York: Harper, 2019.

Showalter, William Joseph. "The Travels of George Washington." *National Geographic Magazine*, Jan. 1932.

Slaughter, Philip. *The History of Truro Parish in Virginia.* Philadelphia: George Jacobs, 1907.

Sloane, Eric. *Our Vanishing Landscape.* New York: Ballantine Books, 1976.

Smith, Thomas E. V. *The City of New York in the Year of Washington's Inauguration, 1789.* New York: n.p., 1889.

Smith, William Loughton. *Journal of William Loughton Smith, 1790–1791.* Edited by Albert Matthews. Cambridge, Mass.: University Press, 1917.

Smith, Zadie. "What Do We Want History to Do to Us?" *New York Review of Books*, February 27, 2020, 10–14.

Smucker, Philip G. *Riding with George: Sportsmanship and Chivalry in the Making of America's First President.* Chicago: Chicago Review Press, 2017.

Sparrow, W. Keats. "George Washington's 1791 Visit to Pitt County." In *Chronicles of Pitt County, North Carolina*, edited by Sandra Hunsucker, 2:72–75. Winston-Salem, N.C.: Jostens, 2005.

Speck, Frank G. *Catawba Texts.* Columbia University Contributions to Anthropology, vol. 24. New York: Columbia University Press, 1934.

Starace, Carl. "Sagtikos Manor and George Washington." In *George Washington's Diary Entries Describing His 1790 Tour of Long Island*. West Islip, N.Y.: Sagtikos Manor Historical Society, 2017.

Stegeman, John F., and Janet A. Stegeman. *Caty: A Biography of Catharine Littlefield Greene.* Athens: University of Georgia Press, 1985.

Steinbeck, John. *Travels with Charley: In Search of America.* New York: Penguin Books, 1986.

Stokes, I. N. Phelps. *The Iconography of Manhattan Island, 1498–1909.* Vol. 5. New York: Robert Dodd, 1926.

Stokes, Sydney N., Jr. "A Visit to Vermont." *Historic Roots: A Magazine of Vermont History*, August 1999, 4–13.

Strang, Alison, and Gail MacMillan. *The Nova Scotia Duck Tolling Retriever.* Loveland, Colo.: Alpine Publications, 2014.

Strom, Adam, Dan Eshet, and Michael Feldberg, eds. *Washington's Rebuke to Bigotry: Reflections on Our First President's Famous 1790 Letter to the Hebrew Congregation in Newport, Rhode Island.* New York: Facing History and Ourselves, 2015.

Struzinski, Steven. "The Tavern in Colonial America." *Gettysburg Historical Journal* 1, article 7 (2002): 29–38.

Stryker, William S. *Washington's Reception by the People of New Jersey in 1789.* Trenton: Naar, Day, and Naar, 1882.

Stryker-Rodda, Kenn. "George Washington and Long Island." *Journal of Long Island History* 1 (1961).

Tagg, James. *Benjamin Franklin Bache and the Philadelphia "Aurora."* Philadelphia: University of Pennsylvania Press, 1991.

Taylor, Susie King. *Reminiscences of My Life in Camp.* Athens: University of Georgia Press, 2006.

Tebbel, John. *George Washington's America.* New York: Dutton, 1954.

Thane, Elswyth. *Mount Vernon Is Ours: The Story of the Preservation and Restoration of Washington's Home.* New York: Duell, Sloan, and Pearce, 1966.

Theroux, Paul. *The Tao of Travel: Enlightenments from Lives on the Road.* Boston: Houghton Mifflin Harcourt, 2012.

Thompson, Mary V. "George Washington Slept Here . . . and Ate Here . . . and Talked Here: Adventures in 18th Century Travel with George Washington and Selected Members of His Family." A talk presented at the Ninth Annual Clothing Symposium on Travel, Taverns, and Attire at Gadsby's Tavern, Alexandria, Va., Oct. 2, 2004.

———. *"In the Hands of a Good Providence": Religion in the Life of George Washington.* Charlottesville: University of Virginia Press, 2008.

———. *"The Only Unavoidable Subject of Regret": George Washington, Slavery, and the Enslaved Community at Mount Vernon.* Charlottesville: University of Virginia Press, 2019.

———. "Taverns Used by George Washington." Archives of George Washington's Mount Vernon, 2005.

———. "They Work Only from Sun to Sun: Labor and Rebellion Among the Mount Vernon Slaves." Unpublished manuscript. 2002.

Tocqueville, Alexis de. *Journey to America.* Translated by George Lawrence and edited by J. P. Mayer. New Haven, Conn.: Yale University Press, 1960.

Trammell, Jack. *The Richmond Slave Trade: The Economic Backbone of the Old Dominion.* Charleston, S.C.: History Press, 2012.

Turner, J. Kelly, and Jonathan Bridges Jr. *History of Edgecombe County, North Carolina.* Raleigh, N.C.: Edwards and Broughton, 1920.

Unger, Harlow Giles. *The Unexpected George Washington: His Private Life.* New York: John Wiley and Sons, 2006.

Urofsky, Melvin I. *A Genesis of Religious Freedom: The Story of the Jews of Newport, RI, and Touro Synagogue.* New York: George Washington Institute for Religious Freedom, 2015.

Vagnone, Franklin, and Deborah Ryan. *Anarchist's Guide to Historic House Museums.* Walnut Creek, Calif.: Left Coast Press, 2016.

Van Horn, Jennifer. "George Washington's Dentures: Disability, Deception, and the Republican Body." *Early American Studies* 14, no. 1 (Winter 2016): 2–47.

Vass, L. C. *History of the Presbyterian Church in New Bern, N.C.* Richmond: Whittet and Shepperson, 1886.

Vogt, Peter. "'Everywhere at Home': The Eighteenth-Century Moravian Movement as a Transatlantic Religious Community." *Journal of Moravian History,* no. 1 (Fall 2006): 7–29.

Waldstreicher, David. *In the Midst of Perpetual Fetes: The Making of American Nationalism, 1776–1820.* Chapel Hill: University of North Carolina Press, 1997.

Wall, Caleb. *Reminiscences of Worcester*. Worcester, Mass.: Tyler and Seagrave, 1877.

Ward, Elizabeth. *Old Times in Shrewsbury, Mass.: Gleanings from History and Tradition*. New York: McGeorge, 1892.

Washington, George. *The Diaries of George Washington*. Vols. 1–6. Charlottesville: University of Virginia Press, 1976–1979.

———. *The Papers of George Washington, Presidential Series*. Vols. 1–8. Charlottesville: University of Virginia Press, 1987–1999.

Waterman, Bryan. "Elizabeth Whitman's Disappearance and Her 'Disappointment.'" *William and Mary Quarterly*, 3rd ser., 66, no. 2 (April 2009): 325–64.

Watson, Elkanah. *Men and Times of the Revolution*. New York: Dana, 1856.

Wayland, John. *The Washingtons and Their Homes*. Baltimore: Clearfield, 2004.

Webb, Samuel Blachley. *Correspondence and Journals of Samuel Blachley Webb*. Vol. 3, *1783–1806*. New York, 1894.

Webster, Noah. *The American Spelling Book*. Boston: Isaiah Thomas and Ebenezer Andrews, 1792.

Weems, Mason L. *The Life of Washington*. Edited by Marcus Cunliffe. Cambridge, Mass.: Belknap Press, 1962.

Wells, Thom Henderson. "Charles Augustus Lafayette Lamar: Gentleman Slave Trader." *Georgia Historical Quarterly* 47, no. 2 (June 1963): 158–68.

West, Rebecca. *Survivors in Mexico*. Edited by Bernard Schweizer. New Haven, Conn.: Yale University Press, 2003.

Whitford, John. "The Home Story of a Walking Stick—Early History of the *Bible Recorder* and Baptist Church at New Bern, N.C., Told in Every Day Talk." 1900. Original manuscript and typescript. John D. Whitford Papers, North Carolina Division of Archives and History.

Widmer, Ted. *Lincoln on the Verge: Thirteen Days to Washington*. New York: Simon & Schuster, 2020.

Williams, George W. *St. Michael's: Charleston, 1751–1951*. Charleston, S.C.: College of Charleston Library, 2001.

Williams, Roy, and Alexander Lucas Lofton. *Rice to Ruin: The Jonathan Lucas Family in South Carolina, 1783–1929*. Columbia: University of South Carolina Press, 2018.

Williams, Thomas. *A Greenville Album: The Bicentennial Book*. Greenville, N.C.: Era Press, 1974.

Williams, William Carlos. *In the American Grain*. New York: New Directions, 2009.

Wills, Garry. *Cincinnatus: George Washington and the Enlightenment—Images of Power in Early America*. Garden City, N.Y.: Doubleday, 1984.

———. *James Madison*. New York: Henry Holt, 2002.

Wilson, Douglas L., and Lucia Stanton, eds. *Jefferson Abroad*. New York: Modern Library, 1999.

Winchester, Simon. *The Perfectionists: How Precision Engineers Created the Modern World*. New York: Harper, 2018.

Wister, Owen. *The Seven Ages of Washington: A Biography*. New York: Macmillan, 1924.

Wood, Gordon. *The Creating of the American Republic, 1776–1787*. Chapel Hill: University of North Carolina Press, 1969.

———. *Empire of Liberty: A History of the Early Republic, 1789–1815*. New York: Oxford University Press, 2009.

———. *Revolutionary Characters: What Made the Founders Different.* New York: Penguin Books, 2007.

WPA. *History of Milford, Connecticut.* 1939; New Delhi, India: Isha Books, 2013.

Yokota, Kariann Akemi. *Unbecoming British: How Revolutionary America Became a Post-colonial Nation.* Oxford: Oxford University Press, 2011.

ILLUSTRATION CREDITS

Page vi: *Reception to Washington on April 21, 1789, at Trenton on his way to New York to Assume the Duties of the Presidency of the United States* by N. C. Wyeth. Courtesy of Thomas Edison State University.

Page xii: John Brown's chariot. Providence, RI. 1782. Wood, leather, metal, textile. Negative number RHi X17 4288. Courtesy of the Rhode Island Historical Society.

Pages 2, 20, 72, 118, 142, 239, 301, 316, 361, and 375: Courtesy of the author.

Pages 8, 19, 287: Courtesy of Mount Vernon Ladies' Association.

Page 38: *Federal Hall. The seat of Congress* / re-engraved on copper by Sidney L. Smith. New York, 1899. The Society of Iconophiles. Courtesy of the Library of Congress.

Page 58: *In a Dream I Meet General Washington*, 1930, by N. C. Wyeth (1898–1945), oil on canvas, 72 ⅜ x 79. Brandywine River Museum of Art. Purchased with funds given in memory of George T. Weymouth, 1991.

Page 74: Photographed by the author with permission from Old Sturbridge Village.

Page 88: Cordwainer's banner courtesy of Revolutionary Spaces.

Page 106: *The Pennsylvania Gazette*, Philadelphia, Pennsylvania, May 24, 1796.

Page 128: *The Tempter and the Traitor—the Treason of Arnold on the Night of September 21, 1780*. Courtesy of The Miriam and Ira D. Wallach Division of Art, Prints and Photographs: Picture Collection, The New York Public Library.

Page 160: Portrait of Moses Brown, c. 1898, Providence, RI, attributed to Henry E. Kinney. Oil on canvas. Negative number RHi X17 3053. Courtesy the Rhode Island Historical Society.

Page 176: © Mark Krasnow of *Lynx* in Nantucket, MA.

Page 192: George Washington's journal courtesy of Virginia Museum of History & Culture (Mss5:1 W2773:1).

Page 214: *Peter Manigault and His Friends*, drawing by George Roupell, Charleston, South Carolina, United States, 1757–1960. Graphite, ink and wash on laid paper, 1963.0073, Museum purchase, Courtesy of Winterthur Museum.

Page 229: *George Washington at Charleston* by Jonathan Trumbull courtesy of the City of Charleston, South Carolina.

Pages 234, 288: Courtesy Library of Congress, Geography and Map Division.

Page 252: Courtesy of Archives, Sandor Teszler Library, Wofford College.

Page 259: © Chas Fagan.

Page 270: © Rob Shenk.

Page 314: © Joanne Hulbert.

Boundary stone at Jones Point, Alexandria.

INDEX

Page numbers in *italics* refer to maps and illustrations.